Coping with India

Robert Wood

Basil Blackwell

Copyright © Robert Wood 1990

First published 1990

Basil Blackwell Ltd
108 Cowley Road, Oxford, OX4 1JF, UK

Basil Blackwell Inc.
3 Cambridge Center
Cambridge, MA 02142, USA

British Library Cataloguing in Publication Data

A CIP catalogue record for this book is available from the British Library.

Library of Congress Cataloging in Publication Data

Wood, Robert, 1953–
 Coping with India / Robert Wood.
  p. cm.
 Bibliography p.
 Includes index.
 ISBN 0–631–16558–4
     0–631–16477–4 (pbk)
  1. India—Description and travel—1981—Guide-books.
I. Title.
DS406.W66 1990   89–32980
915.404'52—dc20   CIP

Typeset in 10 on 11½ pt Garamond
by Photo-graphics, Honiton, Devon.
Printed in Great Britain by Billing & Sons Ltd, Worcester

Contents

Acknowledgements

All cartoons in the book are reproduced by courtesy of *Punch*.

Introduction

Few countries can have had more written about them than India; there is an apparently endless list of travelogues and travel diaries of varying degrees of tedium and inconsequence, novels, accounts of spiritual enlightenment at the hands – or perhaps one should say feet – of various gurus and swamis, and, of course, many guidebooks. Indeed, a minor poet even felt obliged to write a breathless account of his bus-ride through the Ladakh mountains, somewhat in the style of self-help books on creative writing; his picaresque career was, of course, attended by signs and wonders, and the inevitable encounters with ladies from whose hands light shone, 'as if from within'. Alas, the present author, though a frequent traveller in India, has yet to be blessed with self-luminous travelling companions, and so perhaps my authority and fitness to write on the subcontinent could be called into question; indeed, the reader surely deserves some explanation of why I believe that it is worthwhile to add to the already copious literature referred to above.

The *Coping with . . .* books are not detailed regional guides, but are designed to give intending visitors concise, sound, and practical advice about travelling, living, and working in the countries the books cover. It is impossible to do this without devoting considerable attention to the natives – and lest anyone object to the term, let me point out that there is a *Coping with England* which gives just such attention. It is in this respect that I have found most of the guidebooks about India seriously deficient, for few of them treat the Indians seriously at all; at best, the Indians are simply wonderful background colour; at worst, they are a bunch of incompetents who ruin your holiday by their inability to keep their heads down when you're photographing the Taj Mahal. In fact, India is treated as a huge spectacle, a circus; it is not to be taken seriously; it is a vast hot, wet, and often exasperating museum, populated by a music-hall cast of ex-maharajas with soup-strainer moustaches, volatile and seething untouchables riding precariously on the tops of railway carriages, and emaciated religious virtuosos contorting themselves by the banks of holy rivers. India, say all these books, is the world's most populous democracy; it offers unrivalled travel experiences, whatever those are; the people are tolerant, they have an ancient culture, they are hospitable; but they can't run banks, hotels, or post offices, and let's face it, they're all a bit of a joke.

This sort of writing is not only insulting to the Indians, it is unhelpful to Western visitors. No doubt India will always retain its reputation for the exotic and the transcendental, the squalid and the horrific; and the cultural continuity of Hinduism will continue to exert a hold on Western imaginations; but India is also a major military and industrial power, is intent on becoming a regional superpower (at least), and has a space programme, a vast, wealthy middle class, who outnumber the entire population of France, and stockmarkets in the major cities. This India surely deserves the attention and respect of more intelligent travellers, who are not content to allow their impressions of modern Indian society to be formed by occasional unhappy contacts with autorickshaw drivers and hotel keepers.

I am not an expert on India, but an expert could not have written this book; my aim in writing it has been to share my experiences of travelling in India, of dealing with its people, and of trying to understand their society, with new or inexperienced Western visitors. This makes necessary the very unfashionable course of looking at a Third World country from what could be considered to be a Western point of view; furthermore, if the book is to be of serious use to intending visitors, the dark side of India and its people has to be discussed. There are unpleasant, sometimes shocking realities behind all those clichés about the world's most populous democracy and Indian hospitality; all I would say by way of apology for those parts of the book that some Indians might find objectionable is that it was not my intention to be gratuitously offensive in any way, and it was my intention to give a fair and honest picture of contemporary India.

The Indians themselves, of course, love to portray their country in the most lurid terms imaginable; the police are corrupt louts, the politicians are crooked and venial and much addicted to Swiss bank accounts, and the rural masses hopeless and illiterate; the only solace is provided by the gentle happiness of one's family, the bootleg man, and the imported Mercedes. It is hard to take Indian self-criticism seriously for much of the time, not only because of the Indians' evident love of painting their national shortcomings in the direst terms imaginable, but also because no one else can play; foreigners just have to listen. Foreigners voicing criticisms of India or the Indians seem to cause the gravest offence, even when the criticisms are fair, moderate, and justified; indeed, the Indians have a sensitivity to criticism that smacks not a little of jingoism and overweening national pride. How dare *they* criticize *us*? For example, when the BBC screened a not too complimentary documentary about the present Indian Government, a ministerial visit to Delhi was promptly cancelled; a British minister later felt obliged to apologize for the programme, at a private dinner party in Delhi (although how a minister of HM government could apologize on behalf of, and apparently against the will of, an independent broadcasting corporation remains a mystery).

If some Indians are offended by some of my comments about India and her society, I'm afraid that their offence must be akin to that of the authorities in this instance and I repeat that I cannot apologize for causing such offence, beyond saying that it wasn't my intention to be insulting to the Indian people. It is after all much more useful for a book to be written which gives a fair and accurate impression of what a visitor is likely to be confronted with, than yet another eulogy of the Taj Mahal, Rajasthan, or Indian hospitality; there are some 700,000,000 Indians in between all those lake palaces, temples, tiger reserves, and hill stations, and to treat them as amusing and occasionally irritating background colour seems to me to be the worst insult that they could be offered.

In writing this book, my main concern has been to portray the Indian people, and the complexities, problems, and pleasures of being a Western guest in their country. These books are not long by the standards of most guides; and it is inevitable that many generalizations have to be made. Exceptions can be found to almost every statement to be found in these pages, but I have tried to insert 'usually' and 'generally' as often as possible, without, I hope, testing the reader's patience.

To an outsider, Indian society can be strangely impenetrable and paradoxical; you can never quite find your bearings, you can never be quite sure that you've understood what's going on. A highly educated and Westernized Indian businessman will talk to you about the relative merits of Scotch whiskies, then suddenly switch to the wondrous medicinal properties of cow dung, and of how there are hints of advanced technology in the Epics – warriors and sages fly through the air, they communicate across vast distances; was it possible that the ancient Indians had flying machines and something like radios? You have just learned that Hindu weddings last for ever, and that you have to turn up late or no one will be there, when you miss a wedding completely because the ceremony was on time and lasted for all of three minutes; the bride and groom came from a caste whose nuptial rites were quite different from what you'd been led to expect. Cooks are still usually brahmins of some sort, and so are of high caste, and under no circumstances would your bearer (if you have one) do something that was properly the job of the much less exalted sweeper. It all seems hopelessly complicated, something that only a lifetime's acquaintance could unravel.

And yet Indian society is brutally obvious too; as V. S. Naipaul observed, for all the fine distinctions, for all the subtle nuances, some things are simple. Rich men tend to be fat (sometimes a paunch seems to be a status symbol) and poor men are thin. Rich men tend to dress in safari suits or other Western clothes, poor men tend to wear dhotis or veshtis or, if they're really poor, rags. Women, on the other hand, can be harder to place, for almost all of them wear the traditional sari or the Punjabi salwar-kameez; often, the poorer women seem to have the more gorgeous and vivid clothes.

I hope that this book will help visitors – whether long- or short-term, whether employed in India or tourists – make their way unscathed through the labyrinth of India, its people, its institutions, and perhaps above all its internal transport system; for independent travelling, free of the organized tour group, is the best way to explore India and meet Indians.

A last note on organized tours; this book is designed for the independent traveller, and apart from some information on the concessionary travel passes issued by Indian Airlines and Indian Railways, there is no information about package deals; this, after all, you can obtain from any reasonable travel agent, and would be quite out of place here.

Finally, I would like to thank the following people for advice, help, or hospitality during the preparation of this book: John Davey and Mark Allin of Basil Blackwell; Mr and Mrs K. R. N. Menon of Madras; Bikram Grewal and other staff members of Dass Media, New Delhi; Toby Sinclair, also of New Delhi; Shobita Punja; Tanya Luhrmann of the K. R. Kama Oriental Institute, Bombay; Mr S. Muthiah of Madras; the foreign tourist guides at Delhi and Madras Central Railway Stations; and, last but not least, Mr Balaraman Kalyanaraman for an invaluable lesson about the Indian sense of time.

Getting there and back

International travel to India

Alas, the halcyon days of romantic and cheap travel to India are over. The traditional land route, through Iran and Afghanistan, has long been closed, and is likely to remain so for the foreseeable future. A few travel firms organize 'adventure holidays', in which parties of tourists are conducted over the least dangerous parts of the old route, and shuttled by air across the lethal ones, but none of these can compare with the romance of the old overland journey. With tensions still running high between India and Pakistan, much of the land border between them is likely to remain closed, except for a small number of crossing points – notably the road and rail link between Lahore and Amritsar. Finally, even the ferry service between Rameswaram in India and Talaimannar in Sri Lanka has been interrupted because of the civil war in the latter country. Most travellers to India will, therefore, be arriving by air.

Air travel to India from Europe and North America is becoming increasingly expensive; there are certainly cheap flights to be found, especially through the London bucket shops, but many of these are on dubious airlines – Syrian Arab, for example, or Ariana Afghan. Apart from the obvious hazards of the latter, such airlines are very unreliable and are notorious for stranding passengers through overbooking.

The likeliest destinations for most flights from Europe and North America are Delhi and Bombay, both of which are served by large international airports. Calcutta and Madras are served mainly by flights from South East Asia and Sri Lanka, although British Airways has recently begun a direct flight into Madras. The cheapest tickets from London to Delhi or Bombay, on a reliable carrier, are likely to be in the region of £450 for the round trip. All prices given applied in 1989. Air India (AI) offers attractive concessions on flights from the USA and London, but beware of these; the Indian government can requisition AI planes to transport VIPs (see 'Internal travel in India').

Visas

Until fairly recently, citizens of Commonwealth countries didn't require visas to enter India; this relaxed attitude has changed, suffering most, perhaps, in the aftermath of Operation Bluestar in 1984, when the Indian security forces stormed the Golden Temple in Amritsar. The internal security crisis has meant that almost all foreign nationals are required to have a visa, and restrictions are imposed on their length of stay – once it seemed that the Indians were quite happy for foreign visitors to wander around their country indefinitely. All EEC nationals, and citizens of Commonwealth countries and the USA, require visas. To obtain any visa, you must of course hold a passport that will remain valid throughout your proposed visit.

Transit visas

This is exactly what its name suggests, and is valid for a short period only. It is obtainable from Indian high commissions and embassies abroad, but is of little interest to readers of this book, most of whom will, I hope, want to see more of India than airports and transit lounges.

Tourist visas

These are valid for ninety days, and are in principle renewable in India itself at the Foreigners' Registration Offices in major cities (see 'Useful addresses'). Outside India, these visas are issued at Indian high commissions, embassies, and consular offices. Note that the visas specify the number of times you may re-enter the country; for example, if you are issued with a single entry visa, and leave India to visit Nepal, you will not be allowed back in until you have applied for, and obtained, another visa. There are both single and multiple entry visas, and it is of course the applicant's responsibility to request the appropriate version. Holders of tourist visas are not

*'Think of it, luv. In a few weeks you could be plastering mud
from the Ganges on your face.'*

allowed to engage in trade or business, or to accept
any form of employment while in India. Although
a tourist visa might be appropriate for delegates to
some international conferences, holders of tourist
visas are also not allowed to undertake any formal
academic work or research.

Business visas   Anyone visiting India for business purposes, although
they may not actually be employed in the country,
must obtain one of these. Again, like the tourist
visas, they are easily obtained abroad; the business
visa, however, allows multiple entry, and is valid for
any ninety days within a twelve-month period.

Anyone visiting India to undertake research or study must apply for one of these. They are issued for a specific (variable) period, and for a specific purpose. These are obtainable abroad.

Students' visas

These can only be issued in India itself, unlike the other classes of visa; application must be made to a Foreigners' Registration Office.

Residents' visas

In the UK, visa applications are made at the Indian High Commission, India House, Aldwych, London WC2 4NA (tel. 01–836–8484). For non-tourist visas, it is advisable to make your application as far in advance as possible, as these can be subject to some delay. Tourist visas are usually issued on the day following your application. Note, however, that a punitive charge is made for tourist visas, £20 for a single entry and up to £60 for a multiple entry. This fee has to be paid at the time of application, and only cash or postal orders are acceptable; your application won't be accepted unless you pay there and then, so take plenty of cash with you. You will also need two recent passport photographs (of yourself).

Making an application

Applicants in the USA can apply either to the embassy in Washington, DC, at 2017 Massachusetts Avenue NW, Washington DC 2008 (tel. 265–5050), or to one of the regional consular offices in New York, San Francisco, or Chicago.

Make sure that you are applying for the appropriate visa!

When you have obtained your visa, you will notice that as well as a stamp stating 'change of purpose not allowed', there is another that states 'not valid for any restricted/protected area'. There is a surprisingly large number of Indian states in which foreign visitors are not allowed without special permission. Most of them are in the troubled north-eastern frontier, bordering on Bhutan and Burma, but occasionally the Punjab comes into this category; then you find yet another stamp on the visa, 'must travel by air to Kashmir'.

Restricted areas and special permits

Special permits are required for Darjeeling, Sikkim, Assam and Meghalaya, and the Andaman Islands. The other states of the north-eastern frontier are very hard to get into. The special permits can also be issued abroad, at embassies, high commissions, and consulates, but be warned that this can take a long time; periods of up to five weeks have been quoted, so make the applications well in advance of your trip. One problem – or potential problem – is that you will normally be expected to specify the exact dates of your stay in the protected or restricted territory. Application for permits can also be made inside India. Contact a Foreigners' Registration Office, some of which can issue permits, or which will direct you to the appropriate authorities.

Note that permits can be obtained on arrival in Darjeeling and Port Blair (Andaman Islands), but *only* for visitors arriving and leaving by air. (The nearest airport to Darjeeling is Bagdogra.) Government of India tourist offices provide up-to-date information concerning the regulations relating to restricted/protected regions.

Immigration formalities and customs

International flights to India often arrive in the small hours of the morning, and everyone's patience is already exhausted before the process of passing through the immigration controls begins. This is most people's introduction to Indian bureaucracy, and, with customs, can be a somewhat Kafkaesque experience. To be fair to the Indian authorities, immigration and customs clearance have been made much more efficient in recent years. Nonetheless, there are often very long queues, and you can be subjected to eccentric questioning; Why are you visiting India? Where are you going? Where are you staying? Do you know anyone in India? It is not advisable to claim close family relationship with the Gandhis; Indian immigration officers have as little sense of humour as their British counterparts.

In spite of such obstacles, you should have no serious problems if your visa and passport are in order; the latter will be stamped 'permitted to land', and you are now free to face customs. This can be as strange as, if not stranger than, immigration; there's no telling in advance what might happen, although there has been a great improvement in the service since the introduction of red and green channels, the usual 'goods to declare' and 'nothing to declare', at the international airports. There is a duty-free allowance, including alcohol, cigarettes, cigars, and gifts up to a certain value; details of this are given below.

For non-Indian tourists, the following allowances are made; 200 cigarettes, 50 cigars, 250 g of tobacco, 0.95 l of alcohol, and up to 500 rupees' worth of personal gifts. Note that with the rupee at about 24 to the pound sterling, and 14 to the US dollar, Rs500 worth of gifts doesn't amount to very much.

Duty-free allowances and dutiable items

Non-Indian non-tourists are allowed Rs1,250 worth of personal baggage, which again isn't very much.

Goods in excess of the duty-free allowances are subject to duty, which on items like cameras, typewriters etc. is charged on the spot at 175 per cent of the market price of the item; the customs have up-to-date price lists to help them decide on the appropriate charge; there is no escape. Note that the disembarkation card that you are given on the plane has a customs section where you are expected to declare any items in excess of the duty-free allowance.

Most visitors obviously have relatively expensive items with them like cameras, personal stereos etc. In principle, these are dutiable, but duty is waived if such are declared on the TBRE. The point of this exercise is to make sure that they leave India with you, and are not sold. India has a flourishing black market, and you'll be solicited at least five times a day, on the streets, for the sale of your wristwatch and camera. It is pretty hit-and-miss whether you actually have anything entered on a TBRE. Sometimes no one bothers, sometimes a meticulous list of personal possessions is made. If no one picks on you, you can walk through the green channel

The Tourist Baggage Re-Export form (TBRE)

unscathed. If you're selected for special treatment, the form is filled in and your passport endorsed. The whole thing seems pointless, as I've never known officials to take the slightest notice of these endorsements when I was leaving the country.

Transfer of residence to India

There are other waivers for those who are working or studying in India, and transferring their residence there, as the official jargon puts it. These concessions only apply to household effects, and there is no concession for what are deemed to be 'luxury' items – the latter including TVs, video machines, fridges, and air-conditioning units. You must bring the packing list of your goods with you, and upon arrival at the customs, take it to an officer in the red channel and explain that you have unattended baggage, and that you're transferring your residence to India. The appropriate paperwork will then be set in motion.

Note that before your possessions are released, you will have to satisfy the customs that each item is over a year old, or at least looks used. Brand-new objects are treated with deepest suspicion.

Impounding of goods

If a customs officer decides that something is dutiable, the duty is payable there and then. Otherwise, whatever it is will be impounded, and you'll have to return to the airport later to redeem it. If you can, avoid the latter at all costs; the bonded warehouses have a complicated bureaucracy that is staggering even by Indian standards, and the whole process is very time-consuming. The customs have detailed catalogues, listing brand names and current prices of every kind of consumer durable imaginable; and it is from these that duty is calculated. The one interesting feature of a visit to the bonded warehouse is going inside to pick up your possessions; then you will see all the washing machines from Dubai, crates (literally) of Walkmans from Singapore, and suitcases full of cameras that Indians have tried to bring in, all stacked up with rats disporting themselves amongst them. A final piece of advice; if you *do* have to visit the bonded warehouse, allow at least half a day, and take a good book and all of your patience.

The import or export of Indian currency is forbidden. All international airports have twenty-four-hour banks after customs and immigration – usually the notorious State Bank of India (see next chapter). If you have foreign exchange in excess of $1,000 US, you must fill in a Currency Declaration Form (Annexure III to AM circular No. 2 of 1974, in compliance with the Foreign Exchange Regulation Act of 1973). This is not as bad as it sounds, but is another test of your patience when you have to do it at three in the morning. There is usually a booth where both TBREs and currency declaration forms are issued. If you have in excess of $1,000 US, go to the red channel.

Currency restrictions

The Indian government will extort the princely sum of Rs100 (about £4) when you leave, by the simple expedient of not allowing you to check in for your return flight until you have done so. The tax is Rs50 for flights to Afghanistan, Burma, Bangladesh, Bhutan, Nepal, Pakistan, and Sri Lanka.

Airport tax

Money matters and insurance

Indian money The currency is the rupee, abbreviated to Rs. This is divided into 100 paisa (plural 'paise'), abbreviated to p. Both coins and notes are in circulation; coins are 5 p, 10 p, 20 p, 25 p, 50 p, Rs1, Rs2; notes are Rs1, Rs2, Rs5, Rs10, Rs20, Rs50, Rs100.

The banknotes are often in a very soiled and tattered condition, but beware of those that have torn edges, or tears down the creases where they have been folded. People will happily give them to you if you'll take them, of course, but you'll find that for some reason they later turn out to be unusable; they have to be exchanged at a bank; and that might mean a visit to the State Bank of India. Now no one wants to go to the State Bank of India if it can be helped; you can be in there for *weeks*. See the next section for a description of the State Bank's own quaint system of changing money.

It need hardly be pointed out that exchange rates are subject to wild fluctuation; the exchange rate of the rupee is determined with reference to a basket of major currencies, mostly chosen from nations which are major trading partners of India. With the rupee thus floating, the exchange rate can change very quickly indeed. Current exchange rates are Rs24 to the pound sterling, and Rs14 to the US dollar (July 1988). Average values for 1986–7 were Rs19.1 to the pound, and Rs12.8 to the US dollar. Inflation has hit the Indian currency hard; the rupee is now worth only one seventh of its value in 1960; in other words, relative to its purchasing power in 1960, the rupee is now worth only about 14p.

A few other coins are in circulation, other than those mentioned above, but they are rarely found; indeed, small change of any sort is always a problem in India. Prior to decimalization in 1957, the rupee was subdivided into 16 anna; one paisa was then one quarter of an anna. This system is defunct, though some old people still use the term anna, meaning the appropriate fraction of a rupee.

The Reserve Bank of India issues all notes, and it is the Reserve Bank that 'promises to pay the bearer on demand . . .'.

The best way to take your money to India is probably as US dollar travellers' cheques; the US dollar is still *the* hard currency in India, and Indian Airlines has a dollar price list for foreigners paying fares in foreign exchange; the same applies to Indian Railways and the very useful rail passes. Dollar bills are also an extremely useful black-market currency – crooks seem to turn up their noses at Queen Elizabeth's portrait. Pounds sterling are universally accepted in banks and hotels, but other currencies (such as the French franc) can be harder to exchange outside the big cities.

Foreign exchange

Only institutions with permission from the ubiquitous Reserve Bank of India can exchange money; this includes the major branches of all Indian banks (but see the section below on the Indian banking system), the foreign banks, Thomas Cook and American Express (which are probably the best places to change money), and some shops and hotels. The last of these cannot act as general exchange agents, they can only change currency for customers in exchange for goods or services.

There is a flourishing currency black market, of course, and on the street you will be offered attractive rates of exchange. Beware of *agents provocateurs*; illegal money changing is not advisable, and carries heavy penalties.

As stated above, the best – that is, the most efficient – places to change money are Thomas Cook or American Express. Here the transaction will take all of five or ten minutes. The Indian banks, on the other hand, especially the dreaded State Bank of India, can be remarkably slow and cumbersome. You fill in forms at one counter, then wait while a ledger is made up to date; the ledger, your form and cheque then go to a manager, sitting in splendid isolation beneath a slowly rotating fan. Around him are other, lesser functionaries, apparently in a trance as they very slowly put things under other things on their desks or fill in forms in triplicate. Occasionally a telephone rings; sometimes it is answered, but nothing really disturbs the sense of timeless religious repose. At last the grandee at the desk deigns to notice the ledger; he opens it, reads your passport twice, once from the back and once from the front; the cheque is minutely examined; then he appends his mighty signature to the form.

Do you get your rupees now? By no means. You receive a little metal token, with a number on it, and are despatched to the real heart of darkness of the State Banks; the cashier's booth, which could well be on another floor. When you get there, it is like a different planet; gone is religious tranquillity, for the cashier will be surrounded by a seething mob. You console yourself with the number on the disc; your turn will come; but then you realize that no numbers are being called out, people are just pushing their way to the front. You clear your throat, you say 'I say', then 'Excuse me'. No one takes any notice. At last, *hours* later, you stumble out on to the street, your head pounding, your body like chewed string; and as you emerge, a thin little man near the door says, 'Hello friend, you want to change dollar pound sterling? Good rate, good rate? You have something to sell?'

Avoid the State Bank of India if you can. Also, it can be difficult and time-consuming to change money in small towns, especially if they are off the main tourist track. Make sure that you change a reasonable sum of money in a large town before vanishing into the rural fastnesses.

When you exchange money, it is important to keep the form that any legal money changer should give you. The reason for this is that when you leave India, you will not be able to exchange any surplus rupees unless you can prove that they were legally exchanged. Furthermore, many hotels that do not themselves have exchange facilities will demand proof that you are paying your bill with rupees that were legally exchanged. The same applies to the purchase of tickets in Indian currency with Indian Airlines, and international tickets with any other airline's agents.

These are becoming more and more popular in India, and you should have no problem in using a Diners, American Express, or Visa card in hotels and restaurants in the big cities. Master Charge is somewhat less popular, and harder to use. Visa, Diners, and Master Charge have their own Indian agencies – the Indian Master Charge is called a Central Card.

Credit cards

The central institution is the Reserve Bank of India. This fulfils a variety of functions. Of most interest to foreigners is the Exchange Control Department, for this has regulating and licensing powers relating to the commercial and financial activities of foreign nationals. For example, if you are employed by a foreign company, and working in India, permission is required from the Exchange Control Department of the Reserve Bank both to open an office, *and* to live on funds paid from abroad. Foreigners also require Reserve Bank clearance to open bank accounts in India; foreign banks (like Grindlay's – see the next section) will always insist on your obtaining this, but if your sole earned income is in Indian currency, the smaller branches of the nationalized banks probably wouldn't bother.

The Indian banking system

The main office of the Reserve Bank is in Bombay, though there are offices in other major cities. To contact the Bombay office, write to: The Reserve Bank of India, Exchange Control Dept, PO Box 1055, New Central Office, New Central Office Building, Bombay 400023.

There are two main categories of bank in India, the 'commercial' banks and the 'co-operative' banks. The 'commercial' banks include the twenty-eight public sector banks; that is, the State Bank of India, its seven associate banks, and the twenty former private banks that were nationalized in two waves, fourteen in 1969, and six in 1980. Also included in the 'commercial' banks are the eighteen foreign banks, discussed in the next section. There are some Indian owned private sector banks too, but the public sector deals with about 90 per cent of Indian domestic banking transactions. The Regional Rural Banks (RRBs) comprise the last category of 'commercial' bank; these were set up in 1975–6 to aid rural economies by providing credit and other banking facilities to small farmers and agricultural labourers, who would normally be poor credit risks. The 'co-operative' banks fulfil a similar function.

If you opened a normal current (checking) account, it would therefore be at one of the 'commercial' banks. Accounts are maintained in the usual way, and cheque books issued. There is a growing, but still very limited, cheque guarantee card system being introduced; holding a current account in India is rather like the situation in much of the USA; your chequebook isn't much use outside your local area. Some Indian banks issue rupee travellers' cheques, which are a convenient way of carrying your money inside the country.

Foreign banks The main foreign banks are Grindlays (widely represented in large cities), Hong Kong and Shanghai, Bank of America, Standard Chartered, Citibank, Bank of Credit and Commerce International, and American Express's Banking Division. There is a number of other, less well-represented banks, such as the Netherlands' Algemene Bank. The foreign banks generally give a more efficient service than the Indian ones; furthermore, they are definitely better if you are trying to have money transferred from abroad, which at the best of times can be a painful process in India. Some of the foreign banks are trying to set up cash-card (autobank) facilities in major cities, but this service is very limited at present.

Banking hours All banks (foreign and domestic) have very restricted hours; Monday to Friday 10.00 to 14.00 hrs, and Saturday from 10.00 to 12.00 hrs. Banks are open at the international airports either on a twenty-four-hour basis, or to meet international flights.

Safety

You are very unlikely to be mugged in India, but you are quite likely to be robbed. Petty theft, pickpocketing, and bag snatching are fairly common, especially on the public transport systems of large cities. It is therefore a good idea to have a money belt, the kind that fits fairly snugly *under* your shirt/ blouse, and is firmly attached to your person. If this sounds melodramatic, just talk to people who have had their pockets cut off in a crowded train, without their even noticing, or to people who have been deprived of their passports in a fairly out-of-the-way place. It is obviously stupid to advertise the fact that you're carrying, say, several one-hundred-rupee notes by going through your valuables in a public place and rearranging them – as many people seem to do.

Most hotels from the reasonably expensive upwards will have a safe or safe deposit boxes, in which things like your passport can be left. Always make sure that you get a full receipt for anything deposited with hotel management.

The greatest disasters that can befall you in India, short of plague and cholera, are the loss of your passport and/or money. Thomas Cook and American Express provide a reasonably efficient replacement service, and both have an extensive network of offices and agents throughout the country – selected addresses are given in 'Useful addresses'. It is, of course, essential to have the cheque numbers and proof of purchase if a refund on lost or stolen travellers' cheques is to be obtained. Furthermore – something that many travellers do not seem to appreciate – refunds can be seriously delayed if you do not make a prompt report to the local police. You should go to the main police station wherever you are, and ask to speak to the officer in charge. Make sure that you *do* speak to a senior officer. It is most important to obtain a copy of the First Information Report (FIR), a standard police document which records the details of any case or complaint. This will be of great help in dealing with refund agencies, in the case of lost or stolen travellers' cheques, or consulates and embassies in the case of a lost or stolen passport. In spite of their dubious reputation, the Indian police are generally very helpful towards tourists – though of course there are exceptions to this. It is also very useful to keep a photocopy of the essential pages of your passport, including that which has the Indian visa stamped on it.

Insurance All travellers to India should ensure that they have adequate insurance, to cover the loss or theft of personal possessions, but above all to cover medical emergencies. This is, unfortunately, expensive. In the UK, coverage with a standard policy for only two months costs about £80. There are also lots of disclaimers on these policies, and people who are visiting the Himalayas should note that most of these standard travel insurance policies explicitly exclude any cover for injuries incurred while climbing 'with guides or ropes'. So people going trekking should make sure that they are not voiding their insurance cover; of course trekking is *not* climbing, it is walking along mountain paths, sometimes with a guide and porters; but if you fall over a cliff, and survive to make a claim upon your insurance company, they might not see it that way.

The most valuable part of any policy is that which guarantees repatriation, by air ambulance if necessary, in the event of serious illness or injury; so look at the disclaimers very, very carefully before you part with the sums demanded by insurance companies for what can be grudging and indifferent service. Insurance is further discussed in the following chapter, in connection with medical emergencies.

Income tax At first sight, a surprisingly small number of people in India pay income tax; the number has increased from nearly five million in 1985 to over six million in 1987. However, this is not so strange when you realize that the minimum exemption limit is Rs18,000 (about £750) and some 37 per cent of the population are below the official poverty line – that is, their annual income is below Rs3,500 (about £146). Above the exemption limit, the base rate starts at a fierce 50 per cent, which presumably accounts for the

massive tax evasion by both wealthy Indians and
employed foreign residents. All income tax goes to
the central government (as opposed to the state
governments – see 'The modern Indian state' for the
Indian federal system), and forms about 8.5 per cent
of the total revenue. If you are employed in India,
then you are liable for income tax; a PAYE system
operates. The self-employed pay a quarterly tax bill,
which is a percentage of their anticipated annual
earnings; in principle, an annual return should be
filed. India is well supplied with accountants who
will help on tax matters.

Tourists can also run up against the tax authorities.
If you stay in India for more than ninety days, you
must obtain clearance from the tax authorities to say
that you have no outstanding tax liabilities in India
before you leave. For most people, this means
proving that they have been supporting themselves
from their own funds by producing a mass of
exchange forms – you should take care to keep the
forms you are given (or should be given) when you
legally exchange money. To obtain clearance, you
should go to a notary public, who will help you
prepare an affidavit that states you have supported
yourself while in India, and have not been employed
nor engaged in any form of trade. This affidavit,
with your exchange forms, should then be taken to
the Foreign Section (Income Tax Clearance) of the
nearest income tax office. The paperwork can take
three or four days to complete. Some travel agents
will do all the footwork for you, but of course you
will be charged for this.

What you finally get is a grand Tax Clearance
Certificate (TCC). Although the law demands that
you go through this process, the actual document is
rarely examined when you leave; it seems to have a
similar role to the almost redundant sailing permits
issued by the Internal Revenue Service in the USA.
However, if you have been in India for more than
ninety days, it is probably a good idea to get tax
clearance; you could be the unlucky one who gets
picked up when you try to leave. A convenient way
round this is to stay in India for eighty-nine days,

then go to Nepal or Sri Lanka for a break, and come back.

There are tax treaties to avoid double taxation between India and several other countries. Such a treaty exists with the UK, but not the USA. New treaties are, however, being negotiated – the latest being with the Netherlands – so the situation can change quite quickly. Your local tax authorities in your home country will be able to advise you whether a treaty exists, but information about your taxable status in India and claims for protection under the terms of such a treaty are dealt with by the Ministry of Finance, Department of Revenue, Central Board of Direct Taxes, New Delhi.

Other taxes The states of the Indian union raise their own revenue by taxes on commodities and services, amongst others. Sales tax is now the single largest revenue-yielding item in the state governments' budgets, and of course all visitors will end up paying it. It is sometimes supplemented by a luxury tax, which can add up to 15 per cent to a hotel or restaurant bill. The rate varies from state to state, as does the excise duty on alcoholic drinks. In some states (Goa, for example) it is very low, while in others (such as Tamil Nadu) it is very high. Buses and cars are sometimes searched for liquor at state boundaries – especially vehicles coming out of Goa. Note that alcoholic drinks are bottled for retail in particular states; the label might have something like 'Only for sale in Himachel Pradesh' written on it; and smuggling liquor across state boundaries can get you into trouble.

Health, hygiene, and clothing

There are no formal immunization requirements for entry into India, unless you are travelling from an area where yellow fever is endemic. Nonetheless, the following injections are recommended for intending visitors to the country.

Before you go

1   Cholera. Two injections are usually given, the first about six weeks before the date of travel; only one injection is necessary to obtain the immunization certificate. The vaccine is said to be rather ineffective; it lasts for about six months, after which a booster has to be obtained. Be cautious when obtaining this (or any other) injection in India itself; some unfortunate travellers have received more than a cholera shot, they have contracted hepatitis from dirty needles. (See also the section below on AIDS.)

2   Tetanus.

3   Polio.

4   Typhoid. Again, a course of two injections is required, with the first one taken about six weeks before travelling; protection lasts for about three years. Vaccination for the related paratyphoid A and B (the TAB shot) is not normally given any more.

5   Hepatitis. A passive immunization with human immunoglobulin (gamma globulin) should be taken. There is no risk of contracting HIV (the AIDS virus) from this blood product in Europe or the USA, but it is not advisable to have a booster in India or Nepal, where screening procedures are less rigorous. Note that this injection is to protect against hepatitis A, not the blood-borne hepatitis B. A similar injection against the latter can be obtained for those who feel that they are running a high risk of contracting the virus (aid workers, doctors etc.), but hepatitis B is a relatively small hazard for the ordinary visitor, although there is of course some risk in using dirty needles.

*'Sounds adventurous. I read all the brochures but these
diseases are new to me.'*

6 Rabies. A course of two injections is recommended for anyone who will be travelling in
remote rural areas, where they are likely to encounter
infected animals and skilled medical attention is hard
to find. The first injection should be taken about six
weeks before travelling.

7 Malaria. There is no immunization against
malaria. The disease, however, can be very serious
and is sometimes fatal. India spends some 40 per
cent of its health budget on research into, or treating
cases of, this disease. Visitors should therefore take
appropriate anti-malarial drugs regularly, use insect
repellents and mosquito nets, and, if possible, reduce
areas of exposed flesh when the mosquitoes, which

are responsible for transmitting the disease, are active. (See the next section.)

The advice of a doctor should be sought about malarial prophylaxis – especially if a child is to be medicated. British doctors usually recommend two kinds of medication, to be taken together; one is a daily Paludrine (proguanil hydrochloride) tablet, the other a weekly Avloclor (chloroquine phosphate) tablet. These have to be taken for at least two weeks before entering the malarious zone, and four weeks after leaving it. These drugs do not prevent infection, they only inhibit the multiplication of the parasites responsible for malaria in the blood.

The two main health hazards are diarrhoea and malaria.

During your visit

Anti-malarial drugs have already been discussed; however, it is also important to try to avoid the bite of the mosquitoes that transmit the disease. There are two main peaks of malaria in India; from June to the end of August the strain *P. vivax* – the milder strain that produces shivering and sweating – is common. From August onwards there is a peak in the cases of the much more dangerous *P. falciparum*, the coma-inducing cerebral malaria. These seasonal peaks are related to the monsoon, which produces the hot, wet conditions that mosquitoes thrive in. During the day, most mosquitoes hide in dark, wet areas; they emerge at nightfall to find a host. Most are active in the evening and at dawn. Tropical mosquitoes show a marked preference for the feet, wrists, and hands, so long-sleeved and long-legged clothing offers some protection. Apart from this, a mosquito net is almost essential (for comfort as well as for health reasons), and there are several reasonably effective repellents available. Mosquito coils are slowly smouldering spirals that emit pyrethrum vapour (an insecticide); there are also various creams and lotions that can be applied.

Many Indian hotels provide nets, but most are useless as they are riddled with holes. It is really worth taking a reasonable quality net with you from

Malaria

Europe or the USA; the same applies to the cream or lotion repellents.

Diarrhoea The second great Indian health hazard, this can mean anything from a mild stomach upset to cholera. The point to appreciate is that almost all of these conditions are caused by eating or drinking contaminated food or water. *Never* drink untreated water in India; assume that all tap-water is contaminated. Note that the same supply runs to all houses, whether they be those of the rich or of the poor – assuming that the latter have a water supply at all. Very few well-to-do Indians drink tap-water; they too treat it in some way. Furthermore, it is not only drinking water that you must worry about, but also the water in which food, cutlery, and crockery is washed, and even the water you use for cleaning your teeth. *Never use untreated water.*   Two methods can be used to purify your water supply; boiling and disinfection. Water should be boiled for at least twenty minutes. Disinfection is best achieved with iodine solution, or one of the many brands of purification tablets (usually chlorine based, like Puritabs). Disinfection kills (amongst other micro-organisms) the amoebic cysts that are responsible for amoebic dysentery. Purification tablets can be surprisingly hard to find in India, and it is worthwhile taking a suitable supply with you. Also, the tablets are useless if the instructions are not carefully obeyed, or if the treated water is carelessly transferred to an unsterilized container. Take a water bottle with you, and *never* let it be filled with untreated water.

Cheap electric elements for boiling water can easily be bought in India for about Rs30 to Rs50; these are extremely useful. If you are such a rugged traveller that you anticipate having to use highly contaminated water, ordinary purification methods will not be sufficient; you will have to use a filtration device to remove any solid matter that could be the home of the micro-organisms that cause the various gastro-intestinal complaints. Filter appliances can be bought at any good camping and outdoor shop before you go. Finally, be especially careful of the water during the monsoon, for this is the high season for all the water-borne diseases.

Contaminated food can be just as much a danger in expensive hotels as in cheap eating houses; the flies don't discriminate. Indeed, it is sometimes safer to eat at street vendors' stands, where the food is cooked in front of you and can be eaten hot, than to indulge in the cold seafood buffet of a luxury hotel. Salads, fresh vegetables, and seafood are all suspect; and reheated foodstuffs can be very dangerous, especially rice. Dairy products should be treated with caution, including the fresh milk at street stalls (the clouds of flies should be enough to put you off), *lassi* (the yoghurt drink, which often has contaminated water in it), and the lesser known brands of ice-cream and ice-lolly. The same applies to ice cubes – they are no safer than the water used to produce them. Whenever possible, eat only thoroughly cooked food, and never touch rare meat. One of the great delights of the five star hotels is that decent drinking water is available, and things like ice cubes can be used without a second thought; it is wise, however, to be cautious of seafood and salads even in the expensive hotels.

Plates and utensils should be dry; a Swiss army knife is invaluable for, amongst many other things, peeling thick-skinned fruits, which are always safe to eat. A small knife, fork, and spoon set is useful, especially in those areas where you might be expected to eat with your fingers but cannot wash your hands properly (long train journeys in the south are especially bad for this). *Never* allow your hands or fingers to come into contact with your mouth unless they've been thoroughly washed.

Bottled drinks and mineral waters should be properly sealed, and have clean rims. Never drink the contents of the refillable bottles that are replenished by the vendors, rather than the manufacturer; these have the old-fashioned 'float' stoppers. All bottled drinks should have a brand name or label; there are some excellent mineral waters to be found in India – many of them supposedly bottled in the mountain springs of Himachel Pradesh. Soft drinks

tend to be sickly and sweet, but often they are the
only safe things you'll find on the street; reliable
brands include Double Cola, the Indian colas Thums
Up and Campa Cola, Gold Spot, Limca, and the
cartoned mango and apple juices named Fruti and
Appy.

Other   Indian hotel rooms can present hazards of their own.
problems   In cheap places, the bedding (if there is any) will
look very unpleasant; it will smell unpleasant too.
Obviously you want to limit your contact with it,
while getting a night's sleep as well. The solution to
this problem (which only applies to those who are
staying in cheap hotels) is to take a couple of dustbin
(garbage) bags and a sheet sleeping bag, of the kind
used in youth hostels. The latter can also be useful
on overnight trains, when you forget to order a
bed roll or when there are none available. Thong
sandals (flip-flops) are also very useful; they can
protect your feet in unsavoury showers.

Head lice are another problem, and effective lotions
or other treatments seem rare in India. It is therefore
advisable to bring either a lotion or one of the anti-
lice shampoos with you. A dusting powder to repel
bed-bugs is also useful.

The hot season requires especial care; it is essential
to protect your head from the direct rays of the sun,
and to avoid dehydration (see the next section).
Furthermore, it is very easy to become badly
sunburned very quickly; light, long-sleeved cotton
clothes (of the sort the Indians themselves wear) are
far better and cooler than the state of undress affected
by many Westerners.

Finally, take a supply of lavatory paper when you
go to rural areas; it can be hard to find, and the
local methods of avoiding its use are not to everyone's
taste. This problem is one that is wildly exaggerated
in many guides, which give the impression that
outside five star hotels lavatory paper is wholly
unknown; if you venture out into the wilderness
beyond the five star comfort, they imply, you will
have to be attended by a baggage train sweating in
your wake, heaving large bundles of toilet rolls over

the Deccan. Soft lavatory paper is easily found in any large town; the times when it is essential to lay in a supply are when travelling in rural areas, and for long train journeys.

You will probably suffer from nothing worse than a fairly mild stomach disorder during your stay. Don't panic if you get diarrhoea; most gastric disorders clear up within two or three days. If they don't, then you will have to apply some basic first aid; although diarrhoea itself may not be serious, if it is accompanied by pus and blood you could well have dysentery – which comes in many forms. Because of the large number of different kinds of dysentery, self-medication isn't recommended; antibiotics, for instance, will be useless against a viral infection, and may kill off benign organisms that live in the gut. Amoebic dysentery is perhaps the easiest to recognize, for it is not (unlike most of the other forms) accompanied by fever; for this reason, many doctors will give intending travellers to India (and other tropical areas) a prescription of Flagyl, the drug used for treating this condition. In general, however, the most important action that you can take is to avoid dehydration.

The symptoms of dehydration are small quantities of dark yellow urine, a dry tongue, and a curious flaccidity of the skin and flesh; if they are pinched or poked, the indentation will remain, they appear to lose their elasticity. The only remedy that you can apply yourself is oral rehydration; that is, drinking large amounts of fluids. The water should be as clean and pure as possible, but given the serious consequences of dehydration, it is better to use impure water than none at all. If they are available, sugar and salt should be mixed with the water to form a dilute solution; the recommended proportions are four heaped teaspoons of sugar and half a teaspoon of salt to about two pints of fluid. Sachets of pre-mixed rehydration powders (such as that marketed under the brand name Rehydrat) can be found in chemists' shops in Europe and the USA; it is a good idea to take a supply with you, as they are much harder to buy in India.

Treating illness yourself

Medical attention There is no agreement between the UK and India nor between the US and India for the medical care of tourists. Furthermore, although there are some very good hospitals and clinics in India (such as the All India Medical Institute in New Delhi), given the great size of the country and its population, there is a shortage of high-grade medical facilities. It is therefore important, as mentioned in the previous chapter, to have health insurance that will cover the cost of your repatriation in the event of serious illness or injury.

There are many excellent private clinics in India; five star hotels normally have their own doctor on call, and will recommend clinics. In villages and small towns you will be thrown more on your own resources, but there are often 'dispensaries' in the most out-of-the-way places, and these can provide first aid and limited stocks of drugs. Even in small towns you will see doctors' advertisements; try to choose one with what seem to be reliable qualifications. I once found a German-trained doctor in a small town, who treated me for a serious stomach disorder; he was extremely helpful and efficient, and his consultation fee was a mere Rs20. The drugs he prescribed cost more, about Rs30. In general, you can expect to pay anything from Rs20 to Rs100 to see a doctor, depending on the nature of your complaint, and the region of the country you are in.

Take care when collecting prescriptions; chemists' shops often stock drugs in unsuitable conditions. Things that have 'store under refrigeration' clearly printed on them are left on shelves, expiry dates are often long past, and so on. It is as important to obtain a recommendation to a pharmacist as it is to a good doctor.

Finally, remember that consulates also provide advice to their nationals seeking medical care.

AIDS AIDS was long dismissed in India as a disease of Western immorality and decadence. It has recently been acknowledged that the infection is probably quite widespread in the country, although not on anything like the scale of Africa, Europe, and the

19 died of AIDS in India

Raipur, July 13 (PTI): Union Minister for Health and Family Welfare Motilal Vora said on Tuesday 19 persons, including nine foreigners, had died of "AIDS" in India.

The Union Government was very alert and was considering the possibility of bringing a legislation in this respect, besides education people on the dreaded disease, he told newsmen on his arrival from Delhi here.

Mr. Vora said there were now 37 surveillance centres where nearly 1,03,000 persons had been screened. Of them, 300 were found to be positive cases.

Source: *Indian Express*

USA. The official figures (as of August 1988) are 332 people carrying the virus, and 24 deaths from the full syndrome. Homosexuality is a criminal offence in India, and screening facilities are few; since people in one of the high-risk groups are unlikely to come forward for screening, and since screening itself is difficult, the figure for the number of infected persons is almost certainly a serious underestimate. To add to the problem, there is no widespread screening of blood and blood products in blood banks. If at all possible, avoid injections of blood products in India and Nepal. It is also wise to take a supply of sterile, disposable syringes; these can be obtained before you go on a doctor's prescription, but take the prescription with you. A collection of syringes, even when still in their packing, can be treated with the greatest suspicion by police and customs officers.

Note that insurance companies have now introduced yet more nasty little disclaimers into their travel policies; in particular, most policies exclude repatriation of their holders on the grounds of fear of contracting AIDS through local medical attention.

If you are well enough to get back home under your own steam, it is probably better to do so than have any treatment in India that involves blood transfusions or the injection of blood products.

Note that anyone applying for a non-tourist visa must consent to a blood test for HIV antibodies; not all such applicants are actually tested, though they are expected to sign a form giving their consent.

Swimming   Swimming in the sea is generally safe, except near major cities, where vast amounts of untreated sewage are released. No one in their right mind would swim from Chowpatty Beach, for instance, in Bombay. Juhu up the coast isn't much better, it's too close to the city. The same applies to the beach along the marina in Madras.

Away from the big cities, the sea is excellent, but note that there are often strong currents along many of the coasts, and almost no rescue facilities or lifeguards. Still, fresh water is usually so uninviting that no one would bathe in it anyway. Hepatitis and a variety of other unpleasant diseases can be contracted through swimming in it; apart from the possibility of infection through puncture wounds in the skin, swimmers inevitably swallow water too.

Most five star hotels have excellent swimming pools; so too do many of the hotels run by the Indian Tourist Development Corporation. The standards of hygiene in these are high; sometimes they are open, for a relatively small charge, to non-residents.

Snakes and animals   India boasts a number of venomous snakes. Snake bites are at the least very painful, and often fatal. Avoid walking barefoot, particularly at night on dark paths, or through undergrowth. A torch (flashlight) is a great help; snakes will only bite if they are closely approached or trodden on.

With respect to animals, the most dangerous beasts can be the apparently friendly ones; tourists are very unlikely to be eaten by tigers, but they are likely to be approached by the skinny, seemingly friendly pariah dogs. These animals carry rabies, and the disease can be contracted by licking (via puncture wounds or abrasions) as well as biting. Avoid the half-tame pariahs, don't feed them, and certainly don't let them lick you.

Monkeys are very common in India; many of them live in or around temple compounds, where there are also many tourists. The monkeys not only have uncertain tempers, but they too carry rabies. Be cautious when feeding or approaching them.

If you are bitten, clean the wound thoroughly and seek medical advice – do not delay the latter.

Have your teeth checked before you go. Dental treatment in India can be surprisingly expensive, and the work of a low standard.

Dental treatment

India has three seasons, the hot, the monsoon, and the cool. (See 'India, geography and climate'.) You must take clothing suitable to the season, or you will be extremely uncomfortable. An umbrella is a must during the rains; plastic macs can be unbearably hot. During the hot season, a hat to protect your head from the sun is equally important. In the north, it can actually get cold at night during the cool season, and you might find you need a sweater.

Clothing

Many people make the mistake of taking too many clothes from home to India; this isn't necessary, because you can get them made to measure, very cheaply, in India itself. The traditional Indian clothing is also much more practical and comfortable than many Western fashions. A light cotton pajama kurta (that is, the tunic-like long shirt and baggy white trousers worn by many Moslems) can be made before your very eyes on a treadle sewing machine for as little as Rs70; and you will find the pajama kurta much more comfortable in the heat and humidity than Western clothes. It is also easy to launder, for it dries very quickly. A practical and comfortable form of footwear is a pair of chapals (that is, thong sandals); a plastic pair will cost as little as Rs15.

On the other hand, Indians are great clothes snobs, and even if you aren't going on business, but expect to socialize with middle-class Indians, take at least one smart set of Western clothes. Jeans are not only impractical and uncomfortable in the Indian climate, they will mark you out as a freak and a hippy (even though designer jeans are worn by the rich youth of cities like Bombay). Middle-class Indians seem to be obsessed with hippies, they even go on what seem to be pilgrimages to Goa to see the last superannuated specimens rolling about on Anjuna beach.

Women should be cautious about wearing revealing or clinging clothes; you can get away with them in the big cities, but in the country, small towns, and on trains and buses, they will make you the centre of (possibly) unwelcome attention. India isn't as difficult for female travellers as Pakistan, but ladies are not expected to expose large areas of flesh. If you are in male company, you will just be stared at; if you are on your own, you're fair game and will be pestered; pestering can range from indecent proposals to almost violent disapproval. Skimpy shorts, short skirts, sling tops etc, are all inadvisable; don't expose too much leg, shoulder, or upper arm. Finally, don't give skimpy or lacy knickers to the dhobi wallah (laundryman); they either get pounded to shreds on a rock if they're washed by the traditional method, or they never come back at all, evidently being appropriated as souvenirs of Western feminine decadence.

Travellers on business should remember that they will be judged by their clothes as well as by what they say; dress smartly.

The following are best brought with you from home. **Checklist of**
A prescription of the antibiotic tetracycline. **medicines**

Something like Imodium or Lomotil for symptomatic treatment of diarrhoea. These are not cures, they just suppress the most disastrous symptoms. Many doctors say that symptomatic treatments for diarrhoea can make the condition worse. This is all very well, but sometimes temporary relief is vital; how else can you survive long train and bus journeys?

An anti-fungal skin ointment, for treating things like 'dhobi-itch' etc. Daktarin is recommended by many British pharmacists.

Rehydration kits, as mentioned earlier, such as Rehydrat.

General first aid kit, including Melolin dressings; these are invaluable for protecting chafed or badly sunburned skin, and are much more effective than bandages or sticking plasters. They are manufactured by Smith and Nephew, and can be bought at most chemists'.

Anti-malarial drugs, as recommended by your doctor.

Disposable syringes.

An invaluable reference work is the detailed *Travel-* **Further**
lers' Health, edited by Richard Dawood (OUP). **reading on**
This provides specialized advice on many aspects of **health care**
disease prevention and self-treatment.

Before You Go is a Department of Health pamphlet, containing advice on immunization and health care abroad for UK citizens. The pamphlet (Ref. SA 40) can be obtained from doctors' surgeries, some pharmacies, or by phoning 0800-555777. There is an accompanying pamphlet, *While You're Away*, which is also quite useful.

All of the above publications list clinics where immunization can be obtained.

Internal travel in India

By air   There are two domestic airlines, Indian Airlines and
Vayudoot, as well as the Helicopter Corporation of
India Ltd, which provides services to the petroleum
industry, and in terrain too difficult for fixed-wing
craft. (The Helicopter Corporation is usually known
as Pawan Hans Ltd.) The aircraft used by Indian
Airlines (IA) are the Airbus A300 on major routes,
with executive and economy classes, and the single
class Boeing 737, HS-748, and Fokker Friendship.
IA provides some short-haul international services to
Nepal (Kathmandu), Sri Lanka (Colombo), Thailand
(Bangkok), Afghanistan (Kabul), Singapore, and
Pakistan (Lahore and Karachi). Vayudoot started as
a small private airline, but became a public limited
company in 1983. It operates Fokker Friendships,
and started by providing services in the difficult
country of the remote north-east; however, it has
expanded to provide a more extensive service that
supplements that provided by IA.

Booking   Tickets for IA can be booked abroad, although if
you do this you will have to pay the somewhat
higher dollar tariff. All bookings have to be routed
through IA's main Bombay office, so there can be a
slight delay – sometimes more than a slight delay! –
in having your booking confirmed. There are many
horror stories about IA, and I feel obliged to say
that most of them seem to me to be exaggerated.
True, there can be severe delays, but these are often
due to the weather, particularly during the monsoon,
which is something that IA can't be held responsible
for. One of the main drawbacks of using IA is the
occasional chaos caused by the Indian government's
appropriation of aircraft for VIPs. Again, IA can't
help this.

42 AI flights cancelled for VVIP visits

Express News Service
New Delhi, July 11: As many as 42 Air India flights have been cancelled between July 9 and July 22 due to the requisition of planes from the airline's fleet for the foreign tours of the Prime Minister and the President.

It was reported earlier that 20-odd flights were cancelled between July 2 and July 8 for the same reasons, bringing the total number withdrawn on account of the VVIP visits to a stagerring 60-plus.

The President left on a visit to the USSR and Mongolia on July 6 and will return to the capital on July 16. The Prime Minister left on a 4 nation tour on Monday morning (July 11) and will return only on July 20.

These concurrent trips have thrown Air India's schedules completely out of gear "despite its statements to the contrary" particularly during the period where the requirements of the two VVIPs have overlapped. Apart from the 42 cancellations for the fortnight beginning July 22 and this may not be the final figure since changes are occurring day-to-day – a staggering number of flights have been resheduled. No consolidated information was available on the number of rescheduled flights since, according to an Air India official, "many of the changes are taking place at the last minute."

The cancelled flights are on European and Far Eastern routes as well as Air India's lucrative Gulf sector. The airline is attempting to put angry passengers on flights of other airlines to the same destinations – and losing a lot of money in the bargain – but officials admit their helplessness in doing this satisfactorily on account of the sheer magnitude of the problem. "We just cannot cope this time," said an official resingnedly.

The following is the list of flights cancelled between July 9 and July 22. This was provided sources Air India's main reservation office at the Jeevan Bharti Building in New Delhi.

July 9: AI 428, AI 455, AI 811/810, AI 115/A.

July 10: AI 855, AI 852, AI 132A, AI 434/435.

July 11: AI 412A/103.

July 12: AI 863/862, AI 823/822.

July 13: AI 865, AI 165.

July 14: AI 876/87, AI 886/887, AI 129, AI 817/816, AI 804/807, AI 824.

July 15: AI 888/889, AI 128.

July 16: AI 408/415, AI 811.

July 17: —

July 18/19: AI 132A, AI 412A.

July 20: AI 865, AI 825/824.

July 21: AI 817/816.

July 22: AI 818.

Source: *Indian Express* 12 July 1988

Booking a ticket in India itself can be a somewhat painful experience, because the regional IA offices are sometimes chaotic and disorganized. Delhi, for instance, has always been a complete shambles when I've visited it to buy a ticket, whereas the Madras office is clean, efficient, and has helpful staff. It is no good trying to provide a guide to good IA offices, because the situation can change rapidly; and more and more regional offices are being modernized and going on-line. Remember that not all IA offices are on-line, and that if you try to book a ticket, make a cancellation, or reconfirm through one of these, you will have to wait while telexes go back and forth; it is a little reminiscent of the State Bank of India, and you would be advised to avoid IA offices in small towns if at all possible. Travel agents and the travel services of good hotels will, of course, relieve you of the agony of appearing in person at an IA office by making your booking for you.

Cancellations   Cancellation rules are as follows: forty-eight hours or more before the flight, a nominal Rs20 is charged; less than forty-eight hours but more than twenty-four, 10 per cent of the basic fare; less than twenty-four hours before flight but more than one hour, 25 per cent of the basic fare; and less than one hour, 100 per cent. The last also applies to those passengers who simply fail to show up; they will not receive a refund. No cancellation charges are levied against IA international services, or against domestic services when the ticket has been purchased on the dollar tariff. Furthermore, you will find it extremely difficult, if not impossible, to obtain a refund/replacement for lost tickets. Treat IA tickets very carefully, and don't lose them.

The cancellation charges are not as ferocious as they might appear, because they do not apply to that part of the fare called the 'fuel surcharge'; the latter accounts for a substantial part of the price of IA tickets. Nonetheless, cancellation at the last minute can still be expensive, as can the loss of your tickets.

Fares   IA fares are high; a single flight from Madras to Delhi, for example, on the dollar tariff, is around

$160 US. Short flights can be expensive too; it is a mistake to become locked into the IA system, as many tourists seem to do, and to ignore the alternatives – especially the trains, to be discussed in the next section. Many tourists, for example, fly from Madras to the temple city of Madurai, about 460 km to the south. This has always seemed to me to be a shame, because on the Superfast Vagai Express, from Madras Egmore to Madurai Junction, you have a wonderful seven-hour ride through some beautiful country; you actually get to see something of India apart from other tourists and airports. Don't be frightened of the trains (see next section), and don't allow yourself to become locked into IA to the exclusion of everything else.

If you have purchased IA tickets outside India, you should reconfirm your bookings at an IA office on arrival in the country. Snacks and meals are served on IA flights, but no alcoholic drinks are available. Breakfast is served from 07.00 to 08.40, lunch from 13.00 to 14.15, and dinner from 20.00 to 21.45. Hot meals are usually served on jets, because these travel the longer routes, while snacks only are served on the turboprops. The catering is not particularly good, even by the generally low standards of other airlines; usually there will be a choice of vegetarian and non-vegetarian meals, and foreigners who do not express a preference will get non-veg.

IA has a number of low fare packages for tourists. These are: 'Discover India', 21 days' unlimited economy class travel over the entire domestic network, for $400 US; 'Tour India', 14 days of economy class travel, limited to a maximum of six flights, for $300 US; 'India Wonderfares', 7 days of economy class travel on either the north, south, east, or west sectors, for $200 US; 'South India Excursion', which offers a 30 per cent discount on the dollar tariff for certain flights on the southern sector; and 'Youth Fares', offering a 25 per cent discount on the dollar tariff for those between the ages of twelve and thirty. These concessions are available only to foreigners or Indians resident abroad.

By train I must confess to an unqualified love for Indian
Railways; for me, as for many other travellers, it is
the way to see India. The long journeys, the chance
acquaintances, the railway stations at night, the long,
warning wail of the trains' sirens as you lie in your
sleeping berth . . . and the names, the 'Frontier Mail',
'Rajdhani Express', the 'Malabar' and 'Coramandel'
Expresses that ply the west and east coasts respectively; they are irresistible! There are many over-
worked clichés about the 'travel experiences' that
India offers, but I must say that anyone who, while
visiting India, omits to take at least one long train
journey has missed something unforgettable.

Of course train travel is not all romance and
wonderful scenery; sometimes it is boring,
uncomfortable, and grossly inconvenient. Trains in
India never go very fast at the best of times, and
often they stand still for ages, apparently in the
middle of open country, far from even a small village.
Your fellow passengers will explain this in various
ways; 'Sir, I am sorry; it is the monkeys, they change
the signals. They will send a fellow to see to it.' Or
'There is some agitation in the next station. We are
waiting for the agitation to stop.' Or 'The rains have
washed the bridges away. We shall be here for some
days.'

Usually none of these explanations appears to be
correct, but rarely do you ever find out why the
train has stopped. Yet in spite of all this, travelling
by train is certainly the best way to see the country
and meet the people. After a few hours in a
compartment with your Indian travelling companions, you will know all about their jobs, their
homes, and their families, and they will know all
about yours. You'll be told where to stay in the next
town (or wherever else you're going), you'll even be
given addresses and receive invitations. Then there
are the notices; 'All passengers are responsible for
their own carriages. Attend them and beware of bag
lifters', 'Please endeavour not to dirty the seats with
eatables', not to mention the gnomic message on a
fairly remote station in Karnataka, 'Due to some
unforeseen circumstances, the municipal water supply

will not be there. All passengers are requested to allow for this.' My favourite, however, is the stark and somewhat alarming advice offered to drivers not far from Jammu; at the end of a long slope, there is a notice that states 'Drivers should bring their trains back under control.'

Unless you have unlimited time, or are travelling on a fairly tight budget, the best way to explore India is by a judicious mixture of train and air travel. The railway system is quite complicated, and to use it conveniently it is helpful to be aware of the following facts. First of all, there are two classes, first and second. Subtle variations on the basic classes create what are in effect five classes, air-conditioned first, first, air-conditioned chair class, air-conditioned two tier, and second. There are then different categories of train, Mails, Expresses, Superfast, and Passenger. Oddly enough, what you don't want (if you want to actually get somewhere rather than just sit on a train for an indefinite period) is a Passenger train. Passenger trains are often second class only, and if they are day trains, they are the ultimate horror of the Indian Railways, *unreserved second class*. The latter is everything that you might have imagined about Indian train travel from travellers' tall stories. You find that they weren't tall stories at all; there really are limbless cripples up in the luggage racks, cooking fires are kindled in the lavatories, and people really do heave on the communication cord when they're close to home. Undivided Hindu families (that is, parents plus married children) pile out of the carriage ('bogie') and make their way across the paddies with what look like their worldly goods on their heads. The Mails and Expresses are much faster, and stop less frequently. Also, they carry more upper class accommodation.

Finally, there are three gauges, broad, metre, and narrow. The last is of little importance, being confined to a few mountain routes such as the 'toy' train up to Darjeeling, and the similar train from Mettupalayam (near Coimbatore) to Ootacamund in the Nilgiri Hills. All trunk routes have a broad gauge

The railway system

service, while the metre gauge lines tend to be feeders. Broad gauge trains (if you have a choice) are usually faster and more comfortable than the metre gauge ones. The whole network – broad, metre, and narrow gauge – is divided into nine zones as shown in the table.

Zones	Headquarters	Route length (km)
Central	Bombay Victoria	6,371
Eastern	Calcutta	4,238
Northern	New Delhi	10,975
North Eastern	Gorakhpur	5,163
North East Frontier	Maligaon	3,580
Southern	Madras	6,701
South Central	Secunderabad	7,023
South Eastern	Calcutta	7,041
Western	Bombay Churchgate	10,293

Indian Railways is the second largest network in the world, with over 11,000 trains running per day. It is being modernized, but much of the rolling stock – especially that of the lower classes – is very old and extremely uncomfortable. Computerized booking services have been introduced in the major cities, which has had a dramatic effect on the huge queues that used to be the curse of any railway booking office. Furthermore, an extensive electrification scheme is under way, and new designs of rolling stock are being introduced, such as the Pullman-style coaches of some of the Superfast Expresses (like the Vagai between Madras and Madurai), and the double-decker cars on some long routes.

Making a reservation Once you have decided where you want to go, and upon what train, you have to buy a ticket and, if possible, make a reservation. *Always* travel reserved if you can; on some trains, reservation is mandatory, and on others, like the daytime Passenger trains, no reservations are taken. You literally fight not just for a seat, but merely to get into the second class coaches.

The rules for reservation are as follows; reservation is compulsory for travel between 21.00 and 06.00 in upper class accommodation; that is, in anything but ordinary second class. Reservations can be made for daytime travel, but not for journeys of under 260 km unless the train is one upon which all passengers must have reservations. These are trains such as the Superfast Expresses, which are all second class but, with new rolling stock, very comfortable (relative, that is, to what second class usually inflicts upon your body). Second class accommodation can also be reserved, of course, on the Mails and Expresses, many of which make overnight journeys.

Advance reservation facilities are available at many Indian railway stations; reservations can be made up to ninety days in advance, except for some trains where there is a maximum of ten days. Foreigners may reserve (usually through a travel agent) in advance up to 360 days. The reservation system works as follows: each station has a quota of seats or berths allocated to it, which may be reserved by passengers applying at that reservation office. The number of seats or berths in a station's quota depends, of course, on how important the station is; a small town station may well not have a quota at all for an express which passes through. To complicate this further, there isn't a single quota, there are quotas for different classes of humanity; there are VIP quotas, foreign tourists' quotas, a thing called the station master's quota, and so on.

In most stations, there is a board above the reservation desk which indicates the availability of seats and berths on the major trains that pass through or originate at that station. Even when these are apparently showing that no accommodation is available, don't despair; there is always a chance that because you're a foreign tourist some quota will magically open up to you. I have found this to be especially true when I've had an India Rail pass, which is discussed below; the ease with which you can make reservations at short notice, on major routes, is one of the main advantages of the pass.

Actually making the reservation is easy, once you've got to the desk; there are often huge queues, even for the upper class accommodation. It is expected that you will have filled in an application form for the reservation *before* you approach the window; these forms are usually obtained from the enquiry desk. You should know what date you want to travel, and make sure that you've correctly identified the number of your train (they all have numbers allocated to them – these will be displayed on the 'Train Timings', that is, the arrival and departure board), and the class you want. Not every train carries all the five classes; air-conditioned (A/C) first class cars will be carried on most trunk routes, but not minor ones (a good reason for not bothering with the A/C first class rail pass – see below). Similarly, a train might carry the rather spartan ordinary first class sleepers, instead of the air-conditioned first class or air-conditioned two tier cars. Check that the accommodation you want is available on the train you intend to use. Reservation costs are nominal. There are no additional charges levied for sleeping berths in first class, but there are for second; again, for most tourists, these are nominal compared with the cost of the ticket.

Accommodation on trunk routes tends to be heavily booked well in advance; unless you can break into a quota, you might find that a last-minute reservation is unsuccessful. Also, some routes are heavily used during certain seasons – for example, there is an exodus from Delhi up to Kashmir during the hot season, which means that the trains to Jammu are packed solid. It is important to book as far ahead as possible. Remember that any station from which a train is starting will have a very generous quota of berths, while a smaller station, through which a train is passing, will not. As mentioned above, the India Rail Pass appears to give you a much better chance of obtaining a reservation, and booking clerks seem to go out of their way to help pass holders.

Catering Snacks and meals are served on most trains. Furthermore, whenever the train stops, it will be mobbed by the vendors who crowd most Indian stations; there is never any difficulty in getting something to eat. Some of the food will be very unpalatable; blackened, fly-covered bunches of bananas, soggy vegetable cutlets in greasy newspapers, and so on. Nonetheless, you will always find something, even if it is just biscuits and chocolate.

The catering on the crack trains, such as the Rajdhani that runs between New Delhi, Bombay, and Calcutta, can almost be described as lavish in the upper classes.

Most long-distance trains have pantry cars, and reserved coaches have attendants who care for the passengers' needs during the journey. The standard of hygiene in the pantry cars is never very high, and a few precautions are advisable; never eat anything that isn't very hot and obviously freshly cooked, and when you are offered the choice of vegetarian or non-vegetarian meals, choose the former; the meat is tasteless and stringy, especially the chicken.

Always treat drinking water with suspicion. The tea and coffee are safe (usually), but if you ask the car attendant to refill a water bottle, *always* add a purification tablet to it before drinking; I have become ill through drinking the water provided in first class, which the attendant swore blind was pure and safe. Finally, if you are travelling a long distance, it's probably a good idea to bring as much water with you as you can; bottled mineral waters are safe, and make a welcome change from the sweet tea and coffee, or the sickly sweet soft drinks, that you can buy on the train.

In theory, first class passengers should have bed rolls, as should those in the air-conditioned two tier sleepers. There are often not enough to go round, so it is useful to have a sheet sleeping bag. Air-conditioned cars can become very cold indeed at night. In principle you can book your bed roll, which consists of two sheets, a blanket, and a pillow, in advance; to do this you must obtain a slip from the functionary usually known as the deputy station superintendent; but often bed rolls are simply not available.

The different classes

Air-conditioned first class cars are comparatively luxurious; they have recently been revamped on many routes, as the railways try to compete for passengers with Indian Airlines. There are even proposals to install refrigerators and vending machines for coffee, tea, chocolate, and cigarettes; this is unlikely to attract business travellers back to the railways. This class of coach carries accommodation for twenty-six passengers, and is provided with attendants and special catering facilities. They are divided into compartments for up to four people; during the day, the sleeping berths fold into seats.

Ordinary first class is being progressively replaced with air-conditioned two tier cars, which are nominally second class, but which are in fact very comfortable. The old ordinary first class is to be found on many metre gauge lines; the coaches are divided into compartments, there is no air-conditioning, but there are fans – which may or may not work; sometimes the fans have been stolen.

Air-conditioned two tier is probably the best class to choose if you are seeking a compromise between cost and comfort; the A/C two tier cars have semi-private compartments, with a curtain (not a door) between them and the narrow corridor. In these compartments, the seats fold to provide four sleeping berths; on the other side of the corridor, there are pairs of facing seats that provide two sleeping berths at night (one above the other). There is a car attendant and catering facilities are provided. A/C two tier is very popular, and can be heavily booked for days in advance. The main drawbacks of this class are the toilet facilities, which can be dirty and primitive; lavatory paper is usually not provided, even when there is an 'Asian style' and a 'Western style' lavatory; make sure you have your own. Sometimes there is no water in the lavatories either, so cleaning your teeth and washing your hands can be a problem. This is another reason for bringing a decent water supply with you.

Air-conditioned chair cars are perhaps the most variable of the classes; sometimes these can be quite luxurious, sometimes they are dirty and

uncomfortable. The air-conditioning is usually provided by fans, which, as in ordinary first class, may
or may not be there, let alone working. The cars are
like Pullmans, with pairs of seats separated by a
central aisle. The seats are not facing, but are arranged
as in an airliner. In the better cars, these are very
comfortable indeed, and can be reclined; there is a
little folding table in front of you, and you can
actually sleep without too much discomfort.
In the more degenerate cars, the seats are hard, with
head-rests like concrete, and the reclining mechanisms
long broken.

Second class sleepers come in two kinds, two and
three tier. They are very uncomfortable, noisy,
dusty, wet, and hot or cold, depending on the
season. This class of sleeper is for those who choose
to rough it, or who are travelling on a tight budget;
there is also a much higher risk of theft, either in
the crowds who mill round the cars at the beginning
of the journey, or during the journey itself. The two
tier sleepers have the advantage that they're usually
padded; the three tiers are wooden boards. Opinions
differ on the relative merits of these two types; in
three tier, all the seats fold into sleeping berths, so
at least everyone has to go to sleep at the same time.
The car attendant does the same job as his counterpart
in the upper classes, and stops anyone without a
reservation getting in once the seats have been folded
into berths. In two tier, there are still ordinary seats
below the sleeping berths, and people get in and out
and make loud noises with unwieldy items of luggage
in the middle of the night – Indians never seem to
travel without at least one huge tin trunk and a
collection of cooking vessels, all of which make
shattering noises when dropped on the floor of your
compartment. On balance, three tier is probably
more restful if you've brought something to lie on.

Ordinary second class day coaches are primitive and
uncomfortable. They are divided into compartments,
and have hard wooden seats; the number of people
that can be accommodated in the unreserved cars is
simply as many as can be crammed in. A long
journey by unreserved second class is hellish – think

very carefully before doing this. On some routes –
for example, the six-hour journey between Mysore
and Hassan – there is no choice but to travel in this
class; but while short journeys of six to twelve hours
are tolerable, longer ones are not. You will arrive at
your destination half-crippled, with your clothes
filthy, and very out of love with India.

Finally, there are some special second class trains
that are fast and very comfortable; these carry
redesigned second class coaches that are like British
Rail intercity accommodation. Reservation is compulsory on these services.

Guides, maps
and
timetables

To help you find your way around the Indian railway
network, there are a number of publications including
guides, maps, and timetables. The TTK *Map and
Guide to India's Railways* is quite helpful, and can
be bought at most bookshops for Rs9. Local and
regional timetables can be purchased at most railway
stations for a few rupees, but perhaps most useful is
Trains at a Glance; this is not a comprehensive
national timetable, but includes all the fast trains on
trunk routes, and is invaluable if you are planning
a tour by train.

The stations in the major cities have tourist railway
guides (people, not publications), who are almost
always extremely helpful and efficient; they will
advise you on which train to take (you can even say
vaguely 'I want to visit the temple at so-and-so', and
a train will be suggested, with times and dates), and
help you make a booking. New Delhi and Madras
Central stations not only have tourist guides, they
also have booking offices for the sole use of foreign
tourists.

Rail passes

A number of concessionary tickets are available on
Indian Railways, but the most important is the India
Rail Pass. Unless you travel large distances in a short
time, it is probably cheaper to buy ordinary tickets;
however, the Rail Pass has so many other advantages
that it really is worth having. The prices in US
dollars (August 1988) are shown in the table.

Holders of rail passes definitely receive more

Validity (days)	First A/C	First	Second
7	190	95	45
15	230	115	55
21	280	140	65
30	350	175	75
60	520	260	115
90	690	345	150

attention from railway staff, especially booking staff, than other foreign travellers. There always seems to be some quota that opens to you, and I have rarely failed to obtain a sleeping berth (even at quite short notice) when I've produced the pass. It also entitles you to use all station facilities, such as the reserved waiting rooms and the retiring rooms. Railway retiring rooms are discussed in more detail in 'Hotels and other accommodation'; they are very useful places to stay in an emergency.

The first class pass is probably the most sensible purchase; the trouble with air-conditioned first class is that it is very expensive, and of course not all trains carry that class of accommodation. With the first class pass, you can travel in the chair cars and two tier A/C sleepers; you can also use the first class waiting rooms for reserved passengers. Second class passes are not really worth buying; you might as well buy the tickets as you go. The last advantage of any pass, of course, is that it is also a journey ticket; you don't have to join the long queues at the ticket counters, you can get straight onto your train.

Rail passes can be obtained at New Delhi station, Bombay Victoria and Bombay Churchgate, Calcutta, Madras Central (they are not issued at Madras Egmore), Hyderabad, Secunderabad, and Bangalore. Only foreign tourists or non-resident Indians may purchase the passes, and payment must be in foreign exchange.

Fares

Fares on Indian Railways have increased substantially during the last ten years; air-conditioned first class is actually more expensive than Indian Airlines on some sectors. The fares in all classes are calculated on a distance basis (that is, a certain rate per km), with a minimum for short distances. There are different scales for each class, and for Mails/Expresses and Passenger trains; the latter are somewhat cheaper.

A detailed fare list seems pointless, because it would so rapidly go out of date. However, to give some idea of A/C two tier costs, the fares are worked out on a basis of about Rs6 for every ten km. Air-conditioned first class is about double this, air-conditioned chair class about half, and ordinary second about a quarter.

The timetables include distances for every route, so that it is easy to work out an approximate fare for a particular journey. Note that the rate per km decreases with distance.

By bus   The Indian bus network is all too often ignored, except by budget travellers. Fares are very low relative to the trains, but passengers pay for this in terms of discomfort, fear, and outright physical danger. The roads in India are one of the country's major health hazards, and Indian drivers must be amongst the most reckless in the world. Worst of all are the truck drivers, closely followed by the bus drivers; last of all come the car drivers who, because their vehicles are more vulnerable in head-on collisions, have to be a little more careful.

It is possible to travel over the whole of India by bus; there are both state-run and privately run bus companies, and routes are both short- and long-distance. The private firms are very easy to find, because their advertising is prominent and aggressive; in fact, areas of certain towns appear to be almost taken over by private tour operators; Janpath Road in New Delhi, opposite Egmore Station in Madras, the street near the bus station in Bangalore – you can't miss them. Many of the operators also have representatives in the middle range hotels that are patronized by small time Indian business men (see 'Hotels and accommodation').

You can make reservations for long-distance

journeys, especially those that involve overnight travel. Some bus stations in major towns (Bangalore, for example) have even introduced computerized booking, and are extremely efficient; but to make up for this, others are a complete shambles. Madras is a notorious example, where the state bus stand is actually an open sewer, and the Tirruvallur (the privately run bus company in Tamil Nadu) bus station across the road little better. In the southern states, notably Kerala and Tamil Nadu, and to a lesser extent Karnataka, the bus timetables are often in the local language only. After some effort, Hindi bus timetables can be mastered, but the southern languages present problems; Tamil has an alphabet with over two hundred characters.

There are many categories of bus in India, and they are somewhat like the categories of school encountered by Paul Pennyfeather in *Decline and Fall*. There were very good schools, good schools, and simply schools; the scholastic agency through which Pennyfeather was trying to get a job advised him that 'school is pretty bad'. The same applies to Indian buses, for you'll find super-luxury buses, luxury buses, and buses. Buses, like schools, are pretty bad, and this puts the other two categories in perspective.

Categories and seating

The ordinary buses used by the state-owned companies are usually very dilapidated and uncomfortable; they can also become very crowded. Large items of luggage, like rucksacks, have to go on the rack on the roof. If possible, try to load your luggage yourself, because then you can make sure that the tarpaulin has been pulled over it, and that no heavy tin trunks, dead goats etc. have been laid on top of it.

Luxury buses run by private companies usually have pairs of reclining seats, with head-rests, separated by a central aisle. The crew is housed in a separate compartment at the front of the bus, connected to the main cabin by a small door; it is like a small airliner. In such buses, your comfort (or discomfort) won't really be affected by sitting at the front, middle, or back of the bus (although sitting over the back axle can be bad – few Indian buses seem to have any suspension). The state buses are more spartan, and 'luxury' might mean that the seats just have head-rests; otherwise the vehicle is just as degenerate and uncomfortable as the non-luxury ones.

These state buses have seats up next to the driver – *never* sit in them. There is nothing between you and the oncoming traffic except a sheet of cracked perspex, and your nerves will suffer. When the radiator boils, it is you who will be covered with a stream of scalding water, and when the driver tries to pour more into the vent, probably from an old paint pot, it is you who gets splashed with muddy ditch-water. It is your feet and luggage that get burned by the overheated engine just beneath you, and it is your head that would be the first to hit anything in one of the many head-on collisions that seem inevitable. It is best for the nerves and the back to sit somewhere near the middle.

Be warned that this is not a trivial piece of advice. Sitting on the front seat of a bus, coming down the ghat road from the Kodaikanal hill station, was one of the most terrifying experiences of my life. All that I could wish for, after about ten minutes of swerving near drops, and skidding round jeeps and cars coming the other way, was a quick death. It would be so unpleasant to have to join the ranks of limbless cripples who travel in luggage racks.

Short journeys

For short journeys, tickets are always bought on the bus, from a conductor; I have always found the conductors of the country buses extremely friendly and helpful, and they can often speak English. Fares are not only low, they are often a strange number of rupees and paise, and this exaggerates the universal problem of finding change in India. The conductors don't start with a float of change, and so if you proffer a ten rupee note for a Rs6.75 fare, the chances are that he will not be able to give you change. Don't despair! Your ticket will be endorsed with the amount owed to you, and you'll receive it from the conductor at the end of your journey, by which time he will have accumulated enough small coins. Conductors are generally very honest about this.

Finding a seat on a bus is difficult when there is no advance booking; if the service starts from the place where you are catching the bus, then you stand some chance if you are prepared to fight your way on. For a service that has started somewhere else, and is passing through, your chances are more slender, because the bus might arrive completely full. In some places you can buy what's known as a priority ticket, which in theory means that you are allowed to board the bus ahead of anyone who is without one. Some guidebooks make a great fuss about these tickets, but I've never known conductors to take the slightest notice of them.

Services are usually very frequent, and you'll often find that a country bus route has arrivals every half hour or so; if you can't get on the first bus that comes along, you can always wait for the next one and hope for the best. Don't try to be polite, and don't hesitate to push and shove your way on, because all the Indians do, and if you are too delicate to behave like this yourself, you could be left at the roadside for ever. I remember seeing a crowd of Indians literally fighting to board a bus in Madurai; a woman was elbowed in the face by a hefty man as she tried to push her way up the steps, and no one gave this even a second glance. It's everyone for themselves, and you have to behave in the same way or be left behind.

Long journeys

For longer journeys, especially overnight, tickets have to be booked in advance; this can mean anything from days before the journey to a few hours. The bus stations in fairly large towns always have an advance booking office. As with the railways, the only problem in doing this is that you are likely to have to queue for a long time.

If you are making a long journey, the state-run buses are best avoided. To take an example, during my last trip to India, I ill-advisedly took a Karnataka

State Transport bus from Panjim in Goa to Mysore, a fourteen-hour, overnight journey. The bus was optimistically described as 'luxury' at the bus station, but it was a rusty old wreck with the usual hard seats and feeble internal lighting. The driver was more reckless than usual, and succeeded in demolishing the bus stand at Harwar, and running over a stray dog at Arsikere; there were two very long halts to replace headlamps broken by flying stones. Few Indian roads are well surfaced, but those between Panjim and Mysore were particularly bad; I had the feeling of being thrown through a black tunnel of pain and terror, at great speed. Therefore, if you are contemplating a long bus journey by a particular service, you'd be sensible to visit the bus station to see the service departing before you commit yourself, just to see how bad the vehicle you'll be travelling in is.

The private bus companies provide a much more comfortable service for long journeys; a variety of vehicles are used, from air-conditioned coaches to 'luxury' buses. Most of them are in a far better state of repair, and much more pleasant to travel in, than the vehicles used by the state-run companies.

The one drawback of these services is that almost all of them are what are known as video coaches, and Indian video coaches can be torture; all through the night you will be subjected to a series of excruciatingly violent Hindi or Tamil movies, hours and hours of chaste love, indescribably bloody revenges, dacoits (bandits) looting and pillaging apparently impregnable fortresses, and trains plunging into ravines with great loss of life. It's all exciting stuff, but six or seven hours of it, delivered at such a volume that the speakers above your head are distorting, are somewhat trying.

Fares The overwhelming advantage of buses is the low fares. For instance, to get a taxi from Madurai to the hill station of Kodaikanal costs Rs400; the bus is Rs12.50. Fares on the private buses are more than those on the state-run services, but are still much cheaper than upper class train travel. Also, buses provide services where there is no through train – from Delhi to Srinagar in Kashmir, for example. The trains only run to Jammu, where you have to go on by bus anyway; a through bus from Delhi, with one of the many private operators who have offices in Janpath, costs about Rs220 on a video coach. Sometimes the bus system is more convenient than the trains, especially on the popular Goa to Bombay route; the train journey is long and boring, with a whole day's journey down to Miraj, then an overnight train journey from Miraj to Goa.

Madras to Madurai by video coach (a distance of 461 km) costs Rs75, and is Rs55 by state bus; to give an idea of the relative cost of bus and train travel, the 336-km journey from Trichy to Madras costs Rs205 in A/C two tier and only Rs48 on a video coach.

Problems

Beware of the self-styled 'coolies' and luggage loaders who infest many bus stations; they will take your bags almost by force, then try to charge you ludicrous sums of money for roughly throwing them on top of the bus's luggage rack. The charge for stowing luggage should never be more than one or two rupees, and the rates are often displayed (in English) somewhere in the bus station. If you are on a state bus, check your luggage on the roof at the stops.

Both state and private buses make rest stops, often at the roadside dhabbas (the Indian equivalent of a transport cafe or truck stop), and all the men line up for a companionable pee – women travellers should note that things can be quite difficult for them, for Indian lady travellers appear to suspend their bodily functions while in transit. If you are unwell, especially if you have diarrhoea, beware of long bus journeys; you will not find any decent or hygienic lavatories en route.

A further word of advice; at rest stops, keep an eye on the driver, because while on some occasions he will vanish for hours, on others he will pee beside the road, clamber back into the bus, and drive off, in spite of having said 'Ten minutes, ten minutes, please ease yourselves.' It is frustrating, not to say inconvenient, to see the bus vanishing up the road while you are still squatting in the grass or behind a tree, easing yourself.

Organized tours

Apart from scheduled services, there are also tour buses, some of which are run by the Indian Tourist Development Corporation. These can be both good value and a welcome change from the endless queuing and booking that is your lot when you are fending for yourself. There are far too many such tours to give a detailed list here, but a few examples will illustrate what is available.

An organized coach party from New Delhi to Agra (including meals, and guided tours of the Taj Mahal and the Red Fort) costs Rs250 per person. The tour lasts for a whole day, starting out at seven in the morning and returning to New Delhi by about nine at night. The Mysore Tourist Corporation organizes tours that include the Hoysala temples at Belur and Halebed, and a visit to the great Jain shrine at Sravanabelgola; this costs Rs75 per person, and is again an all-day trip. The drawback of most of these organized tours is that they try to cram far too much into too short a time, and this can be very frustrating; the tour to Sravanabelgola is a case in point, and before you buy a ticket for such a tour, look carefully at the map and try to work out how much time you'll spend on the bus, and how much time you'll spend actually looking at Jain shrines or the Taj Mahal. *Don't* ask the people who sell the tickets, they'll tell you anything.

Finding tour operators is easy, because they advertise very conspicuously, and often have someone at the door of their shabby cubby-holes of offices soliciting passers by. Reliable tours will always be recommended by government of India or state tourist offices. This is helpful, because making a choice on the basis of tour operators' advertisements can be difficult. Akbar Travels, of Kodaikanal, attract custom as follows; 'In God we trust inviting you to join daily conducted tours and packace [sic] tours for discover natural beauties. Luch brake. We also assit Air, Rail & Bus tickets booking. Thanking you. Allah is the light of the heaven and the earth.' Who could resist?

Given the discomfort, the poor roads, and the appalling driving, the buses are something of a last resort for many travellers; train travel is more comfortable and less trying on the nerves, but don't ignore the bus system.

By car

There are no self-drive car hire facilities in India. Car hire means that not only do you hire the vehicle, you hire a driver as well. If you want to drive yourself, you can of course buy a car; and you may drive it if you obtain third party insurance and hold an international driving licence.

Driving yourself

Most road users in India are wildly aggressive and reckless, and the road conditions are appalling; not only are the roads along even major or trunk routes poorly surfaced and full of potholes, but they are filled with a solid mass of traffic, from the ubiquitous, creaking bullock carts to the great Tata trucks belching out clouds of black exhaust. The Indian government has never thought it worthwhile to publish anything like the Highway Code, for the rules of the road are but one; give way to the largest vehicle in the middle of the road. This is supplemented by a few secondary maxims, such as always shoot a red light, never change gear when turning a corner, and always try, if possible, to overtake on the inside. Driving in India can be very nerve-wracking, and don't take it lightly; at least have no illusions about what you're in for if you decide to do it.

There is a pecking order on the Indian highways. As outlined earlier, at the top are the truck drivers; next come the buses, followed by private cars. All of these persecute the miserable three-wheeler autorickshaws, and the latter can only persecute the utterly wretched bicycle rickshaws. The only way the bicycle rickshaws can assert themselves is by trying to run over unwary pedestrians.

If you drive in India, you must be prepared to keep your hand on the horn and to be as aggressive as everyone else; if you don't, you could well cause an accident! No one ever seems to be prepared for sane or courteous driving, and to give way throws other drivers into utter confusion; they really don't know how to take such wild eccentricity.

The three main types of vehicle available are the Ambassador, a licence-built version of the old British Morris Oxford, the Premier, a licence-built version of the Fiat 1100 cc, in vogue in Europe in the early sixties, and the new hatchback, the Maruti-Suzuki. The latter is fast replacing the older makes, although the Hindustan Ambassador and the Premier are the most common private cars on the Indian roads. Maruti also produce minibuses, which have become quite popular; there are others, like the Matador, which vaguely resembles the Volkswagen bus. Tata, the huge industrial corporation which makes (with Ashok Leyland) India's trucks and buses, plans to bring out a US-style pick-up truck and a wagon. Finally, there are a number of imported cars, especially Mercedes of various sorts, which are definitely status symbols for the very wealthy.

Car repair and maintenance in India are expensive, you can drive for long distances in rural areas without coming across a petrol (gas) station, and your nerves will suffer. All things considered, it is probably better to hire a car and a driver, for a short or long term, rather than try to drive yourself – unless, of course, you want the adventure.

The AAI and the roads   There is an Automobile Association of India (AAI), which has offices in the major cities, provides first class maps and advice, and has membership treaties with many foreign motoring organizations. It also provides free information and a breakdown service for the cars and motorcycles of members; though how well the latter actually works in rural India is another story. The AAI also provides limited accommodation for travelling motorists in major cities.

The primary road network of India is the system of National Highways; these are not as grand as they sound, and some of them are in a very poor state. They account for only about 2 per cent of the total road length in India, but carry about 33 per cent of the total traffic – which gives some idea of how congested they can be. The National Highways are numbered – National Highway 1, for example, runs north-west from Delhi up to Jalandhar, National Highway 2 runs from Delhi to Calcutta; both of these are part of the old Grand Trunk route of the Raj days.

As mentioned earlier, car hire also means hiring a driver. This is a mixed blessing, because although the driver has the problem of dealing with the Indian traffic, you have the problem of dealing with the driver. On journeys with overnight stops, the driver is supposed to find his own accommodation and to fend for himself; the deal you have with the hire firm may or may not include his subsistence, and it is here that the problem of tipping can arise. The advice of the Government of India tourist office in New Delhi illustrates this; recommended hire cars cost Rs2.50 per km (Rs3.50 for air-conditioned cars), with an overnight retention fee of Rs100 on the vehicle. The question of the driver's upkeep then arises; is it included in the price? No, but if you like the driver then you can give him a good tip – about Rs100 per night if he is a good driver, sir. This is typical of the awkward and difficult situations concerning money and tipping that you'll encounter over and over again in India; whether your driver is good or not, he'll expect a tip, and he'll probably become sour and unco-operative if one isn't forthcoming. This can make a long car journey very unpleasant. A generous subsistence rate for the driver would be somewhere between Rs30 and Rs50 per day, but if you are a foreigner, something higher will be expected. The driver will not hesitate to show his disappointment.

Car hire

If you have the money, travelling by car can be a very pleasant way of exploring India; some guide-books dismiss it for no better reason (it seems) than inverted snobbery. Good hotels (not just the five stars – see the next chapter) can usually recommend a hire service, as can the Government of India tourist offices. Note that hiring through the latter will often be more expensive than hiring through the smaller hotels. If your journey takes you across state boundaries, a surcharge might be added to the basic hire costs to cover state taxes imposed on vehicles at the border.

By taxi Most of the larger cities have metered taxis. There are two problems with this. One is getting the driver to use the meter in the first place – 'Morning time is not a meter time, sir', 'Raining time is not a meter time, sir', 'Evening time is not a meter time, sir' and so on; the times that *are* meter times seem to be very infrequent. The second is that the meters are usually out of date anyway, so the fare you pay is considerably in excess of the meter reading. All drivers of metered cabs should, in theory, carry a conversion card which is available for inspection by passengers. This often remains a theory. The cards are hardly ever shown on request, and it is helpful to have some idea of what the surcharge on the meter reading should be. This changes so rapidly, and differs so much from one city to another, that there is little point in trying to give a list; check at a state or government tourist office. In August 1988, the surcharges in Delhi were running at around 15 per cent, while those in Bombay were a huge 300 per cent.

Metered cabs are black, with yellow roofs; those that aren't are 'tourist taxis', are not metered, and can be much more expensive; they really come into the category of hire cars, but can be better for sightseeing. If you want to hire a car for city tours, ask for advice at a tourist office. Cabs with reliable drivers can usually be found at hotels; New Delhi is the only Indian city where you can phone for a cab. In Calcutta the cabs aren't metered, and the fare is calculated on either a time or a distance basis, depending on which one is most to the driver's advantage.

By autorickshaw These strange little three-wheeled vehicles, also known as scooters, are powered by two-stroke engines, have seats for two or three passengers, have drivers who all seem to be petty crooks (except for the notorious 'Auto' Shankar of Madras, who made the big time by strangling his fares with a towel), and are noisy and uncomfortable. On the plus side, they are easy to find, cost only about half of what a cab would for the same journey, and are good at weaving through densely packed traffic. Occasionally, of course, one sees an autorickshaw that has come to grief beneath the wheels of a large bus or truck, but you just have to hang on and hope for the best. It is often more difficult to get auto drivers to use their meters than it is to persuade the cab drivers to do the same; indeed, during rush hours, and early or late in the day, or if you are at a disadvantage (if it is raining, for example), you'll find it impossible. Then you will have to negotiate a fare.

Never accept the first figure that the driver suggests, because you can be sure that it is ludicrously inflated; haggle, even make as if to walk away. Sometimes the driver will go away too, but often he'll shout, 'No, no, friend, master, come, come, what will you give, sir?' This means that real negotiations can begin.

If you have some idea of the distance you want to go, it is easy to work out roughly what the true (metered) fare should be; most autos have the rates painted on the metal plate behind the driver's seat, and this will be a basic hire charge of about Rs2 or Rs3, then a charge of about Rs1 to Rs1-50 for every additional kilometre after the first. If you do have to negotiate a fare, it's obviously up to you to decide on what you'll accept as a reasonable compromise. Sometimes you will have the shock of finding a driver who flags the meter without your even asking; after some time in India, this can strike you as utterly bizarre, even frightening; you feel that there must be something wrong with the man. I always make a point of giving generous tips to those few drivers who use their meters without a struggle.

If you have a bad time with auto drivers, walk away from areas that are obviously associated with tourists; for instance, in Connaught Circle, in New

Delhi, there is a class of drivers who prey upon the many tourists who congregate there. Few of these will ever ask for a reasonable fare; if, however, you walk a comparatively short distance away, you'll find less rapacious drivers, some of whom will flag the meter without an argument. This applies to every city or town throughout the country; getting an auto near a tourist trap is going to be expensive.

By pedal rickshaw   Pedal rickshaws are a complete waste of time and money. Most of them are operated by emaciated old men who never seem to know their way round their own cities, are frequently dishonest, and are unable to pedal up even slight inclines. It is understood that you will get out and help push the apparatus up steep slopes. Most of the drivers are also illiterate and non-English speakers.

It can be fun (in some ways) having a ride in a pedal rickshaw, but as a serious method of transport, they are useless. The old traditional rickshaws, pulled by malnourished coolies, are now only found in Calcutta.

By bicycle   It is often easy to hire bicycles in India, especially in villages, and cycling is a convenient and interesting way of exploring country areas. Bicycle hire is cheap, often only a few rupees per day, and you are rarely asked for a deposit. The debit side is the type of machine you'll be given, for although they are usually in reasonable mechanical condition, the Ludhiana manufactured Hero cycles are very solid and heavy, somewhat like the old fashioned British village policeman's bike; they can be hard work on a hot day, especially uphill.

Nonetheless, I thoroughly recommend hiring a bike to explore the surrounding country, if you stay in a village. About 17 km from the coastal temple village of Mahabalipuram, for example, is the little-visited town of Tirukalikundram, which itself has a large temple complex, and where two kites descend to be fed by the priests twice a day; cycling out there, through groves of coconut palms and fields of sugar cane, through little hamlets and past old temple tanks, is one of my happiest memories of travelling in India.

Beware of cycling at night; few bicycles are equipped with lights, which makes it dangerous enough; but if you have a white face you can also become the target of a certain amount of harassment from Indian motorists; trucks swerve towards you, the men who always travel in the back throw things, and the mood is quite different from that of the daytime.

One of the great problems with public transport is explaining where you want to go, and making sure that the driver has understood this. (The officials in railway booking offices almost always speak and understand English perfectly – so do the attendants on the trains; the language barrier, if you yourself have no Indian languages, is one that you will encounter with the drivers of taxis and autorickshaws.) Many taxi and rickshaw drivers will drive you away without understanding where you actually want to go; their first priority is to grab you as a fare, and they will sort out the problem of where you want to go later. This is especially true of the pedal rickshaw drivers, and is another reason for avoiding them.

When you ask a driver whether he understands where you want to be taken, you'll receive the reply 'Achcha, achcha!', that all-purpose Indian expression that means almost anything, but usually something like 'Okay, okay', then, a little further on, he will stop and jump out to buttonhole a pedestrian whom he believes can speak English; the pedestrian will be brought over to the cab or rickshaw, and you will have to tell him where you want to go, and this will be translated for the driver. This is where you can have a surprise, because often the translation isn't a translation at all, it is just what you said in the first place. You could have been saying 'Railway station, railway station!' over and over again, and even making engine noises, with no luck; your pressganged interpreter will simply say 'Railway station!' to the driver, and his eyes will light up and he'll exclaim,

Problems with public transport

Making yourself understood

'Ah, *railway* station!' The problem is, I imagine, one of pronunciation, but the strange thing about all this is that often the destination is pronounced by the interpreter in exactly the same manner as you did; the difference is that now the driver understands!

A similar problem can arise when trying to find a particular place; a driver will take you on without knowing where it is, and will navigate by dead reckoning and frequent stops to consult passers by and traders at roadside stalls. Many tourists get annoyed by this, and have the vague idea that they are being cheated, but this is stupid; in fact, the driver is being polite, and is going to some lengths on your behalf. The occasions when this *is* annoying usually involve the pedal rickshaws, the drivers of which can take you miles out of your way and never succeed in finding the right place, even with guidance from passers by.

If a driver doesn't understand you, and can't be bothered to make the effort to find out where you want to go, he'll ignore you and pick up someone else; this usually happens when there are lots of other fares available, during rush hours, for instance, or when it's raining. If passengers are in short supply, great efforts will be made to solicit your custom and get you to your destination.

Complaints   The threat of reporting a driver to the police is often greeted with derision; sometimes, however, it is effective. If you have good reason to believe that you are being wildly overcharged, one of the best ploys is to refuse to pay anything when you get to the other end, but take down the cab or rickshaw's number; if you're going to your hotel, you can explain to the driver that he knows where to find you, if he wants to complain about your non-payment of the fare, and that you're going to report his number to the police and the tourist office. Obviously you have to use your sense and judgement; if the driver is built like Tarzan, and it is late at night, it wouldn't be a good idea to try this; on the other hand, most rickshaw drivers (but remember 'Auto' Shankar and his towel!) will back down and accept a more reasonable fare. Sometimes drivers become so terrified by this that they refuse to take a fare at all, and you are put in the ridiculous position of having to force the money upon them.

It also helps to kick up a noisy fuss, and attract attention, for many Indians are very sensitive about guests to their country being rooked in any way; if you start a noisy argument, passers by will almost always side with you. Again, however, use your common sense about this; while this last statement is true in an area where there are a fair number of middle-class passers by, it obviously isn't in an area where most of the people are from the same class as the rickshaw driver himself. Educated, English-speaking Indians will always try to help you out, and if they see that you are in trouble, they will go to great lengths to do so.

Many streets and roads in Indian cities have two names; an old one dating from the days of the Raj, and a new one designed to remove even the memory of the colonial past. This can cause some confusion, because some cab drivers and rickshaw wallahs don't seem to know the new names, while others refuse to understand the old ones. Some residents cling to the old names out of nostalgic affection. For example, Mount Road in Madras is now the Anna Salai, but many people still refer to it as Mount Road; and Wellington Street in Calcutta has become Nirmal Chunder Street.

Changing the names of streets

Hotels and other accommodation

Hotels: general

There is a very wide range of hotel accommodation in India, with luxurious and air-conditioned five stars at one end, and filthy doss houses at the other. At the top end of the market in the cities, prices can be almost as high as those in New York or London, while at the bottom end hotels are often not called hotels at all but are known as 'lodges'. 'Hotel' at the lower end of the market usually means a traditional Indian eating house.

Your choice of accommodation depends on how much you want to spend, but even if you don't have to make economies, you should think carefully about whether the five stars are really worth it. Do not allow yourself to be unduly influenced by snobbish books like Louise Nicholson's *India in Luxury*; my own feeling is that most of the five stars are simply not worth the money you part with, and lest I be accused of inverted snobbery, let me emphasize that I say this because I have stayed at many of them, and have not been impressed.

The five stars

Indian five star hotels can be divided into two categories; the international 'business' hotels that are usually towers in the major cities, and the supposedly opulent palace hotels in tourist centres, like the lake palace hotels of Rajasthan.

'Business' hotels

Of this category, little can be said except that they are much like their counterparts anywhere else in the world, and offer air-conditioned comfort, a wide variety of services, and sometimes staggering prices. If you are an international business traveller, and need the facilities they offer (conference rooms, valet services, and the like) obviously you will go to them. None of them is particularly exciting, and none of them has any atmosphere, although they are subject to some eccentricities (like the sudden breakdown of the electricity supply that is euphemistically called load-shedding) that their counterparts in, say, London and New York are not. The city hotels are usually run by one of the big chains, of which the most important are the Oberoi Group, the Welcomgroup, the Taj Group, the Ambassador Group, the rather smaller Clarks Group, and the Centaur Hotels that are run by a subsidiary of Air India.

Examples of this type of hotel are the Oberoi on Nariman Point in Bombay, where a single room costs Rs1,650 per night and a double Rs1,800, and the Chola Sheraton in Madras, where a single is Rs890 and a double Rs1,010; taxes and service charges must be added to these figures. Suites at the Bombay Oberoi can cost up to Rs9,000. From this it should be clear that the international business hotels are relatively expensive; so are their restaurants and other services.

The dubious five star hotels are those in the great tourist resorts. Although many of them are owned by the same chains that run the city hotels, and they are supposed to offer unparalleled luxury and romance, they usually rely on grand exteriors and location (such as the Rajasthan lake palace hotels) rather than quality of service or the standard of their rooms. Because of this, many – if not all – of them offer poor value and can be disappointing.

Tourist resort hotels

A specific example is the Lalitha Palace Hotel near Mysore, which is one of the former Maharaja's palaces and resembles the Capitol in Washington, DC. Once you've got over the romance of staying in what was once a maharaja's palace, there isn't all that much to be said for the place when the cost is taken into account. It is of course agreeable to have chilled drinking water and cold buffets readily available, but the place has a run-down atmosphere, and is somehow disappointing. The nearby Rajendra Vilas Palace hotel on Chamundi Hill doesn't just have a run-down atmosphere, it *is* run down and decaying. This is often true of the luxury hotels outside the international business class, and almost all seasoned travellers in India seem to come to the conclusion that five stars represent poor value, are disappointing after the build-up they receive in Indian and foreign tourist literature, and insulate you from the country.

The services and facilities at expensive resort hotels are often no better than those to be found at far cheaper places; the differences are sometimes purely cosmetic, and you end up paying vast sums of money for things that don't really add to your comfort – such as the potted palms in the foyer and the gilded door knobs.

The good and the bad Some of the five stars are, of course, superb; a notable example is the Taj on the Apollo Bunder in Bombay, which is perhaps India's finest hotel. Others do have beautiful locations and you would be missing a lot if you were not to visit them once. For many visitors the most useful services offered by the five stars are the English language bookshops and the twenty-four-hour coffee shops. The former stock foreign papers and magazines (see 'Services, communications, and the media') while the latter, although expensive, usually offer Western breakfasts and the sort of snacks for which you can develop a wild desire after weeks of eating an Indian diet. The Taj in Bombay not only has what must be the city's best bookshop, but it has cool, comfortable bars overlooking the harbour. Non-residents can use these facilities, and such places can be havens of cleanliness and sanity if you have been experiencing budget traveller's India. The five stars also have swimming pools, hairdressers, and sports facilities; the latter are rare in India outside the private clubs. The offices of many major airlines are inside the large hotels – Pan Am has an office in the Bombay Taj, for example.

On the debit side are poor service and overpricing; my pet hate is the Hotel Imperial in New Delhi, which has a silly restaurant called The Verandah, full of somewhat tasteless Raj memorabilia, where a

bunch of underemployed 'waiters' literally menace
you for tips that they don't deserve. The food is
poor, and expensive for what it is. Then there are
the shopping arcades; apart from the bookshops,
almost all of the luxury hotels have their own shops
which deal in handicrafts, jewellery, painting, rugs
and carpets, brasswork, silks, and other Indian
curios. These are outrageously overpriced, as a rule,
and their one possible advantage – that at least you
are buying genuine ivory or silk – is illusory. You
are as likely to be sold junk in one of these arcades
as you are in a street bazaar. (At the Hotel Imperial,
one of the shopkeepers has been known to sell
polyester as 'chiffon silk'.) Unless you want to waste
money, avoid the shopping arcades in the five stars,
and go to the state-run 'handicraft emporia' and
other regulated outlets, if you want to buy good
silks, pictures etc.

Then there is the company that you will find at
the five stars; again, this is a matter of taste, but
surely few people really want to spend their time
in India in company with pink English yuppies,
brandishing their copies of *India in Luxury*, or
groups of Americans visiting the local Ramakrishna
Mission, or parties of Japanese tourists buckling
under the weight of complicated photographic apparatus.

As a final note to this diatribe, I must give an
unqualified recommendation to one luxury hotel that
is really luxurious no longer, having fallen from
fashion and glory into decay. This is the Fernhill
Palace in Ootacamund, the hill station in Tamil
Nadu, which is surely unique. This, like many other
celebrated hotels, is a former maharaja's palace, but
absolutely nothing has been done to capitalize
on this; it is an endearing ruin, uncomfortable,
mysterious, often deserted out of season, with walls
adorned by sepia photographs of the Fernhill Hunt,
and where almost everything on the menu is unavail-
able. The rooms are grand in the sense that some
Scottish country houses are grand, a grandness that
has nothing to do with comfort or convenience; the

old ballroom is now the restaurant, and here you can dine in solitary splendour while bits of the gilding from the ceiling plop into your mulligatawny soup. Up above the ballroom, on balconies, are the smoking room and the billiard room; in the former is a small library containing such titles as *Polo in India* and *Juvenile Crime in Southern India*, while in the latter the moths have done for the billiard table, but there is still a wonderful antique scoring machine and a notice warning that 'Beginners are not allowed to play.'

Alas, I fear that the days of the Fernhill Palace are numbered, and that it will go the way of the Carlton in the other hill station, Kodaikanal, which has been knocked down and turned into a modern five star that for all the world looks like a midwestern motel. The Fernhill tariff is only Rs100 to Rs200, while at the Carlton you'll pay about Rs700. If you go to Ootacamund, go to the Fernhill; and go quickly, before it's destroyed. There is nothing else like it in India. The bar is run by a born-again Christian, Brother Pannelrselvam Edgar.

The middle-range hotels

If you are seriously interested in meeting Indians, the best places to head for are the hotels that are patronized by middle-grade Indian businessmen. These usually (but not always!) represent excellent value for money, offer extremely good services and facilities (like car hire without inflated 'tourist' prices), and always seem to have a bar (or 'permit room' as they are called in the south) with a drunken customer in it, who will be only too happy to provide instant and garrulous company. It is in these places that you will meet ordinary Indians – that is, ones not connected with the tourist trade – who will always be friendly and hospitable, and often offer to show you round or give you tips for the next place you're visiting. I must emphasize that not every middle-range Indian hotel is like this, of course; you'll find the ones that are either by luck or by talking to chance acquaintances – of which there is no shortage in India.

A good middle-range hotel would probably have

at least some (if not all) air-conditioned rooms, room service, hot water for at least part of the day, laundry services, a restaurant, and car hire arrangements. The drawbacks are that often there are no telephones in the rooms, and the restaurants may not serve any Western food. This can be miserable at breakfast time, as any Westerner who has breakfasted on *idli* (see 'Food and drink') for a week will tell you. A good hotel in this class compares very favourably with the five stars. For example, the Hotel New Victoria, near Egmore station in Madras, has fully air-conditioned rooms, hot water all day and night, a good restaurant, full telephone and telex services, and even televisions in every room; this is for Rs270 per night for one person.

Facilities

Be cautious when choosing a hotel room; *always* ask to look at it first, and if the hotel prominently advertises certain facilities, don't take them on trust, make sure that they are actually available. Most cheap Indian hotels that want to attract Westerners advertise facilities and services that are simply non-existent; 'Western flushes' and 'daily hot and cold running at all times night the same' are among the firm favourites. Others are more subjective, such as 'heavenly stayings with joy-full ness day and night through attentive staffs. God bless you.' Many Indian hotels will ask you for a substantial deposit when you check in; sometimes this deposit is more than the tariff for the room. Make sure that you're happy with the room *before* you part with any money, because if you change your mind when horizontal jets of water appear from the 'Western flush' and rodents scramble out of the bed when you try to get in, you won't get your money back. Don't be impressed by the mere presence of pipework and electric cables; make sure that water flows through the former and electricity through the latter, and not vice versa.

Within the range of hotels discussed here come the 'Hindu style' or 'Asian style' establishments; these are often huge places, somewhat grim and barrack-like, set round courtyards, and patronized

by Indian businessmen and Indian tourists. They can
be very noisy and spartan, and some of them have
only Asian style lavatories, that is, the ones you
squat over rather than sit on; some of them are coy
about matters such as lavatory paper, so be prepared
for all this if you stay in one.

Many cheaper hotels have, like the more expensive
ones, safes or lock boxes for guests' valuables; these
are worth using, but always make sure that you get
a detailed receipt for anything that you leave with
the desk. It is never a good idea to leave valuables
in your room; cheaper hotels often have a flimsy
hasp and padlock on the room doors rather than
proper locks.

Finally, do not be impressed by grand foyers,
plastered with Visa and Master Charge stickers;
Bombay hotels, especially the ones on Marine Drive,
go in for this sort of thing. The foyers are very
encouraging, all air-conditioning and potted palms
and travel posters; and all this stops quite abruptly
when you are taken to the stairs or the lift, for the
actual hotel is a decaying pile held together by the
layers of grime on the walls. Again – *always ask to
see the room before you commit yourself!*

Prices   The prices at these hotels cover a wide range,
depending on location; in a large city, a hotel like
the New Victoria in Madras is Rs270 for a single; in
a smaller town, the prices are much lower, a typical
example being the Hotel Aarathay in Madurai (in
Tamil Nadu), where an air-conditioned single is only
Rs49. It is worth pointing out that this last hotel is
probably the best for value in town; Madurai has
the famous Meenakshi temple, and attracts many
tourists and pilgrims. There is a luxury Ashok hotel
several kilometres south of the river, which is
expensive, far away from the temple and the city
centre, and really a drab and indifferent place. The
Aarathay, on the other hand, is about five minutes'
walk from the temple, is actually behind a smaller
Vishnu temple, and offers excellent services and
facilities.

This book is not the place for a thorough guide to Indian hotels, but I hope that these examples illustrate my point; the choice of accommodation is similar to that of method of transport. Sometimes Indian Airlines is the logical way to travel, but you will miss a lot, as explained in the previous chapter, if you don't explore India by train; similarly, sometimes it is a good idea to stay in one of the five stars, but even if these are well within your budget, it is a great shame to get locked into the system of luxury hotels to the exclusion of the alternatives.

The lower end of the market fades into a strange oblivion; there really are some horrible, filthy, insanitary, and downright dangerous hovels in India that are optimistically called lodges or hotels. In spite of this, many of the very cheap hotels are clean, have friendly service, and are in beautiful places; you do not have to be a budget traveller to enjoy them.

An example of this is the Taj Lodge in Kodaikanal; by the standards of cheap places it is actually relatively expensive, at Rs75 per night, but the reasons for this are firstly that Kodai is a major tourist resort, and secondly, that from the windows of the Taj Lodge there is what must be one of the most beautiful views in India, down a 2,400 m drop to the plains. The Lodge is an old bungalow or cottage, built by a British resident of the hill station in the early years of this century; the rooms are clean, you get a bucket of hot water in the morning, and the people that run the place are extremely friendly and helpful (they are a Moslem family named Khan). The Carlton in Kodaikanal has already been mentioned, and is not worth staying at; nor is the quite dreadful Paradise Inn. Again, the lesson is as before; don't judge by first appearances, and don't pay large sums of money for purely cosmetic features of a hotel that don't actually add to your comfort or convenience; the Taj Lodge is by far and away the best place to stay in Kodaikanal, even if washing with a bucket of hot water at 8 a.m. doesn't appeal to you.

The only way to find decent budget accommodation is by word of mouth, or by using the *Lonely*

The really cheap

Planet guide to India, which makes great efforts to
keep an up-to-date gazetteer of such places; one of
the problems in doing this, of course, is that Indian
hotels can change hands quickly, and their standards
can change dramatically.

Many of the budget hotels and lodges are terrible
places to stay; you really will see cockroaches as big
as skateboards, and have rats standing on your head
to nibble the light cord; all this and more awaits you
in the numerous Lakshmi Lodges, Ringo Guest
Houses for delightful stays and wonderful boardings,
and Mountbatten Lodges with full flush and running
hot and colds for a delightful stay at all times.

In cheaper hotels, the bedding is often badly
stained, and if it doesn't actually stink it will probably
smell unpleasant. It's a good idea to carry some
plastic garbage bag liners to place between you and
the bed linen, and a sheet sleeping bag will add to
your comfort. Beware of showers – a cheap room
with attached bath means that there is a dank little
cubicle adjoining your gloomy bedroom, where a
rusty shower rose sprouts from the wall, the floor
is covered with strange glistening excrescences, and
there might only be an Asian style lavatory (without
any paper, of course). It's wise to wear thong sandals
in the shower, and when in bed to be prepared for
bed bugs – take a supply of dusting powder with
you, because these nasty little insects can make your
life misery.

The cheapest Indian hotel rooms have an amazing
display of electric switches, cables, junction boxes
etc., but few of these are connected to anything or
have any function; so the ground rules elaborated in
the previous section apply *a fortiori* to the budget
hotels; *always* ask to see the room, and *always* check
that the plumbing and lights work. If the fixtures
are there, you are paying for them; they might as
well *do* something.

Cheap hotel rooms are the places where you get
eaten by mosquitoes; a net is very useful, and if you
don't have one, at least use a smoke coil or cream
repellent. Don't leave food lying around, because
this will attract rodents and insects.

Every Indian railway station and bus stand has its
complement of self-styled guides and hotel touts who
will ruthlessly invest you from the moment of your
arrival; they are very insistent, could not as a rule
care less about your comfort or convenience, and
are interested in only one thing – money. Their
attentions can be frightening when you are tired or
ill, because they will pick on you when they see that
you are at a disadvantage, and won't let go. Many
touts have arrangements with local hotel owners; a
particularly bad example is the Paradise Inn in
Kodaikanal (see the previous section). A tout will
expect a commission for taking you to a hotel; this
commission is often paid by the hotel keeper himself,
but sometimes the tout will expect baksheesh from
you too.

This system often comes close to one of extortion.
For instance, you arrive at a small town by bus,
shrug off all the touts at the bus stand, and find
yourself a taxi because you think you know where
you want to go; you ask the driver to take you
there, he agrees, and all seems well. Then you notice
that two other men are approaching the cab, and
they pile into the front seat beside your driver. Who
are they? They are 'guides'. You ask the driver, who
are they? He tells you they are his friends. And they
may be his friends, but they aren't yours; because
although you knew where you wanted to go, and
although you asked the driver to take you there,
these 'guides' are going to insist that they took you
to the hotel, once you've arrived, and are going to
extract a commission from someone. They are able
to do this because most Western tourists or visitors
speak none of the Indian languages, and won't be
able to follow what's being said when they get to
their destination.

The real problems start when the hotel keeper
tries to pass on the responsibility for paying the
commission for these 'guides' to you – you are under
no obligation whatsoever to pay it – by slipping it
onto your bill. Even the most miserable doss house
will have a vast ledger, and make out complicated
bills in triplicate, so unless you check, you may not
see what's happened. Furthermore, the 'guides' may

well try to harass you for baksheesh as an extra, to reward them for their great efforts on your behalf. You will not receive much help from small-time hotel keepers when you resist this, because most of them are – or claim that they are – somewhat in the power of the touts; that is, the touts will keep people away from any hotel where the manager or owner doesn't co-operate with their games.

The payment of the tout's commission can also be a problem if you suddenly decide not to stay somewhere after having committed yourself and parted with money as a deposit; you won't get it back, because the hotel keeper will rage and scream about how much he had to pay the tout for the honour of bringing you to his miserable hotel in the first place. This is why you should make sure that you're happy with a room before signing anything or parting with money.

Sometimes the touts have their uses; they often know where the last free rooms are, when things are crowded (as, for example, many towns that are objects of pilgrimages can be), and at such times their services can be invaluable. If, however, you know where you are going, or have some idea of where you want to go, get rid of them. They're a pain in the neck.

Other short-term accommodation

Many Indian railway stations have what are known as retiring rooms. These are fairly spartan but clean dormitory rooms, or, in some cases, single or double rooms, which are for the use of railway passengers. You are entitled to use them if you have a valid ticket or rail pass, although sometimes the rules are bent for foreign tourists in distress (but don't count on this). Retiring rooms are relatively cheap and good value; a further bonus is that you'll often meet travelling Indian businessmen, who will take you under their wing and give you advice, show you round, and generally provide good company. If the retiring rooms are full, there is always the first class waiting room; these have benches and things like primitive sofas that are not too uncomfortable to sleep on.

Another type of accommodation is the PWD Bungalow. PWD stands for Public Works Department, and the bungalows are really for travelling government officials; however, it is sometimes possible to find a room in one of these, and they can be quite pleasant places to stay. If you want to try this, you should contact the local assistant engineer at the PWD. A variety of accommodation that is also meant in the first instance for visiting government officials, but in which tourists can sometimes find a room, goes under many names; Dak Bungalows (*dak* means postal service), Rest Houses, Circuit Houses etc. Rest and Circuit Houses are unlikely to find room for tourists, being reserved for government VIPs, but the PWD Inspection Bungalows and the Dak Bungalows are always worth a try; sometimes they are the only accommodation available. Note that the Dak Bungalows can be exceedingly primitive.

There is also a certain amount of government-run accommodation specifically for tourists; most common are the Tourist Bungalows, which can vary widely in quality and price. Often they are good bargains, and in some states, such as Rajasthan, they are especially good. Accommodation offered is usually either dormitory style, or double rooms, although some of the more luxurious places have more facilities.

Finally there are various lodges, hotels, and beach resorts run either by the Indian Tourist Development Corporation or the various state authorities, such as the Tamil Nadu Tourist Development Council (TTDC). The former category includes many Ashok hotels (such as the Hotel Varanasi Ashok – but be careful, because there are many other Ashok(a) hotels *not* run by the government), which are in the upper bracket. However, many of these government- or state-run enterprises are cheap and very good. The ones run by the TTDC, usually named Hotel Tamil Nadu, are especially useful places to head for if you are uncertain of where to go, or are being plagued by 'guides'.

India has some good youth hostels and camping grounds. At the very bottom of the range, you can often rent a room in a village with a family; this can cost as little as Rs100 per week. You'll have to negotiate about meals etc., and be warned that the sanitary arrangements will almost certainly be primitive. Some people still build palm frond huts on the Goan (and some other) beaches, where they become tourist attractions in their own right; 'hippy revels' are actually mentioned in Goan tourist literature!

Flats and houses

Rented accommodation can be extremely hard to find, and surprisingly expensive, in India's major cities. Bombay is probably the worst, followed by Delhi, Calcutta, Madras, and Bangalore. If you are a long-stay visitor in India, it is best to find an Indian contact (a business associate or representative, a friend etc.) to arrange your accommodation for you, rather than to try to do it yourself. Rents in fashionable parts of New Delhi or Bombay are comparable to those for similar accommodation in London or New York, so be warned.

If you do try to find something on your own, you should employ a broker (house agent); in fact, you should employ the services of several brokers, because their fees are only due when a specific rental agreement has been made. The fee is usually fifteen days' rent. Most brokers provide an efficient and reliable service, but if possible, try to get some recommendations. Once contact has been made with a possible landlord, don't hesitate to bargain and haggle with him yourself, because of course the broker, with his fee in mind, will not want to push the rent down too far on your behalf.

The catch in renting is that often a year's rent may be demanded in advance, and this can be a huge sum of money by anyone's standards. The reason for this is that your landlord, or prospective landlord, will, like most wealthy Indians, be trying to cheat the Indian revenue service. A rental agreement will be drawn up that quotes a rent far less than the actual rent, so that the landlord can avoid paying tax on most of it; to be sure of getting his money, given this low figure in the agreement, he will therefore ask for a large sum (usually a whole year's rent) in advance.

Having said this, I must repeat that it is extremely hard to find accommodation in Bombay and New Delhi; if you don't want to stay in a hotel for ever, leave the arrangements to a local contact. Rumour has it that the manager of a major Western airline has been living in a hotel in New Delhi for over a year, so difficult is it to find somewhere to rent. Furthermore, there is no escape from paying large sums of money in cash in advance; even the embassies in New Delhi are said to do this.

Household equipment

Most lets are unfurnished, and it will be up to you to find domestic equipment; some things are best bought in from abroad, and import duty can be waived on some items for those who are transferring their residence to India (see 'Getting there and back'). Duty is still payable on those imported household appliances deemed by the Indian government to be luxuries, such as TVs, videos, refrigerators, and air-conditioning units; nonetheless, it is still worth thinking about bringing them with you if you intend to stay for a long time, because in India they are harder to buy than in most Western countries, and they are liable to a special sales-tax, the so-called luxury tax. Expatriates to whom I have spoken have suggested that long-stay visitors bring with them appliances ranging from microwave ovens and food mixers to washing machines!

Indian products are usually licence-made versions of rather antiquated foreign models, and are relatively expensive. For example, in Spencer's department store in Madras (one of the few Indian department stores with departments), a Washtex twin tub washing machine sells at Rs5,540, while licence-built Kelvinator refrigerators are Rs8,100; gas cookers are Rs5,935, electric cookers Rs6,200. One of the welcome effects of the Indian government's policy of economic 'liberalization' has been the appearance of more consumer luxuries on the open market, and the price, quality, and availability of Indian-made goods could change quite rapidly in the near future.

(In the summer of 1988, Uptron TV sets, a new single tub washing machine, and Moods condoms – 'made by the Hindustan Latex Company with the latest Japanese technology' – were the subjects of aggressive advertising campaigns!) Bed linen and furniture are easy to obtain in India itself, and are relatively cheap. Air-conditioning units can be hired in most large towns.

Utilities   Rental agreements usually last for slightly less than a year; the services and utilities are generally left in the landlord's name, and the bills will be passed on to you as the tenant. Electricity bills are issued monthly, telephone bills bi-monthly. Always remember that just because somewhere has become your home (temporarily), it doesn't mean that the water is safer there than it is anywhere else; at least boil the water before drinking, and if possible both filter and boil it. *Never* drink tap water!

Servants   Few homes in India are without servants; indeed, life in India would be almost unimaginable without them. This can be a problem for many foreign residents, for few of them are used to dealing with domestic staff, still less Indian cooks, gardeners, and those mysterious functionaries, bearers. In major cities, there is a special class of domestic servant that caters for the foreign community; this is especially true of New Delhi, because of the large number of diplomats and their families. These servants speak English fluently, and can cook Western food. You are very unlikely to inherit servants with a house or apartment, so you'll have to hire them yourself. Diplomats in New Delhi run a semi-official hiring ring from the British High Commission and the US Embassy; Indian contacts can obviously be a great help too.

The number of servants you employ will depend on the size of your house and the amount of entertaining that you do. A cook is very useful, and he will often double as a bearer, which office is best described as a sort of butler; a bearer would serve drinks, shop for you, and undertake general tasks of household management. A cleaner is useful, because you cannot expect a bearer to clean the lavatory; that is the job of the cleaner, who will be a man or woman of a lower caste. If you have a grand establishment, you might also have a gardener and a chauffeur. The servants who cater for foreigners charge twice what they would were they working in an ordinary Indian household; a typical wage could be between £50 and £80 per month.

Living with servants can be a trial. Some of them, such as the cook or bearer, might well live in, and you will therefore see a lot of them (most expensive Indian houses have servants' accommodation). They can also be very temperamental and given to prima donna's high strikes, for they know that it is their market, and that good servants are hard to find. Many people who have had to deal with Indian servants suggest that you keep the booze locked away; this is not so much because their employees were given to drunken orgies in their absence, but more because of the temptations offered by the high prices that imported liquor commands on the black market.

Food and drink

There is no more a single Indian cuisine than there is a single Indian language, for the food, like the languages, shows sharp regional variations. Western Indian restaurants are not as a rule very good introductions to Indian cooking; most of them have only a rather pallid imitation of the northern Indo-Pak meat dishes, and the southern vegetarian tradition is hardly ever represented (though there used to be a very good South Indian restaurant in Chicago!). In Indian restaurants in the West, there are things on the menus that are unknown in India; no one in Madras, for instance, would know what a Madras curry was; and the Vindaloo, offered as a strong curry in Western Indian restaurants, is in fact a Goan pork dish, owing as much to Portuguese as to Indian influence.

The first point to appreciate is that there is no such thing as curry; the term was coined by the British, from the Tamil word for sauce (*kari*) as a catch-all for the spicy sauces that accompany most Indian meals. Furthermore, not every Hindu is a strict vegetarian; the strictly vegetarian sect is the Jains, who represent only a small percentage of the population. Nonetheless, the strong meat-eating tradition in the north owes much to Moslem influence.

Indian food can be delicious; it can also be absolutely foul. It might be surprising for those who have not spent long in India to learn that it can also become very boring, especially at breakfast time, when you can be reduced almost to tears for want of a decent Western breakfast. Western food (often called Continental Cuisine) is in general not very good, even in expensive places, and in cheap ones the Indian imitations of foreign dishes can be quite horrific. The best alternative to Indian food is provided by the large number of Chinese restaurants throughout India, which range from small, independent places to the excellent Szechwan Golden Dragons in the Taj group's hotels; the latter are very good indeed, especially those in the Taj in Bombay and the Taj Coramandel in Madras. Other major hotels also have Chinese restaurants, such as the Sagari Roof Garden in the Madras Chola Sheraton; these restaurants seem to be a favourite meeting place for India's upper classes.

The following chapter is not intended to be an exhaustive guide to the many regional cuisines and specialities of India, but it should help you find your way round a fairly basic Indian menu. The cheap and popular Indian 'meals' restaurants are always worth a visit, and so are the many 'hotels' (that is, cheap eating places – see 'Hotels and other accommodation') for they serve good food and are good value; but it helps if you know what you're ordering!

Basics – wheat and rice

The Indian climate, particularly the distribution of rainfall, divides the country into mainly wheat-growing and mainly rice-growing regions, although there is, of course, considerable overlap, especially in Uttar Pradesh. The main wheat-growing regions are in the dryer north-west, or centred in the Punjab and Haryana, with smaller regions in north-east Rajasthan and northern Madhya Pradesh. Rice growing is concentrated in a broad belt sweeping up from West Bengal along the Himalayan foothills into Uttar Pradesh, in Orissa, a belt running down the Coramandel Coast with a major centre at the delta of the River Cauvery in Tamil Nadu, and on the west coast in Kerala. Although rice and Indian breads are eaten in both the north and the south, this agricultural division means that rice is traditionally more important in the south, and the breads – naans, chapattis etc. – more important in the north.

Roti is the general term for Indian bread. The chapatti, familiar to anyone who has been to an Indian restaurant in the UK, is a small, circular flat

cake of coarse unleavened bread baked on a griddle.
The larger naan, often served in Indian restaurants
with tandoori food, is leavened and baked in a clay
oven, a tandoor (or tandur). Other ingredients or
methods of preparation give more breads; the paratha
is a fried, unleavened wheaten pancake, and is
sometimes stuffed with spiced vegetables; the deep
fried version is called a poori or loochi, while
papadums are deep fried crispy pancakes that are
often served as a sort of appetizer in Western Indian
restaurants.

Other ingredients such as millet or lentil flour can
also be used, and the pancake of lentil flour is called
a *dosa*; this forms the basis of Indian fast food, the
dosa meal, a *masala dosa* being a dosa wrapped
round a collection of spiced vegetables. These are
delicious and cheap, and can be a good staple when
you're travelling; they're also what you'll get in
Indian offices if someone sends out for a snack.
Dosas can come in various shapes and textures, the
latter ranging from the very soggy to the hard and
brittle, like that of a papadum.

Normally you would use your bread to mop up
the sauce that accompanies your meal; in the south,
this is done with rice rather than bread, the most
common manifestation being *idli*, a steamed rice cake
that is often served as a snack with a sauce or
chutney. *Pongal* is similar but is itself spiced, often
with peppercorns. You'll often have to make do with
idli and its accompanying sauces for breakfast in the
south, and this can be very unpleasant; few Westerners want to eat strongly spiced food first thing in
the morning.

Spices   Strongly spiced sauces, with or without meat or
vegetables, are a universal feature of Indian cooking,
and gave rise to the term 'curry'. An Indian cook
has a huge range of spices in his or her armoury,
and most of them find their way into the food; the
term 'masala' (as in 'masala dosa') doesn't mean a
meat or vegetable but a certain combination of these
spices. The Portuguese were responsible for enlarging
the range of spices by introducing chillies, amongst

other condiments, to Indian cooking, and in Goa
they created a unique Indo-Portuguese cuisine.
(Incidentally, 'masala' is not to be confused with
'*mashallah*', which means 'let God's will be done.')

Amongst the most common spices are: turmeric,
a member of the ginger family, the powdered root
of which can also be used as a dye; saffron, which
is also used as a dye and which gives some rice dishes
their characteristic yellow colour; ginger; coriander;
cumin; cardamon; and cloves. Garlic is heavily used,
and this, with the spices, gives Indian food its rich
flavour but leaves you with a rather unpleasant and
lingering aftertaste.

'Chutney' is one of the many Indian words that
has passed into English; chutneys are often served
with meals, and a chutney is a relish made from
pickled fruit or vegetables with vinegar and spices.
Chutneys deserve to be treated cautiously, because
many of them are very powerful and rather than
hurting your mouth, they simply numb it; the pain
comes later.

Main dishes

The main divide in Indian cooking is between the
north and the south. The Moslems have left their
meat-eating habits in the north, and the cuisine is
often described as Moghul (after the line of Emperors
of India) or Mughlai; this embraces the bread-and-
meat cuisine of the Punjab, commonly represented
in Indian restaurants abroad by the tandoori menu.
In south India, there are a fair number of 'Punjabi'
restaurants where northern food is served. Otherwise,
the south remains a bastion of orthodox vegetarianism.

A proper Indian meal has no starters as such; those
served in Western Indian restaurants are offered as
a concession to local custom. Usually a selection of
food is ordered in a restaurant, or served at home,
and delivered in communal dishes from which you
take what you want.

Northern cooking

A north Indian meal would typically consist of: a
dry meat that has been marinated and cooked over
charcoal in a clay oven (tandoor); a curry (to use the

Western term), which could contain meat or fish; a vegetable; *dal* of some sort (see below); a yoghurt or curd dish to neutralize the effects of the curry; and an Indian bread or rice.

Dal is a porridge-like dish of lentils or split peas, or some other pulse; among the dals are *dal urad* (a rather creamy dish made with black lentils), *dal arhar* (made with red gram), and *dal moong* (made with green gram). Often a dal and roti will be served alone as a snack. Common vegetables include the aubergine or egg plant (*brinjal*), okra or ladies' fingers (*bhindi*), potatoes (*alu* or *alloo*), peas (*mutter*), chick-peas (*chana*), and spinach (*saag*); *sabzi* is a term for greens, and is also used to mean a dish of curried vegetables.

Gosht is meat; *kofta* means spiced meatballs, while *kurmas* or *kormas* are very creamy, rather rich dishes of braised meats. Meat in India can be something of a disappointment, especially chicken, for all Indian chickens appear to have devoted their lives to strenuous exercises in an attempt to keep fit and lose weight. Mutton and lamb are fairly common in the north, especially in Kashmir, while beef and pork are often hard to find. Beef is, of course, objectionable to the Hindus, while pork is forbidden to Moslems. The best meat dishes that I have eaten in India have been Kashmiri lamb and mutton.

On some menus you will see something called 'Country Captain'; this is really chicken and rice, and is a British legacy. In the days of the Raj, officers and officials who were on the road satisfied their desire for meat by eating chickens, which were easier to obtain than the other meats, and were in no way objectionable to the Indians; this chicken and rice dish became an Anglo-Indian institution, and still lives on in the menus of some older hotels and restaurants. Unfortunately, the chickens that end up as Country Captains seem just as emaciated and lacking in flesh as the ones that go into tandoors and curries; they are disappointing. It is possible, of course, that since chickens are the most vulnerable of all Indian fowl and beasts, being objectionable to no religious group, they have cultivated anorexia as a means of self-defence.

Other common dishes are *biryanis* and *pilaus* (or *pulaus*), both rice based and served with meat and a curry sauce, and the various *dopiazas*, which are a kind of korma with a large amount of onion in them ('dopiaza' means 'two onions'). Fish is used in a large number of Indian dishes, especially in Bengal and around Bombay and Goa. A Bombay Duck is not a bird, but a small fish called a bummalo, and is often used as a relish.

Southern cooking

In the south, there is a strong vegetarian tradition, best represented, perhaps, by the Udipi Hotels, eating places which are run by Udipi brahmins, are always spotlessly clean and are always good to eat at. The most common meal in the south is the so-called *thali*, which in fact takes its name from the Hindi word for a plate; this is why the thali meals are often called plate meals, for that is exactly what they are. ('Thali' is a confusing word, because in Tamil it means 'thread'; the *mangalasutra*, the thread or necklace worn by a married Hindu lady, is called a *mangalathali* in Tamil Nadu. It has no connection with food!) A thali meal is served on a big metal plate, and consists of rice, usually in large quantities, papadums, a number of vegetable curries, relishes, curd, and sometimes a sweet, usually a sticky ball of boiled milk, ground almonds and coconut, and syrup, with something of the consistency of treacle pudding. Thalis are a staple in the south, and this is what you will get at most of the hotels that advertise 'meals' or 'meals ready here'. They are certainly very filling, for someone will come round replenishing the pots on your plate without your even asking, and usually without any extra charge; thalis are sold on an all-you-can-eat basis! If you are low on cash, thalis are a good way of surviving, for a complete thali meal with soft drinks and coffee can cost as little as Rs10 to Rs15. Of all Indian food, the thali can jade the Western palate most quickly, and leave you longing for a Western meal; then it's time to find a 'Punjabi' restaurant, or go to one of the many Chinese places. You will never find that good Western meal, I'm afraid, unless you are very lucky.

Other food   There are a number of other extras or side-dishes that might be encountered, among which are mulligatawny soup, a thick, strongly spiced curry soup that originated in Tamil Nadu and became something of an institution during the British Raj; *sambhar*, a soup-like mixture of lentils and vegetables; *pakoras*, fried pastries stuffed with spiced vegetables; and the related samosa, which is a triangular pastry parcel filled with spiced meat or vegetables. *Cachoombar* is a sort of spiced onion salad, while *achoori* is best described as spiced scrambled eggs – the thing that you can rely on Indian food for is the spice. *Panir* means cheese, as in *mutter panir* – peas with cheese.

Sweets and   Indian sweets and desserts make much use of boiled
curds   milk and sugar. Many of them are far too sweet for most Western tastes, but many are delicious, once you've got used to them. Among the sweetmeats and desserts made of boiled milk are *barfi*, *peda*, and the Bengali sweet called *sandesh*. The basic method of preparation is to boil or simmer milk until most of the liquid has evaporated, then to mix the residues with various ground fruits or nuts, adding syrup or sugar. Ground almonds, cashews, coconut, pistachios, rice, and chopped dried fruits can all be used. *Jelabi* is a little (only a little) like a saffron-coloured doughnut soaked in syrup; in the south, especially, there are many desserts that are like rice-pudding. Many sweets and sweet pastries are sold in very thin silver or gold wrappings, and you are supposed to eat these along with the contents.

Curd is often served with curries, as mentioned in the previous section, because it is the only thing that can kill the effects of the spices on taste buds; water is useless. Buttermilk is used to produce the drink called *lassi*, which can be tasty (but it should be treated with some caution when sold on stations or by roadside vendors, as I've said before; it sometimes contains contaminated water). *Dahi* is a general name for curd drinks, and raita is curd and chopped vegetables.

India produces many delicious ice-creams; *kulfi* is the special milk-rich Indian ice-cream, while there are good brands of Western-style ice-cream, such as Kwality and Gaylord. Beware of street vendors selling home-made varieties, for they will contain (or are likely to contain) contaminated water; the same goes for ice-lollies. The well-known brands just mentioned are safe and very good, coming in a variety of flavours. Nirulas also produces wonderful ice-cream, and their ice-cream parlour in Connaught Circle, New Delhi, must be one of the best in India, a sort of Indian Vivoli's.

Cakes are hard to obtain, but there are some good confectioners in the big cities; again in Connaught Circle is Wenger's, which sells an amazing (and good) selection of sweets and cakes and has become something of an institution for thousands of visitors – not to mention the residents of New Delhi, who also seem to patronize the place in large numbers.

It is possible to find Western foods, or imitations thereof, but they are often somewhat strange, and not infrequently inedible. Some of them take a certain amount of courage to order, such as mashroom tostes; then there are wondrous inventions like sheepburgers, even buffaloburgers (which I found surprisingly digestible), not to mention those rare delicacies rice padding and bernana filters. In general, unless you are in an expensive hotel, the breakfast menu is the only Western cooking worth trying. Breakfasts can be very good, including scrambled or boiled eggs, toast, porridge (the Indians clearly have a nostalgic affection for all that army mess food), omelettes and the like. Boiled eggs come in many forms, full boiled, half-boiled etc., and when you order them you will be questioned minutely about how you want them. Toast usually comes with butter and preserves, sometimes even with marmalade. Bombay toast is something like French toast, and always delicious. Cereals, mainly a strange kind of cornflake, are also available at breakfast time, but these are not such a success as the eggs and toast; they tend to be small things swimming in boiling milk, and trying to eat them is what I imagine chewing on a mouthful of gravel would be like.

Western food

Chips (French fries) are popular in India, and many of the Western-style beach cafés that have sprung up in resorts like Kovalam in Kerala and Mahabalipuram in Tamil Nadu serve them with good seafood. Chips are often called 'finger chips' on Indian menus, and watch out for the finger chips at places like the Silver Sands Beach Resort in Mahabalipuram; they have 'grilled fish and finger chips' on their menu, which raises expectations that are dashed when the meal arrives with only about four or five 'finger chips' on the plate (though the fish is a reasonable size). I have encountered this again and again in India, in such middle-range places with pretensions; whenever chips are advertised, you get a very small number of them. The best chips in India are prepared by an old man who runs a stall opposite the gate of the International School in Kodaikanal, and you can have *as many as you want*.

Drink

Alcoholic drinks

Alcoholic drinks are popular in India, and come in two general categories: imported liquor, which is very expensive unless you have contact with the local bootleg man; and the stuff called (somewhat paradoxically) Indian Made Foreign Liquor, or IMFL for short. Indian-made rum and gin are not too bad – in fact the latter is often pretty good – but the scotches are undrinkable. The strange thing about the scotches is that so many of them are made, and they are all so terrible, in spite of their grand names; 'Bag Piper – a legend comes alive', 'Diplomat – the measure of a man', and the mysterious 'Hag Wards' and 'Aristo Crat'. It's obvious what an Aristo Crat is meant to be, but what is a Hag Wards? A 30 ml measure of these elixirs will cost about Rs8, but imported scotches are extremely expensive, and are only obtainable in the bars of luxury hotels. Imported scotches are usually Johnny Walker or some other blend, and cost about £4 or £5 for a 30 ml measure. It's best to stick to Indian gin; though some of the vodkas aren't too bad.

Indian beers are good, resembling continental lagers, and are often available cold. Good brands include Black Label, UB, Golden Eagle, and Rosy

Pelican. There are even brands called Old Guru, Merry Old Monk, London Special, and Old London, though I can't pretend to having tried these myself. The beers go down very well with hot or spicy food, whereas most wines certainly do not. Outside really expensive hotels, table wines are unobtainable anyway, so if you want to drink you might as well stick to beer; it is sold in 650 ml bottles, draught beer being almost unknown outside the bars of the top hotels.

India suffers from occasional outbursts of prohibition, usually on a state-wide scale near state elections (prohibition tends to be very popular with long-suffering Indian women), but sometimes on a national scale. Some states are dry all the time, notably Gujerat; Tamil Nadu swings back and forth, but is currently tolerant of alcohol. When prohibition *is* declared, tourists can still drink if they obtain a liquor permit. This can be done inside the country, at Government of India tourist offices, where All India Liquor Permits are issued; permits for Gujerat can be obtained at Gujerat state tourist offices.

If you are adventurous, you might come across the local moonshine called *arrack*, which is also known as country spirit; it is made from the fermented sap of various palms. In Goa there is a variant, distilled from coconuts, called *feni*. In newspapers you will often read that badmashes (rascals and louts) had been indulging in mighty quantities of country liquor before they did whatever it was that got them in the paper. Feni can also be made from cashews, and can taste reasonably pleasant; the great drawback seems to be the variable alcoholic content of these drinks, which sometimes seem innocuous, and at other times like petrol.

Soft drinks

There are also many brands of soft drink. Coca-Cola was booted out of India long ago, and this spurred the Indians to produce their own colas; among these are Thums Up, Campa Cola, and more recently the American-style Double Cola, which is the best. Reliable soft drinks include Gold Spot, Limca, Spencers, and Bisleri bottled soda water. Bisleri (the name is that of the Italian firm whose products are licence-made in India) produce a still mineral water in a plastic bottle. Finally, there are a number of aerated mineral waters, such as Golden Eagle; these are very good, and make a welcome change from the sweet soft drinks.

Cartoned fruit juices have recently made an appearance in India, the mango juice being called (unfortunately) Fruti ('Rich and juicy – got to be Fruti' as the advert goes) and the apple juice Appy. In spite of their names, they are both good and appear to be safely packaged.

When buying a bottled drink, always make sure that there is a brand label on it, that the top is securely in place and not too rusty, and that the bottle is reasonably clean. Never drink anything out of the refillable 'marble' bottles, which have a rubber float stopper (the 'marble'). You never know what went in them.

Indian menus   Some of the strange spellings of English words that can appear on Indian menus have already been mentioned. Another problem with interpreting them is that Indian words can be Anglicized in a confusing variety of ways. A papadum can be a pooperdum, a popperdum, a poppderm, a pappadam, and so on; menus are a happy hunting ground for those who are fond of Indian English. A magnificent example is the following, from a hotel in Tamil Nadu; 'The live-li ness of the music right amidts you would beckon you once again to indulge yourself just this once in our Gulabd and Black Forests, and the very goodliest of our confectionary items.' You will also find old English favourites like caramel castered and the somewhat aeronautical plane castud.

Tea and coffee   Tea (*chai*) and coffee can be quite revolting because they are often served with milk and vast amounts of sugar already added to them. Furthermore, the tea has often been stewing for ages, especially on railway station stalls, and this doesn't improve its flavour; sometimes it can almost be undrinkable. South India is the home of Indian coffee, but this too can be a let-down; all too often the coffee you'll be served is instant of some sort, and again with milk and sugar added. In good hotels decent tea and coffee are easy to find, but outside these finding a palatable hot drink can be a problem.

Asking for a pot of coffee with 'separate milk and sugar' sometimes works; separate tea, milk, and sugar is called 'tray tea', but 'bed tea' is early morning tea!

In middle- and upper-class homes and in most reasonably expensive restaurants, ordinary Western crockery and cutlery are provided, and are used in the British fashion (as opposed to the American style of scooping with the fork in the right hand). In very traditional households, many rural homes, and in many of the 'meals' restaurants, this is not the case; the plates are metal, because there is crushed bone in porcelain that is objectionable to the Hindus, and knives and forks that have been used (possibly) by someone else are suspect from the point of view of ritual defilement. The origins of all this lie in the Hindu preoccupation with ritual cleanliness, especially with respect to food.

Table manners

The thali meals will always be served on a beaten metal plate, with pots called *katoris* on it that contain all the various bits and pieces; sometimes the plate is made with hollow depressions stamped in it, and these are used instead of separate katoris. In very traditional, rural, or expensive and pretentious places, a thali will sometimes be served on a fresh banana leaf, which is presumably the earliest form of throw-away plate. Hindu chauvinists can therefore claim that their ancestors not only invented aeroplanes and telephones (see 'Introduction'), but also, with a little more credibility, disposable crockery.

In a traditional restaurant or household you may sometimes be required to eat with your fingers. This is also true on some train journeys in the south, and leads to the obvious problem of washing your hands; *never* touch food with your fingers unless they have been properly washed. In the 'meals' restaurants, there is often a bucket or basin for this purpose, but the contents don't always inspire confidence. Washing your hands on lower-class train journeys can be impossible.

The left hand is unclean, because it is the one used for unclean purposes (see 'The modern Indian people'); you therefore eat with the right and the right only. In the north, the tips of the fingers are used, not the rest of the hand, and the roti is used as an edible scoop. In the south, where the food tends to be more liquid, the whole hand is used, and in place of the roti, rice is used to absorb and scoop liquids. Eating with your hand is actually easier than it sounds, once you've had a bit of practice; as mentioned before, the main problem is one of hygiene. *Don't risk your health through trying to be polite and eating with dirty fingers.*

Tipping   Tipping in restaurants can be something of a problem, because, in spite of the large (usually 10 per cent) service charge that most of the expensive places add on, waiters can become almost menacingly vulture-like when you pay your bill, especially when the change comes back, and all in the hope of coercing you into giving them a big tip.

In the better restaurants, the conventions for tipping are much the same as those in other countries; if there is no service charge, give between 10 and 15 per cent; if there is a service charge but you were particularly pleased with the service, then give a tip as a gesture of appreciation; but whatever you do, for the sake of other visitors, don't be *bullied* into giving one where it isn't deserved. Tipping can absorb a surprisingly large part of your budget once it gets out of hand.

In smaller restaurants, there usually isn't a service charge, and the waiters – often young boys – don't seem to expect a tip, even from tourists. Obviously it's a pleasant gesture to give something for the service, but you don't have to be too generous; a few rupees represents a substantial sum to many Indians. This might sound mean, but if you feel generous one day, and the next day go back to the same place, you'd better still feel generous, because a failure to keep up the previous level of baksheesh will not be appreciated. In the 'meals' restaurants, although there is no service charge, you'll often find strange little additions have appeared on your bill; always check the bill against the menu (if there is one) and your memory of what you had to eat.

Fruit is easy to buy, at street stalls, from roadside vendors, and at railway stations. Vendors will often board trains and buses with grapes, bananas, oranges, and mangoes. Fruit with thick skins or rinds are always safe to eat, and can be the mainstays of many a thirsty bus or train journey. Coconuts are often sold by roadside traders, who will sit in the shade of a large tree with a machete and a pile of nuts beside them. For about Rs2 or Rs3, you buy a coconut which the vendor slashes open with a machete so that you can drink the milk; the vendor then cuts it open and scoops out the white meat for you to eat.

Fending for yourself

Apples and soft fruits can be found in the northern and mountainous areas (Kashmir, for example), and Himachel Pradesh apple juice is sold all over the country; most large railway stations have one of the booths ('A Government of Himachel Pradesh enterprise', the signs say) selling it by the glass.

Western bread can sometimes be found in ordinary shops, and many towns have bakeries, but the quality of their product can range from the reasonable to the very bad; cheese and butter are fairly easy to find, though not in all areas; everywhere dried pulses and nuts can be bought if you are desperate for something to eat that isn't full of spices.

Services, communications, and the media

Electricity The Indian national supply is 220V AC at 50 Hz. The supply is very unreliable even in the big cities, and is subject to the frequent interruptions that are called load-shedding; Bombay is better than most places, because the supply there is in the hands of the Tata Corporation. If you are using any equipment that is sensitive to sudden voltage fluctuations, you should take steps to protect it with a buffer transformer. The plugs are round three-pin, like the old-fashioned ones in the UK; visitors from the US should note that the plugs and sockets are like British ones in that the plugs are not bonded to the cables, and that the socket includes a switch which is usually (but not always) off when the switch is up. Finding adaptors can be difficult; the size of the Indian plugs and sockets doesn't match the old British ones. Good hotels have the standard two-pin razor sockets.

Weights and measures India uses the metric system. Some conversions are given in the boxed area.

Weight is measured in kilograms (kilos, kg) and grams (g).

1 kg = 1,000 g = 2.2 lb avoirdupois

Distances are given in kilometres (km) and shorter lengths in metres (m) and millimetres (mm).

1 km = 1,000 m
1m   = 1,000 mm (1 centimetre [cm] = 10 mm)
1 km = 0.62 miles
1 m   = 3.3 feet

Capacity is measured in litres (l).

1 litre = 0.88 Imperial quarts or 1.06 US quarts

Temperatures are given on the Celsius scale.

If you are not familiar with the metric system, it is worth memorizing some of the conversions, because food is sold by weight in markets (do you really want a kilo?) and cloth by the metre (do you really need four metres to make a pair of trousers?).

Counting and numbers

You will encounter the terms *lakh* and *crore* in India. A lakh is 100,000, sometimes written as 1,00,000, while a crore is 10,000,000, sometimes written as 1,00,00,000. The use of these terms is very common in newspapers and advertisements.

Time

Indian Standard Time is five and a half hours ahead of Greenwich Mean Time, and nine and a half hours ahead of Eastern Standard Time in the US. There are no internal time zones within India.

The telephone system

The Indian telephone system is being modernized, and has greatly improved during the last few years with the introduction of new technology and subscriber trunk dialling (STD) for both national and international calls. Local services, which still rely heavily on antiquated electromechanical exchanges, are more hit and miss, and you could well find that it is easier to get a call connected to London than it is to an office a few miles away.

The handsets range from futuristic push-button trimphones to black bakelite things familiar to devotees of 1940s' films; the latter type is often to be found in the rare public callboxes (phone booths). Although the telecommunications system has been decoupled from the postal service, the post office is often the place where you can find a public phone that works, especially if you wish to make a long distance or international call.

Public telephones

There are three general types of public phone in India. First, there are the old coin boxes (phone booths) which can be found at railway stations, in some museums and art galleries, and sometimes on the street, though these will often have people living in them who will resent being disturbed. These phones are useless for anything except local and transferred charge (collect) calls – if they work at all.

The coin boxes are small, and only take a 50 paise coin, which doesn't buy you very much time.

To operate these, first check whether the wire to the handset is joined to anything; if it is, then place the relevant part of the handset against your ear and listen for noises. Often public phones are not dead, but neither can they be said to be alive, for instead of a dialling tone (a continuous clicking, like the old dialling tone in Britain) you will hear all manner of strange noises, hisses, whistles, random clicks, and very distant Indian voices saying, 'Hello, hello, hello? Are you there Calcutta? Hello?' Never mind, rattle the cradle and try again; sooner or later you'll get a dialling tone.

Keep your 50 paise coins handy as you dial, because you have to insert them as soon as the other party has answered. If you haven't got the right person, it's quite simple; don't put the coins in and you'll be cut off. Unfortunately, you are often cut off even when you *have* got the right person on the other end of the line, and when you've put your coins in. Just be patient and try again.

The second type of public telephone has no coin box, but has an attendant who will dial the number for you – usually the wrong one unless you write it down – and time your call. (Many of these booths are staffed by disabled people through a Government of India scheme to give employment to the handicapped.) A few – and a *very* few – of these booths are set up for long-distance STD calls, both domestic and international, but these are a rare discovery. Most of them are restricted to Rs1 local calls. As usual in India, there will be a queue in front of them, and you have to push and shove like everyone else; otherwise you'll never get near the thing. Always have the number you want clearly written down before you reach the operator; if you pause when you reach the head of the queue, you will simply be pushed out of the way, and have to start all over again. These booths are often found in or near railway and bus stations, and sometimes near small post offices.

> # NUMBER
> # BUSY
> # ?
> # DIAL AFTER
> # SOMETIME
>
> ## OBNOXIOUS CALLS
> A subscriber making or allowing to make obnoxious calls is liable to lose his telephone connection permanently.

Source: New Delhi telephone directory

The third type of public telephone is found in large post offices and airport terminals; these are similar to the continental European staffed booths (like the Italian SIP service, for example), where you make the call yourself in a cubicle, and an attendant outside monitors a meter and calculates the charge. These are extremely useful, because they offer full STD services for both national and international calls, and are often open (at airports, for example) twenty-four hours a day.

When no such service is available, you must go to the post or telegraph office and book a call through the operator, which is more expensive. (See the section below on calls through the operator.)

Private telephones

There is a long waiting list for telephone connections in India, and the length of this list is something that provokes the average Indian into extraordinary exaggerations, backed up by all sorts of obviously apocryphal stories. However, there is no doubt that obtaining a brand-new line can take a long time. A deposit of Rs8,000 is charged for a new service, and there is a bi-monthly rental charge for a private line of Rs136. Billing is also bi-monthly. If you take over a house that has no telephone connection, and you want one, then give up hope unless you intend to be in India for a very long time.

As mentioned earlier, all sorts of fancy and futuristic handsets are now making their appearance, and seem to be something of a status symbol.

Calls through the operator   If STD doesn't work, or if for some reason you can't use it, then you will have to go through the operator. This is not only time-consuming, but also more expensive than STD, and can be very expensive if you inadvertently get a priority service – the Indian telephone network is overloaded (which is why STD calls can just give the busy signal for hours, forcing you to try the operator), and in an attempt to alleviate this, calls can be made with various priorities.

First of all, there is the ordinary trunk call, which has to be booked in advance. This can take some time, several hours being common. Then there are Urgent Calls, which are supposed to be connected more quickly, and which are charged at twice the normal tariff; and there are Lightning Calls, which in theory are connected immediately, and are very expensive indeed, at eight times the normal tariff. There is also something called a Demand Call, which is available between a limited number of stations in India, and internationally only to the UK; a Demand Call is supposed to be as quick as a Lightning Call, but is only charged at the Urgent rate. If you are lost, you'd better study the front of an Indian telephone directory, where all this is set out in great detail.

The above calls are all charged in units of three minutes; that is, once you're connected, you pay for three minutes (so you might as well use them), then the pips sound and another three-minute charging period begins. Urgent and Lightning Calls are often restricted to six minutes' duration to ease the load on the lines.

When making an operator controlled call, it is therefore very important to make clear what service (that is, what priority) you want. Another refinement is the Person-to-Person (PP) facility, which is quite useful; you book the call and ask to speak to a particular person, and charging only begins when the operator is satisfied that that person is on the other end of the line. The PP facility is *not* available with Demand Calls, and in general a 50 per cent surcharge is added for its use with Urgent and Lightning Calls.

These can be made by STD or via the operator. The PP facility is available, and Demand Calls can be made to the UK. It is usually cheaper to make international transferred charge (collect) calls, and this can be done to the US, UK, Canada, Australia, and New Zealand. If an international call is booked through the operator, it will often take about an hour for the connection to be made.

International calls

Luxury hotels provide STD phones in their rooms. In others, calls have to be routed through the desk, or made from the lobby. Making a call from a hotel has certain advantages; you don't have to queue, and the surroundings are pleasant. Unfortunately, hotels will add a service charge of their own to your bill, just for making the call; for example, an extra Rs40 was added to the cost of a Rs360 call I made to the UK from a Mysore hotel. Sometimes a higher charge is made, and when this is done on a percentage basis, it can make the cost of international calls prohibitively expensive.

Calls from hotels

These apply on ordinary calls, made through the operator, between 10 p.m. and 5 a.m. on weekdays, and all day Sunday and during the three fixed public holidays on 26 January, 15 August, and 2 October. There are *no* concessions on Urgent or Lightning calls.

There is a concessionary STD rate between 7 p.m. and 8 a.m. on weekdays, and all day Sunday and during the three fixed public holidays. There are no concessionary rates for international calls, whether made STD or via the operator.

Concessionary rates

The larger cities have well-laid-out phone books, with useful information pages prefacing the directory.

Telephone directories

Recorded information services and the usual emergency services are listed. You can even send greetings telegrams if you wish, with messages like 'Heartiest Diwali greetings', 'Wishing the function every success', 'Heartiest Pongal greetings', and best of all, perhaps, 'Greetings on the occasion of "Pary Ushan", a day of universal forgiveness.' The big cities also have a yellow pages (classified directory).

The general rule when trying to make a phone call is, as with many other things in India, *be patient*. Telephone lines come to those who wait.

Fax and telex   India has an efficient domestic and international telex service. Fax services are becoming more common, and there are even plans to provide fax services at some airport terminals for the benefit of business people. Most luxury hotels will have a telex service.

Postal system   The domestic postage service is quick and efficient. All domestic mail should include the PIN code (the Indian postal or zip code) in the address; lists of PIN codes can be found at post offices. Airmail letters are Rs6.50 per 10 g. Domestic letters are charged at two rates; lettercards (a sort of postcard) are 15 paise, while sealed letters are 70 paise for weights up to 10 g.

The speed of the service depends on where your letter is posted; an air letter to the UK or USA posted from a country village can take well over a week to reach its destination, whereas from a large city post office, it will take only four or five days. If you have a letter to post, and know that within a few days you'll be in a fairly large town, it is probably better to wait until you've arrived there before you post it; otherwise it might simply vanish for a long time.

Post offices   Indian post offices, like other official organizations in India, have very strange methods; be prepared for long waits, because you might have to have a letter weighed at one counter, where the charge will be written on it in pencil or ballpoint, buy the stamps at another counter (and make sure they give you *all* your change), and hand the thing (letter plus stamps) in at yet another counter to be franked and stuffed in a postbag. If you are very unlucky, there'll be a long queue at every counter, and you'll wish you'd never written to anyone in the first place.

Nothing can compare with posting a parcel, however; this is a major operation which makes queuing for stamps and so on a mere bagatelle. For a start, the parcel must be enclosed in linen, stitched, and sealed along the seams with sealing wax. You'll see many of these dirty white linen packages at the parcels counter in any Indian post office; parcels will *not* be accepted unless they have been wrapped in this fashion, and no amount of brown paper or scotch tape will do. To get your parcel sewn into a linen bag, either you can approach a tailor (most Indian tailors are used to being asked to do this), or, in larger cities or at large post offices, you may find someone sitting on the steps outside, with linen and thread at the ready, who is prepared to do this for a moderate sum of anything from about Rs8 to Rs15.

Once the thing has been sewn into the linen bag, you can return to the parcels counter and go through all the usual formalities – if it is going abroad, then a customs declaration form has to be filled in. One catch is that although the parcel will be weighed at the parcels counter (with which you will have become very familiar by this time), and the charge calculated, you will probably have to go somewhere else – a stamp counter – to buy the stamps. When you've put the stamps on your parcel, you'll have to go back to the parcels counter to post it. It's all somewhat reminiscent of the State Bank of India.

Some shops will offer to post things abroad for you. Be wary of this; the government-run places are usually reliable, but not all of the independent businesses are so by any means; if it is possible, bring expensive souvenirs and gifts with you on the plane when you return. The export of antiquities over 100 years old is strictly forbidden; the value of a parcel to a foreign address can be up to Rs1,000, and to a domestic address, Rs500.

Post offices are open six days a week, and are closed on Sundays in common with most other Indian businesses. Counter service starts at 10 a.m. and usually finishes at 5 p.m., although in large cities the main post office will have extended hours. Letters can be posted by handing them over at a counter, where they'll be franked, or by posting them in the very inconspicuous letter boxes on the streets; these bear a faint resemblance to the old red British pillar boxes. All large hotels have their own arrangements for the collection of guests' mail.

Indian stamps don't stick, and have to be encouraged to do so by the use of glue; you'll find a pot of this, with a brush with which to apply it, on the desks in most post offices. The same is true of Indian envelopes, for they either have effective glue, which means that, because of the humidity, they are already sealed up (empty) when you buy them; or they are impossible to seal at all without another glue. Don't be alarmed by this, just use the stuff they provide in the little pots.

Radio and television   Radio broadcasting in India started in 1927, and television was introduced in 1959 in Delhi. The Indian Broadcasting Service became All India Radio (AIR) in 1936, and since 1957 has been called Akashvani.

Radio   The national radio channel broadcasts at 1566 kHz, from about 7.45 p.m. to 1.30 a.m. daily; programmes are usually sports news, financial news, concerts of both Indian and Western music, and various features in Hindi and some other regional languages. There are one or two channels in large cities. In Delhi, for example, there are Delhi A and Delhi B, which broadcast from around 6 a.m. until midnight; programme schedules can always be found in national papers, most of which have local editions (see the next section). There is a surprising number of English language programmes, a fair number of news bulletins, but very little in the way of radio drama or detailed political analysis.

News coverage tends to be as superficial as that

on US radio stations, with the added disadvantage that government control pushes it very close to outright propaganda; this is especially noticeable in the reporting of foreign affairs, which can be little short of scandalous, especially where the US is concerned. You will hear the newsreader baldly state such things as, 'The US today blocked a new proposal for world peace at the United Nations in New York.' Such offerings are made without any explanation or amplification. It is hardly surprising that many educated Indians listen to the BBC World Service's Hindi broadcasts (and, of course, the English language broadcasts).

There are also limited FM stereo transmissions, often for only one or two hours in the evening; these tend to be Indian or Western music, and are well worth listening to if you have a radio.

Television – Doordarshan – is organized in a similar *Television*
fashion, with one or two channels in large cities, which transmit local and national programmes. Transmission is divided into two periods, one of which starts fairly early in the morning and lasts up to noon, and the other in the evening. In lesser cities the transmission time may be more limited. There are relatively few films, the news deserves the same comments as those made earlier about the radio news broadcasts, and many of the other programmes tend to be of the educational or public service type. Indian television can be quite interesting as a window on the country – or at least on official thinking about how the country ought to be – but its entertainment value is even more limited than that in the USA or UK.

Doordarshan recently screened Ramanad Sagar's spectacular serialization of *The Ramayan*, the ancient Sanskrit epic supposedly composed by the sage Valmiki, which tells of the exile of Prince Rama with his faithful wife Sita, of Sita's abduction in the forest by Ravana, the demon king of Lanka, and of her rescue by her husband with the aid of the monkey army led by the faithful monkey general Hanuman. This was originally scheduled for fifty-two weekly episodes on Sunday mornings, but was later extended to seventy-eight, the last of which ended on 31 July 1988. The serial gained a remarkable popularity, and streets would empty at 9.30 a.m. every Sunday morning as everyone crowded round the nearest TV set; in Uttar Pradesh, villagers even pooled their resources to buy communal black-and-white sets, and as the series drew to an end there were strikes and disturbances in various parts of the country from enthusiasts who wanted yet more episodes.

The discussion that surrounded the filming is very interesting, because it illustrates many of the tensions in contemporary Indian society: historians advised the producer that Sita would have worn a topless costume, as would all the female courtiers; but verisimilitude was sacrificed to protect the modesty of Indian womanhood, and Sita appeared throughout in a sari. Even more sensitive, perhaps, was the issue of the monkey army itself, the *vanars*; the term was probably applied to the jungle tribes of the south, and whatever its connotations at the time, it is hardly likely to be seen as a complimentary epithet nowadays. The monkey army therefore remained just that, men in monkey outfits looking for all the world like every Indian child's vision of the monkey god-general, Hanuman. To criticisms from Indian women's groups that Sita appears weak, the producer retorted that in his version the long-suffering heroine cries for only about a fifth of the time she does in the original story, which Indian feminists may or may not have found consoling.

Many hotels provide closed-circuit TV in the rooms, with a non-stop diet of appalling US films and soaps; you can lie in your room in Nirula's hotel in New Delhi and watch *Cagney and Lacey* when you're bored with the Red Fort and the Chadni Chowk. You'll get *Where Eagles Dare*, *Batteries Not Included*, *Space Balls*, and other such masterpieces of the Western cinema; after them, Hindi movies don't seem so bad after all.

Newspapers   India has a long history of English-language journalism. Some of it is good, much of it is indifferent, and most of it is appalling. There are 138 English dailies, compared with 554 in Hindi. The number of dailies in other Indian languages can be judged from the total of dailies, which is around 1,600. Most of these papers are privately owned, and can be categorized by their attitude to the present Indian government; some are sympathetic and 'establishment', others are wildly critical and are 'opposition'.

In September 1988, Rajiv Gandhi antagonized the press (and many other influential groups) by his blatant attempt to introduce a kind of censorship. A bill was introduced in the lower house, the Lok Sabha, with new press laws slipped into it. Because of the Congress's huge majority, it was passed without too much difficulty; the trouble only started later, when journalists realized what was being done to them. Rajiv Gandhi's friends had been featuring in various press stories relating to graft and corruption with increasing frequency: the bill tightened the rules relating to defamation, and in particular placed the burden of proof on the journalist who was responsible for writing anything which anyone else objected to. It provided that original documentary evidence would have to be produced (journalists would thus be unable to protect their sources), and introduced heavy fines and prison sentences as penalties. This produced a wave of protest that forced Rajiv Gandhi to accept defeat by not introducing the offending bill into the upper house (the Rajya Sabha) for ratification; if this is not done, bills automatically lapse after six months. The Prime Minister's remarkable achievement was to unite almost the entire press against him, including such men as Mr Girilal Jain, editor of the prestigious *Times of India*, and Mr M.J. Akhbar, editor of the Calcutta *Telegraph*, both of whom would usually be regarded as pro-establishment figures.

Indian daily and weekly papers can be quite boring for anyone without an active interest in, and fairly detailed knowledge of, Indian domestic politics, because this provides most of their material; foreign news coverage is almost non-existent.

*English-
language
dailies*

Of the major English-language dailies that are worth reading, *The Times of India* has Delhi and Bombay editions, but is available all over the country. Many people would regard this as the acme of Indian journalism, and its measured, magisterial tone is indeed reminiscent of the English *Times* before Rupert Murdoch. It is generally regarded as establishment; that is, it would be pro-Congress and pro-government on most issues. As stated above, it was a measure of Rajiv Gandhi's folly that he turned *The Times of India* against him.

The *Indian Express* is probably the most interesting and lively of the dailies; it is radical and virulently anti-government, has some excellent pieces of journalism, and even a foreign news section – although the latter is very sparse. Although the crucial papers were published by *The Hindu* (see below), it was the *Indian Express* that led the campaign against the government over the Bofors affair in 1988; this scandal concerned allegations that government officials and others had been raking in huge kick-backs from Bofors in return for arms contracts. The offices of the *Indian Express* have frequently been raided, and the paper's editorial tone is splendidly sardonic and irreverent. It claims to have the largest circulation of any daily, although it is not the dominant paper in any particular city; editions are produced in Ahmedabad, Bangalore, Bombay, Chandigarh, Cochin, Delhi, Hyderabad, Madras, Madurai, Pune, Vijayawada, and Viziangaram.

The Hindu is the great south Indian paper, printed in Madras, Coimbatore, Bangalore, Hyderabad, Madurai, and Gurgaon. The standard of journalism is good, and although the paper would perhaps be regarded as conservative and establishment, it was *The Hindu* that published Swiss bank documents relating to the Bofors scandal. Like the other papers, its front page is almost entirely taken up with domestic affairs, whatever has been going on in the rest of the world; it also carries a huge number of advertisements.

The *Hindustan Times* is printed in Delhi and Patna, and is really a north Indian newspaper;

although there is full national news coverage, the paper is rarely found in the south. Other papers are *The Statesman* (Calcutta, Delhi), *The Telegraph* (Calcutta), the *India Post* (Bombay), the *Free Press Journal* (Bombay), and *The Deccan Herald* (Bangalore). The Calcutta papers are interesting, for Bengalis have always been in the forefront of Indian writing; Bengal's internal politics are fascinating, as it is one of the states that has a communist government, which is not to the liking of the conservative *Telegraph*.

Coverage

Indian domestic politics is a strange labyrinth. The main problem of interpreting what you read in the papers is knowing what all the initials that are used for the multitude of opposition parties stand for. You might read all about the leadership struggle in the AIADMK between the Janaki faction and the Jayalalitha faction; unless you have a serious interest in Indian politics, you won't really want to read this every day at breakfast. One of the things that is almost shocking about Indian papers – which is a reflection of Indian political life – is that national issues are rarely debated or analysed in any depth. Few politicians ever seem to talk about policies or ideas; most seem to spend all their time verbally abusing each other. So even when you have learnt to crack the code of the AIADMK, the DMK, the CPI (M), the Cong(I) and the Cong(S), you are likely to have discovered very little about what really goes on in India.

Most of the papers have readers' letters, and these are always very interesting; there are also daily guides to radio and TV programmes, diaries of local events and public engagements, and general entertainment guides. At weekends many newspapers have supplements carrying feature articles and Western comic strips, and perhaps it is these that give the Indians their sense of spiritual superiority; the *Indian Express* Sunday magazine has Spiderman, Mandrake the Magician, Peanuts, 'The Small Society', and 'Bringing Up Father'. Apart from the comic strips, the only other mentions of the United States are when it gives arms or support to Pakistan, when new crime figures are published that show New York is uninhabitable, and in the 'matrimonials' columns, in which parents advertise on their child's behalf for a suitable spouse. These are worth studying, for they reveal much of the truth behind the clichés about Indian spirituality and tolerance. 'Wanted suitably qualified beautiful, homely girl, having green card/visitor's visa for States for handsome Garg, Manglik boy, 25 yrs, 172 cms, MBA, employed in States (green card holder).' 'Girsikh match for slim, smart, beautiful, convent educated, Honours Graduate, Delhi University, 23/ 159 girl belonging to respectable Girsikh Khatri family, income high five figures monthly, only very well placed, decent, Girsikh families need correspond.'

Some foreign newspapers are available, usually in the bookstalls of the major hotels. *The Times, Daily Telegraph, Guardian, The Independent, Herald-Tribune* (Singapore edition), and *Wall Street Journal* (Asian edition) are fairly easy to come by, but are rather expensive; Indian dailies cost about Rs1.20, with a 20 paisa air surcharge where applicable; foreign papers cost from Rs18 to Rs20. British papers are of course a few days out of date; in Delhi or Bombay this will only be by one or two days, but in Madras and Calcutta three or four. In Delhi, around Connaught Circle, the street vendors also sell British papers; for some reason very ancient copies of *The Sunday Telegraph* seem a firm favourite.

Time, Newsweek, a surprising range of English women's magazines, and a few stray copies of *Paris Match* and *Brigitte* can also be found in the bookshops of the luxury hotels. No other European or American papers or magazines seem to make it to India.

Indian glossy magazines Indian glossies have become a craze, with titles like *Indian Today, Sunday* etc. Many of them are *Time* look-alikes, but again without any foreign news coverage. (The exceptions to this are the reports about Pakistan and Sri Lanka; the former has always been of absorbing interest as India's devil incarnate, while the latter has become newsworthy because of the civil war and the presence of the Indian Peace Keeping Force.)

India Today is a very interesting and detailed fortnightly magazine dealing with Indian social, political, and economic issues; it appears to pursue a tough and independent editorial policy, and has been severely critical of the Gandhi administration *and* the opposition. It is available all over the country, and costs Rs7.

Others worth reading are the weekly *Sunday*, the cultural fortnightly *India Magazine*, *The Illustrated Weekly of India*, the monthly *Gentleman Magazine* (which in spite of its title has no dirty pictures but does have some interesting articles), *Bombay* (which is effectively a city update, and a very useful entertainment guide), *Frontline* (a Madras-based fortnightly), and *Destination India*. The last is a monthly which features special articles on travel in India, and carries useful information such as changes in facilities or services at domestic airport terminals etc. Finally there are a number of smaller magazines that provide only information, such as *Bombay Calling* (a complimentary copy will often be found in Bombay hotel rooms), and *Delhi Diary* (which is a very useful guide to entertainment and eating out in the capital).

Financial journalism

Financial Express is a stablemate of the *Indian Express*; other business papers include *Economic Times* and *Business Standard*. There are also a number of magazines that deal with financial and business affairs, *Business India*, *Business Update*, and *Business World*. *The Economist* can be found in hotel bookshops.

News agencies

India has four news agencies, Press Trust of India (PTI), United News of India (UNI), Samachar Bharati, and Hindustan Samachar. The PTI was created in 1947, and now has 124 news bureaux throughout the country.

The Press Council of India dates from the Press Council act of 1978, and is intended to safeguard freedom of the press, and to monitor and improve the standard of newspapers and news agencies.

Indian films   Moving pictures arrived in India on 7 July 1896, courtesy of the Lumière brothers (Auguste and Louis), who put on a show at Watson's Hotel in Bombay. Their short films had titles such as 'The arrival of a train' and 'A demolition', but in spite of this possibly inauspicious beginning, the Indians took film and the cinema to their hearts and have never looked back; now India produces more films per year than any other country in the world, and the Indian film industry's output dwarfs that of Hollywood. Few of these ever reach the West, because most of them are so appalling – even by the standards of American cinema. The Indians themselves acknowledge this, and the shocking violence depicted in many Tamil and Hindi movies has become a matter of concern for the educated middle classes, who, like their counterparts in the West, spend much time playing prophet and seer and tracing the roots of all manner of social ills to cinema violence.

There is a sharp divide in the Indian film industry between the minority urban 'art' cinema, exemplified by the work of Satyajit Ray and Mrinal Sen, which tends to reach Western audiences, and the great mass of what are sometimes called 'masala' films – that is, the ones you'll see advertised in the huge hoardings that line the streets in Bombay and Madras.

Popular films   The stories, such as they are, in these films are either sentimental and trite to the point of inanity, or terrifyingly violent, or both. It is these films that you'll be subjected to in video coaches, and they are, like the matrimonials columns, an interesting window on India.

Few people would argue that popular films draw a realistic portrait of contemporary Indian society, but what they do contain are reflections of the hopes, fears, and frustrations of many ordinary Indians. A recurrent theme in the Hindi movie (and for that matter the Tamil movie) is a violent, antisocial outcast, who becomes a hero by his struggle against corrupt and oppressive institutional authority. The frequency with which this story-line recurs is one of the first things you notice on a long video coach journey; if I were an Indian politician, I'd take a warning from this. The nemesis of the corrupt and oppressive (whether they be gangsters, politicians, or businessmen) is usually terrible and bloody – not to mention painful. Such themes are usually mixed up with those of star-crossed love, where the women are (like Sita) tearful, somewhat ineffectual, and faithful with a touching canine devotion to their men; one longs for these women to do something other than pout, flutter their eyelashes, burst into tears, or swoon.

Recent Indian films have tended to lose even these threads of a story, and portray violence simply because the audience likes watching it. Then there is a strain of very unpleasant nationalistic films; Indian *Rambos*, as it were. These feature a kind of religious revivalism combined with an unnerving nationalistic fervour. Anyone who wants to take India and its people seriously should not only see at least one Hindi movie, they should see it at a cinema; the reactions of the audience are far more interesting than the film.

The Indian 'art' cinema produces first class films, but unfortunately they are hard to see outside Calcutta (which is the centre of the great Bengali film school) and some of the other major cities. Indian film critics give this type of film various appellations, New Film, New Wave Film, Regional Cinema, and so on. For most Westerners, the name of Satyajit Ray is synonymous with Indian intellectual cinema, but there is a large group of like-minded film makers whose products are well worth making a great effort to see. From Ray's era there are Mrinal Sen and Ritwik Ghatak; later Bengali film makers in this tradition are Tapan Sinha and Tarum Majumdar. Bombay is the capital of the popular film industry, yet it has also produced Basu Chatterji; the south too has a crop of first class films, for Madras is another major centre of the industry.

The 'art' cinema

The film industry

A total of almost 1,000 films are produced in India every year, and about 75,000,000 Indians are estimated to go to a cinema every day! Ordinary cinemas are easy to find, and in a town of reasonable size, there'll be one on every street. If you go to one yourself, be prepared to be stared at; many in the audience will watch you instead of the film.

Popular film stars are national heroes and heroines, and their lives and loves are avidly followed by many people. *India Today* has what is virtually a gossip column in the back, where pouting actresses explain their private agonies over the reception of their latest film, or hulking actors in shiny lurex sequined jackets coyly talk about their 'mature relationship' with their leading ladies.

Film stars have even made the big time in politics; Andhra Pradesh has as state prime minister the colourful ex-star N.T. Rama Rao, who runs a bizarre party called the Telegu Desam; until his recent (and lavishly mourned) death, the Tamil star M.G. Ramachandran was minister in Tamil Nadu. Such things are by no means confined to California and Washington.

If you want to have a part in a Hindi movie, hang round the YMCA in Bombay; sometimes you'll be approached by film makers who are looking for Western extras. You'll probably end up playing a hippy on a beach, who corrupts an otherwise decent Indian boy, who is rescued by his big brother (with the aid of martial arts and large quantities of explosives).

Geography and climate

The principal physical features of the Indian subcontinent are shown on the map. Traditionally, the term 'India' included what are now the politically separate entities of Pakistan and Bangladesh, and these two countries contain much of two of the great Indian rivers, the Indus (of old the boundary of India upon the west) and the Brahmaputra. The land borders with Pakistan and Bangladesh do not correspond to major geographical divides, and this adds to the artificial, makeshift character of the frontiers with the two Moslem states. All of India's borders are troubled, and even the great mountain wall of Himalaya provides less protection than might be imagined, for here the Indian army confronts both the Pakistani and Chinese armed forces.

The lie of the land

Modern India is nonetheless vast, and it is easy to underestimate its size on the globe, for the south-jutting, triangular peninsula seems dwarfed by the great mass of Asia hanging above it; yet it is over 2,000 km from Simla in the north to Cape Comorin in the south, where the Bay of Bengal meets the Arabian sea; and from the desert city of Jaisalmer in the west, to Calcutta in the east, it is over 1,600 km across the wide top of the subcontinent. Those who imagine that they can 'do' India in a couple of weeks should take a careful look at the map.

The land is as diverse as the people who inhabit it. It is hard to describe a typical Indian landscape; indeed, there is no such thing. What scene is recalled when India is named? An early morning on a houseboat on Nageen Lake in Kashmir, with the call to prayer floating through the mist across the still water, the Hatrabal Mosque as white as the flame-like Himalayan peaks that rise behind it? Or a day of heat and pilgrimage in some southern temple city,

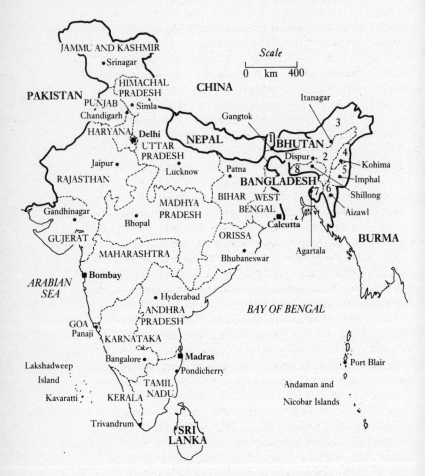

Key to the North East Frontier

1 Sikkim
2 Assam
3 Arunachal Pradesh
4 Nagaland
5 Manipur
6 Mizoram
7 Tripura
8 Meghalaya

JAMMU AND KASHMIR
• Srinagar

PAKISTAN

HIMACHAL PRADESH

PUNJAB
Chandigarh • Simla

CHINA

HARYANA
Delhi

UTTAR PRADESH

NEPAL

Gangtok

Itanagar

3

1 BHUTAN

Dispur • 2

8

Kohima

Imphal

Shillong

Aizawl

Scale
0   km   400

Jaipur •

Lucknow

Patna

RAJASTHAN

MADHYA PRADESH

BIHAR

WEST BENGAL

BANGLADESH

Gandhinagar •

Bhopal •

ORISSA

Calcutta

BURMA

GUJERAT

MAHARASHTRA

Bhubaneswar

Agartala

ARABIAN SEA

Bombay

• Hyderabad

ANDHRA PRADESH

BAY OF BENGAL

GOA
Panaji

KARNATAKA

Bangalore •

Madras

Pondicherry

Port Blair

Lakshadweep
Island

Kavaratti •

TAMIL NADU

KERALA

Andaman and

Nicobar Islands

Trivandrum •

SRI LANKA

"I hear the England XI won't be touring India this winter."

where soaring, cow-horned gopurams rise above the palms, and sacred kites drift down on lazy wings to be fed by white-robed priests? Or rain slanting down over teeming villages in Uttar Pradesh as your train slowly lurches past, an ox-drawn plough in a field, a line of swaying women walking by the railway track, brass water-pots balanced delicately on their heads? There are deserts, plains, mountains (not just the Himalayas), great rivers, forests, and jungles. Surely no other region except South America exhibits India's richness in wildlife and vegetation, set in a landscape that varies from arid plains to the world's highest mountain range.

India may be divided into seven major regions. These are: (1) the Himalayas, and the associated mountains and foothills of the north-east; (2) the Indo-Gangetic plain, which is the Hindi heartland, where you'll see the worst things that foreigners tend to associate with India as a whole in the crowded, poverty-stricken villages of Uttar Pradesh and Bihar;

(3) the Central Highlands, ranging from the Aravalli Range on the borders of the Thar Desert in the west to the Chotanagpur Plateau on the borders of Madhya Pradesh and Bihar; (4) the Peninsular Plateau (the Deccan) and the far south; (5) the west coast and the Western Ghats; (6) the east coast and the Eastern Ghats; (7) the islands, such as the Andaman and Nicobar groups.

The Himalayas

The Himalayas form a natural boundary in the north, but they are one of India's most troubled regions; a war was fought here with China in the early sixties, and Kashmir has long been a major cause of Indo-Pakistani antagonism. The hills in the north-east are politically one of India's most volatile regions, with trouble flaring up periodically between the local indigenous population and refugees from Bangladesh. The Himalayas are not a single range, but a number of parallel chains of mountains with deep valleys between them – like the Vale of Kashmir, for example. These mountains are the birthplace of three of the Indian rivers, the Ganga (Ganges), Indus, and Brahmaputra.

The Indo-Gangetic Plain

At the foot of the Himalayas lies the Indo-Gangetic Plain; in the far west this becomes (in Pakistan) the Indus plain, and to the south-west, the Great Indian or Thar Desert. It is upon these rich alluvial plains that many of the great events of Indian history have been played out, especially to the north of Delhi. Battles both historical and legendary have been fought all along the route of the national highway that once ran up to Peshawar when it was the old Grand Trunk; for this is the way to the north-western frontier, and from here all of India's many invasions have come. Even the great battle at the climax of the Mahabharata war was fought along here, at Kurushetra, some 100 km north of Delhi. The plain is flat and monotonous, and the journey across it, from Delhi to Calcutta, is very tedious; besides, the plain always seems to be at some extreme – unbearably hot or unbearably wet, or overwhelmed by yet another natural disaster. From the train, the tumbled

villages seem not to be the work of human hands,
but, in the monsoon, strange fungoid growths sprung
from spores buried in the mud in which they founder.
Along here you will see India at its worst, especially
in Bihar, once the centre of two great Indian empires,
and now one of the poorest and most backward
states of the Indian Union.

In the south-west, the plains run into the Thar
Desert, which is divided by the border between India
and Pakistan. The Thar Desert has the atmosphere
of the Arabian Nights, especially the somewhat
inaccessible towns of the far west like Jaisalmer.
Southwards, where the border between India and
Pakistan reaches the sea, is the Rann of Kutch, a
sterile marsh where the salt-laden soil prevents the
growth of vegetation. During the monsoon, the
Great Rann (which actually separates India from
Pakistan) is like a vast lake, the monotony of which
is relieved by a few islands where vegetation can gain
a foothold. During the hot season, it can dry out
altogether and turn into a huge salt pan. South of
the Ranns and the Kutch peninsula is the larger
Saurashtra Peninsula or Gujerat, with a small plain
(the Gujerat Plain) lying inland.

South of the alluvial plains of the Indo-Gangetic
basin, the land rises in ranges such as the Aravallis
to the Central Highlands. The Himalayas are supposed to be one of the world's youngest mountain
systems, formed by the collision of India (a fragment
of the ancient continent that included Africa, South
America, and Australia) with Asia; the Aravallis are
said to be amongst the world's oldest. They lie on
a north-east to south-west axis on a line from the
city of Ahmedabad to Jaipur in Rajasthan. The
present range is said to be but a remnant of the much
higher ancient range, whose peaks once thrust well
above the snow line; now the Aravallis scarcely rise
above 1,200 m, although at their highest, near Mount
Abu, they reach 1,700 metres.

The foreland of the Central Highlands is interrupted by the basin of the north-flowing Chambal River,
which joins the Ganga–Yamuna system in the plains,

*The Central
Highlands*

then comes Bundelkhand and its hills, which rise to about 500 m; the foreland continues eastwards with the Baghelkand and Chotanagpur Plateaux. South-wards is the Vindhya range of hills, which have an average height of about 300 m and traverse almost the whole of peninsular India in a great sweep from south-west to north-east; in the south-western extremity of this range lie the ancient cities of Indore and Ujjain. The Narmada river forms the southern boundary of the Central Highlands, which are sometimes called the Malwa Plateau.

The Peninsula Plateau

Peninsular India consists of the Deccan Plateau, which for the most part is somewhat arid and barren, and the Eastern and Western Ghats, the long chains of hills along the coasts. The Deccan actually consists of a number of linked plateaux, such as the Teladgama near Hyderabad, and the Karnatakan plateau to the south-west. This country contains some of India's most haunting and lovely scenery, and here you can look round and wonder where the teeming hordes of Asia are; indeed, much of the Deccan seems empty and deserted. Karnataka has many strange, boulder-strewn hills, known to geologists as granite inselbergs, which rise abruptly from the surrounding flats like huge anthills; these are one of the most striking features of the southern landscape, and it is upon one of these that the great monolithic statue of the Jain saint, Bahubali or Gomateshwara, stands near Sravanabelgola.

The Western Ghats

The Western Ghats form the western border of the Deccan, and run right down the coast from the Tapti River, which reaches the sea at Surat, to Cape Comorin in the extreme south; their average height is about 1,200 m. This range exerts a powerful climatic influence on the thin coastal strip between it and the Arabian Sea, because the hills intercept the monsoon winds from the south-west, which causes heavy rains to fall on their western slopes; these are therefore often covered with lush tropical rain forests, while their eastern slopes are bare and relatively arid. The train journey from Bombay to

Goa begins in the humid, wet coastal plain, takes you over the Ghats to Pune, then through the semi-desert on the other side where the country seems almost empty; finally, in the first light of dawn, you look out of your sleeping berth to see rain forest outside the window as the train crosses the Ghats again, this time from east to west.

The Eastern Ghats, which form an irregular eastern border to the Deccan, are broken up by large rivers such as the Krishna and the Godavari; all the great rivers in the Peninsula and the far south flow from west to east, rising on the eastern slopes of the Western Ghats.

The Eastern Ghats

In the far south, the Ghats end in the boss of hills named the Nilgiris, made famous because of the hill station of Ootacamund; to the east and south is the Tamilnad Plateau and the basin of the Cauvery, the great river of the south. Beyond all these is the continuation of the Western Ghats in what is sometimes called the Southern Ghats that stretch down to Cape Comorin. The other famous southern hill station, Kodaikanal, lies on a long ridge on the northern edge of this group, at an elevation of about 2,000 m.

The rivers in India may be split into three groups, corresponding to the three principal watersheds of the Himalayas, the Vindhya range, and the Western Ghats.

The rivers

The main rivers of the first group – the Indus, the Ganga, and the Brahmaputra – have already been mentioned. The major Deccan rivers are the Godavari, which flows east across peninsular India to the sea in a complicated delta near Rajahmundry; the Krishna–Tungabahdra system, which again flows east and reaches the Bay of Bengal in a delta near Vijayawada; the Cauvery down in Tamil Nadu, which also has a fertile delta that is the rice bowl of the south. The Periyar, Narmada, and Tapti rivers are notable in that they flow westwards, and empty into the Arabian sea; the Narmada is of some historical significance, as it was the traditional divide between the Deccan and the north. For example, when Harsha unsuccessfully attacked the Chalukyan Deccan kingdom in the middle of the sixth century, he was eventually forced to accept the Narmada as his southern frontier.

The northern rivers

The three great northern rivers are rich in historical and mythological association. The Indus, called the Sindhu by the Aryans, was traditionally the boundary of India upon the west, and indeed gave its name to the whole country. The Ganga is *the* holy river for the Hindus, and flows east to the Bay of Bengal through a complicated system of shifting tributaries, the main ones being the Yamuna (upon which Delhi stands), the Chambal, and the Son upon the right bank, and the Gomati, Ghaghara, Gandak, and Kosi on the left. This vast river basin occupies one quarter of the total area of India, and it is therefore not surprising that the Ganga has figured so greatly in Indian life and thought, and is personified as a goddess; the Ganga is also held to flow from the matted locks of the somewhat wild god Shiva, who is said to spend much time in his Himalayan home smoking joints. The Ganga has produced what was once a very fertile alluvial plain, and it was this (with the fertile plains of the Punjab, that are in fact part of the Indus plain) that has attracted wave after wave of invaders into the country.

The climate

Nothing in India is ever as simple as it might at first appear, and the climate is no exception. The simple description is that there are three seasons, a cool season (which is also *the* tourist season in much of the country) from about October to the middle of February, the hot season from mid-February to mid-June/early July, and the rest, which is the wet or monsoon season. This basic programme is subject to many regional variations, which can seriously affect travelling or simply enjoying your holiday; don't forget that India stretches from 37° 6' to only 8° 4' in latitude, and that significant climatic changes are going to take place as you move from north to south; also, as mentioned in the previous section in connection with the Western Ghats, mountains and hills can have a drastic effect on the local rainfall.

This is without doubt the best time to visit much of India, for then even the northern plains are bearable, being neither a humid bog nor a sweltering oven. In northern cities such as Delhi, the nights can become quite chilly; further north in the mountains, Dal Lake in the Kashmir will be frozen over, and the road to Leh in Ladakh (the part of the Tibetan plateau that is under Indian control) is blocked by thick snow. The cool season can be a good trekking season, notably in the Darjeeling region (October, November, and the beginning of December) and in Nepal as soon as the monsoon finishes.

The cool season

The south is probably at its best during the cool season, for although the temperatures never sink to the point where the air feels cold (even at night), the days are never too hot; this is the best time to travel in Tamil Nadu.

This is a good time to visit the northern Himalayan regions, and it is when the great northern hill stations like Simla have their season. The heat is terrible on the northern plains, where temperatures of over 40°C are common during the day. Peninsular India and the far south are more bearable because of the moderating effects of the surrounding sea, but in Bangalore daytime temperatures in May can rise to 33°C; this is not a pleasant time to travel, for the air will be full of fine dust, everyone seems to be asleep in the shade or throwing a fit of bad temper, and you'll have to take great care to drink as much as possible to avoid dehydration. If you go to India between late February and late June, head for the Himalayas (Himachel Pradesh or Uttar Pradesh) and the hill stations, or go to Kashmir and Ladakh. (The road into Ladakh should be open by early June.) The one place to avoid at all costs is the Ganga plain, where the temperatures are highest, the population densest, and everything at its worst.

The hot season

The monsoon   Towards the end of May, the monsoon begins to make its appearance, and the television and newspaper weather forecasts chart its progress in great detail, for the whole economy of India depends upon this annual spectacular. For the last few years, there have been failures of the monsoons, which spell near disaster for Indian farmers; given that most of the population is rural and works the land, a disaster for the farmers means a disaster for the Indian people.

The Indian government has contingency plans for drought relief in the event of a failure of the monsoon, and these worked magnificently in 1987 when there was one of the worst droughts since that of 1965. The effects of the drought were alleviated by the huge buffer stocks of foodgrains – about 23 million tonnes – and by the large area under irrigation, which has doubled since 1965. The successful efforts made to protect the Indian people against the periodic droughts and famines that have plagued them in the past must surely be one of modern India's greatest achievements. Although contingency planning can save lives, the failure of the monsoon means a great loss in cash crops and has a serious effect on the Indian economy; fortunately, the monsoon in 1988 was very good, and to some extent has offset the failures of the previous year.

The monsoon is often said to have shaped the Indian mind, and lent to it that somewhat fatalistic tendency that goes with the notions of karma (the fruits of one's works in a previous life showing themselves in the present one), and dharma (one's destiny and road to fulfilment), to both of which human life is inescapably bound. The monsoon also brings destruction as well as rebirth, another consistent theme in Indian religious thinking; the Lord Shiva is both a creator and a destroyer. During the rains, villages are washed away, fields are flooded, bridges are brought down, buses fall into water courses and many people are killed; yet this is also the time when new life springs almost miraculously out of the parched, sear ground that has been baked by the sun during the hot season. It is hardly surprising that the rains have been celebrated in

Indian prose, poetry, and dance, the coming of the monsoon to the country often being likened to the approach of a bridegroom to the bride.

Causes The causes of the monsoon are complex, and many distant phenomena seem to be associated with it – the Pacific current called El Niño, for example. The basic mechanism is the summer heating of the great Asian land mass to the north of India, the temperature of which rises faster than that of the Indian Ocean; large low pressure areas are created over 'hot spots' in Rajasthan and central India. Over the sea, temperatures are lower and the pressure higher, and this causes a reversal of the normal wind direction as large masses of moisture-laden air are sucked up from the south-west. A major shift in the pattern of the south-east trades also occurs as these too are sucked into the monsoon system.

Progress The first true monsoon rains can be expected in late May or early June, in the south of the country; heavy rains fall in Kerala on the Western Ghats, then move over the Deccan to Madhya Pradesh where they are joined by a second branch of the monsoon winds that pushes out into the Bay of Bengal and turns back north-west and over the coasts of Andrha Pradesh, Orissa, and Bengal. The latter winds then move up the Ganga valley, reaching the Delhi area in late June; by early July, the monsoon, if good, is covering the whole country.

Distribution of rainfall Although most of the country (with the exception of coastal Tamil Nadu) receives the bulk of its rainfall during the monsoon, the distribution of rainfall by region is very uneven, and contrary to many first-time visitors' expectations, it doesn't rain solidly all day even in those areas where the rainfall is high. The monsoon begins with sombre rolling clouds and heavy electrical storms; at first, instead of cooling the country down, the rains just make it humid. A pattern then develops of periods of heavy downpours, followed by clear spells in which the sun can break through. Although travel

Temperature (°C) and rainfall (cm)

	Jan.	Feb.	March	Apr.	May	June	July	Aug.	Sept.	Oct.	Nov.	Dec.
Delhi												
Av. daily temp.												
Max.	21	24	31	36	41	39	36	34	34	34	29	23
Min.	7	9	14	20	26	28	27	26	24	18	11	8
Av. rainfall	2.5	2.2	1.7	0.7	0.8	6.5	21.1	17.3	15.0	3.1	0.1	0.5
Calcutta												
Av. daily temp.												
Max.	27	29	34	36	36	33	32	32	32	32	29	26
Min.	13	15	21	24	25	26	26	26	26	23	18	13
Av. rainfall	1.3	2.4	2.7	4.3	12.1	25.9	30.1	30.6	29.0	16.0	3.5	0.3
Bombay												
Av. daily temp.												
Max.	28	28	30	32	33	32	29	29	29	32	32	31
Min.	19	19	22	24	27	26	25	24	24	24	23	21
Av. rainfall	0.2	0.1	0.0	0.3	1.6	52.0	70.9	41.9	29.7	8.8	2.1	0.2
Madras												
Av. daily temp.												
Max.	29	31	33	35	38	38	36	35	34	32	29	29
Min.	19	20	22	26	28	27	26	26	25	24	22	21
Av. rainfall	2.4	0.7	1.5	2.5	5.2	5.3	8.3	12.4	11.8	26.7	30.8	15.7
Cochin												
Av. daily temp.												
Max.	32	32	33	33	32	29	29	29	29	31	31	32
Min.	22	23	25	26	26	24	23	24	24	24	24	23
Av. rainfall	2.3	2.0	5.1	12.5	29.7	72.4	59.2	35.3	19.6	34.0	17.1	4.1

can be difficult, and the drinking water is at its most dangerous (this is the season for all the water-borne diseases), I have often found this to be a quite beautiful time to be in the country; the Rajasthan lake palaces are definitely at their best now, and the southern rivers, which can dwindle to streams during the hot season, are strong and swift-flowing; this is the busiest time for the farmers, and in the paddies rich green shoots emerge from the black water. The monsoon is not a good time to visit those areas where the rainfall is exceptionally heavy, a notable example being the Keralan coast.

The monsoon retreats in reverse order, leaving the Punjab in mid-September, moving back down the Ganga valley to the delta by the end of October, and leaving the peninsula by November. Sometimes the post-monsoon period from October to November is considered to be a fourth season, and the weather can be very pleasant although the humidity remains high. During this time, coastal Tamil Nadu receives the bulk of its rainfall. Tamil Nadu also has rains in December and January caused by winds that blow from the land mass of north-western India towards the Indian Ocean; these are sometimes called the north-east monsoons.

After the monsoon

When planning a trip, it is important to take the regional as well as seasonal variations in rainfall into account; to help you with this, the table gives monthly rainfall and temperature figures for important cities.

History and the development of religions

There are many features of later Hinduism for which
no roots can be traced in the cults and traditions of
the Aryan invaders who, in religious compositions
such as the Rig Veda, gave India its earliest literature.
Many of the features of contemporary Hinduism –
for example, the veneration of the female aspects of
the major deities (their *shakti*, which lends them
creative force), the veneration of cattle, the doctrine
of metempsychosis or the transmigration of the soul
– have no place in the religious thinking of the early
Aryans; and like so much in Indian culture, these
things appear to come from nowhere. Traditionally
there has been a tendency to dismiss such things as
borrowings (the Indians are by no means the
only people to believe in reincarnation), but the
comparatively recent discovery of the highly sophisticated urban civilizations of the Indus valley has
suggested a possible source of so much that is
unexplained, or for which no precedent can be found,
in the long Indian religious tradition.

The cities of the Indus valley lay undiscovered
until the late nineteenth century, when Alexander
Cunningham, the Archaeological Surveyor of India,
visited the site at Harappa, which is about 160 km
south-west of Lahore (now in Pakistan). An earlier
visitor had reported a 'brick castle', but this had
been used as ballast for the new railway line.
Cunningham noted that there were still many of the
bricks lying around, and the place seemed to merit
further investigation. However, it was not until the
1920s that work started in earnest on the Harappan
site, under Sir John Marshall, and while this was
under way one of his colleagues, R.D. Banerji,
discovered a similar site far away to the south in the
Sind. This also became known by the name of a

nearby contemporary settlement, Mohenjo-Daro, and proved as rich a discovery as Harappa. Many other sites of the Harrapan culture have been discovered, most of them along the Indus or the course of the old Sarasvati river.

Excavation has revealed a highly developed urban culture, with large towns of almost identical brick houses arranged in a precise grid pattern. Sophisticated arrangements were made for drainage and sanitation, and one of the most surprising things about the Harappan sites is their uniformity; the settlements are all remarkably similar, even if they are several hundred kilometres apart. This has led to speculation that the cultural conservatism of the Harappans is evidence of the theocratic nature of their society, but very little is really known about the people or their beliefs. Buildings in the cities have often been given names – the granary, the baths etc. – but no one has ever been sure that the functions of the various structures (except for what are obviously dwelling houses) have been correctly identified.

Harappan culture

There is no extant literature from the Harappan cities, but the Indus people were certainly literate. One of the most common finds in the cities were steatite seals, usually in small rectangular plaques. These carry an as yet undeciphered script, and there have been suggestions that it is everything from a primitive form of Tamil to a precursor of Ashoka Brahmi, the earliest of the Indian scripts of the historical period. As interesting as the inscriptions are the pictures on the seals, many of which appear to represent cult objects, religious scenes, or deities. One recurrent theme is especially noteworthy, and this is the strange creature who has become known as 'Lord of the Beasts' or 'Proto-Shiva'; some of the seals depict a horned being who sits in the posture often adopted by Indian holy men of later times (that is, squatting, with legs drawn up and heels touching). His (or its) large horns are buffalo horns, not those of ordinary cattle, and the face is very strange; indeed, it isn't even certain that the face is

a human one, and there are curious projections at
the sides that have led to suggestions that in fact
there are three faces, as in some later Indian deities.
This being is attended by various animals. In other
seals the humped bull is represented (though never
with the 'Lord of the Beasts'); the bull Nandi was
later the vehicle of the Lord Shiva.

All this has led to the suggestion that in the
Harappan culture we see the early religious traditions
that survived the Aryan conquests and later reasserted
themselves not only in Hinduism itself, but in the
heterodox cults of Buddhism and Jainism; much in
the later yogic and transcendental cults is believed
to have its early roots in the Indus valley. Furthermore, it is to the legacy of Harappa that the Indian
devotion to mother goddesses is often ascribed; crude
figurines of what is apparently a mother goddess
have been unearthed at many of the Indus sites.
Perhaps the most interesting find of all is a small
bronze statuette of a girl in a provocative pose, who
is often called a dancing girl – though again, no one
is really sure whether she was. She bears no
resemblance to the big-busted, waspy-waisted
heavenly maidens of later Indian iconography, but
is nonetheless sensuous and unambiguously sexually
attractive.

Decay   The decay of the Indus valley civilizations is also
shrouded in obscurity, though again there are
tantalizing hints. There appears to have been a
breakdown of life in the cities, some evidence of
burning, and further evidence of occupation by less
civilized people who nonetheless had better weapons.
It is about this time, the second half of the second
millennium BC, that the Aryans are supposed to
have made their appearance in India, and it is
therefore likely that they at least had a hand in the
collapse of the Indus valley urban civilizations. One
of the Aryans' more boisterous gods, Indra, is said
to have conquered and overthrown many strong
places, and is occasionally eulogized as 'the destroyer
of cities'.

The Aryans must have been a part of the larger group of migratory peoples who seem to have caused chaos in the civilized world in the second millennium BC. Although they were less sophisticated than many of the peoples they conquered, they possessed the advantages of better weaponry and light, two-wheeled chariots. The Aryan incursions into India must have been spread over a considerable period, rather than a single apocalyptic invasion, but the loosely federated tribes eventually established control over the north and began to penetrate southwards.

The Aryans and the Vedic age

The religion of the Aryans, as revealed by the collection of religious compositions, the Rig Veda, was a rather elemental affair, at once fearful, ferocious, and joyful, in which the sky, storm, and other natural phenomena were personified and worshipped or propitiated. In common with other Indo-European peoples, they had a sky god, Dyaus, but his importance was fast declining in the early Vedic age. The principal Aryan god of the times seems to have been Indra, a storm and war god; Indra was a jolly and amoral character, much given to vast binges and intoxication. He could, as a storm and war god, be fearful, but generally this ferocity seems to have been directed at the Aryans' enemies.

Early religion

Other important early Vedic deities are Agni, the fire god, who became increasingly important as the sacrificial cults in which fire played a vital role became more significant; Varuna, a somewhat austere god of cosmic order and justice who was later relegated to the sea as a kind of Poseidon; Surya, the divine personification of the sun; and Soma, the deity who presided over the mysterious intoxicating drink of the same name. Soma (the drink) evidently played a large part in the religious life of the Aryans, though its nature remains obscure. It couldn't have been alcoholic, because the references to its preparation make it clear that there was no time for fermentation to occur. It could, though, have been a hallucinogen, because the references to divine and human experiences under its influence are obviously similar to those induced by consciousness-expanding drugs. Many other lesser gods receive a mention, in particular Rudra, a solitary and rather dangerous deity who is sometimes taken to be the early Vedic forerunner of the Hindu Shiva.

Culture The Aryans established themselves in north-west India, and from there their power spread through the Ganga plain. They had a strong sense of tribal identity, especially with respect to the aboriginal inhabitants they subjugated, whom they called *Dasyus*; the descriptions of these people as dark, with broad noses and thick lips, corresponds to the present-day Dravidian inhabitants of south India. The origins of caste are sometimes attributed to the Aryan desire to maintain their racial purity from these despised aboriginals (though this is to oversimplify the institution grossly).

The Aryans appear to have maintained a loose tribal federation, where each tribe (or group of tribes) was ruled over by a chief or king, a *raja*; the office was hereditary and passed through the male line. The early Aryans were almost certainly illiterate, and the early Vedic compositions, such as the hymns of the Rig Veda, were preserved through oral tradition. There are no historical works or epics from this early period, and the only hints about the life of the early Vedic peoples are those given in their religious outpourings. The Vedas are four in number, with the Rig Veda being the earliest; then come the Sama, Yajur, and Atharva Vedas. The first is a compilation of verses from the Rig Veda for ritual purposes; the second is a book of sacrificial formulae that owes much to material in the Rig Veda. The Atharva Veda is a collection of magical spells, some of which seem very ancient indeed, whose meanings are obscure.

The Aryans were clearly not vegetarians, and they had no particular reverence for cattle; their society was patriarchal, and scant regard was paid to mother or other female deities. They were accomplished horsemen and charioteers, pastoral rather than urban, and although their kings were usually hereditary, they were sometimes chosen by election and ruled with the aid of a council known as a *sabha*. (The

present Indian parliament has two chambers called
the *Lok Sabha* and the *Rajya Sabha*.) This practice
has led to exaggerated claims from some Indians
about the extent of democratic institutions in early
Vedic society; this Indian cultural chauvinism is a
reaction to the tendency of many Western historians
(especially during the Victorian era) to ascribe every
significant Indian achievement to foreign influence.

Vedic religion revolved around a complex sacrificial   *Vedic religion*
cult. Vedic myth described (in the Hymn of the
Primeval Man) how the universe was brought into
being as a result of an ancient sacrifice, that of a
primeval man; the myth has affinities with those
found in other places, notably the primeval sacrifice
of the giant Ymir by the sons of Bor (one of whom
was Odin) in Norse mythology. Vedic religion never
seems to have had either a clearly defined creator
god, nor an unambiguous creation myth, apart from
this mystical veneration for sacrifice. Eventually
sacrifice by the priests attained a new significance,
and instead of offerings to the capricious gods in
return for their favours, sacrifices came to be seen
as a priestly reenactment of the primal sacrifice that
had brought the very universe into being. This
presumably led to an enhancement of the prestige of
the priestly class, the *brahmans*. A highly complex
mysticism was built up surrounding sacrifice, and
sacrificial cults in a sense eclipsed the worship of the
Vedic gods themselves; the gods were less powerful
than the priest who could call them down to the
place of sacrifice, who uttered the sacred syllables
which he alone fully understood, who sustained
cosmic order by his reenactment of the primal
sacrifice. Such ideas as elaborated in the *Brahmanas*,
treatises on sacrifice appended to the *Mantras* (as the
fundamental part of each of the four Vedas is called).

The *Upanishads* are later mystical and speculative   *The*
writings that also form a part of the Vedas, and   *Upanishads*
number about 108 in all. They were probably
written between 800 BC and 500 BC. The above
components, *Mantra, Brahmana* (and certain writings

called *Aranyakas* or 'forest-books', which were to
be studied in the seclusion of the forest hermitage),
and *Upanishads* go to make up each of the four
Vedas; and the whole is referred to as the Veda (the
word means 'knowledge'). The Vedas are that class
of writings known as *sruti*, or inspired revelation, as
opposed to those that are *smitri*, traditional learning
that is not revelation or the result of inspiration.

The *Upanishads* represent a vast amount of religious
and philosophical speculation, and it is in these
writings that many basic doctrines of later Hinduism
appear; karma, the transmigration of souls, and the
elaboration of the identity of the individual soul with
the Universal Self – the Atman–Brahman equation
that is so fundamental to Indian religious teaching
(see the chapter on 'The religions of modern India').
Salvation in the *Upanishads* is the realization of this
identity, which, not as a piece of knowledge but
as an intimate mystical experience, liberates the
individual soul from the illusion of its individuality,
and leads to freedom from the cycle of rebirth.

Throughout the Upanishadic period, the Aryans
had been expanding through north India, and their
influence was being felt southwards. Towards the
end of the period, they had been in India for almost
a thousand years; their religions and social institutions
had been developing under the influence of the beliefs
of the indigenous population, a strong element of
which must have been the remnants of the Indus
valley peoples, and the Aryans' own mystical and
philosophical speculations upon their supernal sacrificial cults.

**The
Brahmanic
age**

The Brahmanic age is considered to be that period
from 900 BC to around 500 BC, and corresponds
to the period of the Upanishads; it ends with the
appearance of many heterodox cults that developed
from the early religious beliefs, notably Buddhism
and Jainism. The centres of power had shifted from
the Aryans' first settlements in the Punjab and the
north-west to the Ganga plain; the old pastoral
character of Aryan life was lost with the growth of
fortress cities, the memory of which presumably

inspired those described in the later Epics. There was no paramount ruler, and it was not until much later that the first true Indian empires were founded, with their capitals near the present-day Patna in Bihar.

Much of the difficulty in understanding modern Hinduism results from the complexity of the pantheon. This has its roots in the shifts in status suffered by the Vedic gods during the Brahmanic period, for many of them were demoted, notably Indra, and the prestige of gods in general suffered at the expense of the sacrificial cult, to which the gods eventually became secondary. Furthermore, their position was not helped by the intense speculation about the ultimate fate of humanity after death. The old Vedic beliefs were fairly straightforward; there were two destinations for dead humans, the heaven named 'The Abode of the Fathers', and the rather gloomy 'House of Clay', which seems somewhat akin to the Mesopotamian House of Shadows or the Jewish Scheol. For those who went to the House of Clay continued existence meant a shadowed life of regret and poignant longing – something less than a fully human life. On the other hand, as mentioned in the previous section, the Upanishads show that much mystical speculation concerning the meaning of human life and the unravelling of the enigma of mortality were entertained during the long years of the Ayrans' expansion into the Ganga plain. Metempsychosis is suggested, and striving towards the great creator of the universe begins; for creation in the Vedic writings is a vague business, and there is no evidence of a supreme architect who creates *ex nihilo*.

The old gods suffered from this preoccupation with death and meaning, and other gods gained prominence. Brahman, the universal and impersonal world spirit, the immediate consciousness of which as residing in one's own soul spells salvation for many Upanishadic writers, became personalized as the demiurgic god Brahma who is responsible for the reordering of the cosmos after the periodic cataclysms of Indian mythology. Shiva, now one of the major gods of Hinduism, has a complex beginning both as the fierce and unpredictable Rudra, and in the pre-Aryan god of the Indus valley. Vishnu has affinities with Varuna, and he too began to become increasingly important. Many priestly legends were generated to translate the changes in gods' relative positions to the people, and these account for the vast number of often confusing and apparently silly stories about episodes in the lives of the later Hindu gods.

Little actual historical detail emerges from this period, and nothing is known about the secular life of the people except for what is contained in the religious writings. Nothing like reliable lists of kings or chiefs was compiled, and no buildings from this period have survived. Even the palaces of the later Mauryan emperors (see below) were built of wood, and these too perished long ago.

The Epics   This period also includes the age when the Epics, the Ramayana and the Mahabharata, were first produced.

The Ramayana   This tells of the voluntary exile in the forests of Rama, the righteous son and heir of the old king Dasaratha of Ayodhya. Sita, his virtuous wife, accompanies him (as do his brothers), but she has the very great misfortune (for a virtuous woman at any rate) of being abducted by a demon, Ravana, who is also king of Lanka. Most of the epic is taken up with the vicissitudes of the sundered lovers, with Rama waging war against Ravana and his island fortress to recover Sita, and Sita waging war against Ravana's attempts to put their relationship on a more intimate footing. Eventually Ravana is overthrown and Lanka taken; Sita is liberated, and all should be joyful; but doubts are raised about Sita's conduct while imprisoned by Ravana. Sita suffers a fire-ordeal in order to prove beyond all doubt that she behaved herself, and she is vindicated.

This, however, is not the end of the affair, for after the royal couple's return to Ayodhya, aspersions are once again cast on long-suffering Sita, and she is banished. Eventually Rama asks her to come back, and to prove once again her purity before an assembly of the people; Sita returns, and calls upon the Earth (her mother, for Sita was born in a field-furrow, being originally a sort of goddess of crops and agriculture) to give everyone a sign. Her wish is granted when the Earth opens a great cleft and swallows her up, thus putting an end to all of her misfortunes. Sita, the long-suffering, faithful, and utterly spotless woman and wife is often held up as a model of wifely love and self-abnegation.

The Mahabharata This is a longer work, and concerns the great war between the Kauravas and the Pandavas, which culminated in the battle of Kurushetra in which representatives of every people in the subcontinent were said to have taken part. Many claims have been made for the historical veracity of the war, and some enthusiasts even date it as early as about 3000 BC. That the epic may

'How can I be sure the money will reach the snake?'

contain the memory of some great civil war is possible, but it can't be regarded as a historical account, and has evidently been subjected to many revisions and interpolations over the years. Perhaps the most famous of these is the Bhagavad Gita, or Song of the Lord, which is the nearest thing to a Hindu equivalent of the Bible. This is the discourse between one of the main protagonists in the war, Arjuna, and Krishna, an incarnation of God (Vishnu). Krishna effectively preaches a sermon to Arjuna concerning the workings of moral law and destiny in the lives of men, and this culminates in a wonderful theophany that is all the more moving because it is on the eve of the final battle; Krishna has chosen to play the part of Arjuna's charioteer. The theism of the Gita belongs to the later devotional Hinduism rather than the earlier Brahmanism.

Buddhism and Jainism

Indian history emerges from the shadows in the seventh century BC, because of the passing references to social and political conditions made in the Buddhist and Jaina scriptures. Of all the mystical and philosophical schools that sprang up at the end of the Brahmanic age, only two survived sinking into oblivion or absorption into orthodoxy, and these were Buddhism and Jainism. The founder of the former is, of course, the Buddha; his near contemporary, Mahavira, may be considered to be the founder of Jainism, although to orthodox Jains Mahavira is only the last in a long line of religious virtuosi called *Tirthankaras* (or 'ford-makers'), which stretches back into the remotest antiquity. Mahavira (the name was given to him by his followers, and means 'great hero'; his true name was Vardhamana) was a historical character, and whatever previous traditions he drew upon, he can reasonably be regarded as the founder of Jainism.

North India was divided into a number of autonomous states during this period, and there was no paramount power. Some of these states were ruled by monarchs while others appear to have had some sort of republican government. The main centres of power had shifted eastwards, towards the borders of the modern Bengal and Bihar, and the kingdoms of which most is heard are those of Kosala, Magadha, Vatsa, and Avanti. The last was not in the Ganga plain but to the south-west, near the city of Ujjain, in the region that was later called Malwa. Magadha, in what is present-day Bihar, was to become the nucleus of the first great Indian empire under the Mauryan emperors. Of the kings of Magadha, Bimbisara is notable, because he was on the throne during the lifetime of the Buddha. He was an energetic and ambitious ruler, and laid the foundation of the power that was later to expand over almost the whole subcontinent.

Mahavira was a member of the powerful Lichchavi tribe, whose lands were in north Bihar and whose capital was Vaisali. Mahavira came of noble stock, but he early renounced his own social position for a life of asceticism; like the Buddha, he became dissatisfied with this, and in middle age began his own preaching and teaching, pursuing a career as a religious leader that lasted for about another thirty years. By the time of his death, traditionally given by the Jains as 527 BC but probably somewhat later, he had accumulated a body of followers who adhered to his teachings, and had the benefit of royal patronage from great kings such as Bimbisara and his parricide son, Ajatasutra. *Mahavira*

The Buddha belonged to the Sakya tribe, and was born in Lumbini to the wife of the Raja of Kapilavastu. He belonged to the second of the traditional castes, that of the Kshatriyas; his name was at first Siddhartha Gautama. While still a young man Siddhartha renounced his noble birth and took to a life of austerity and religious devotion. This reached a climax when he achieved enlightenment and became a Buddha; he devoted the rest of his life to preaching and teaching, and to founding and caring for the order of monks that was at the heart of the movement. *The Buddha*

 Buddha's life is surrounded by almost certainly apocryphal stories, and his teachings have been amplified and interpreted by others; there is therefore not only some doubt about what he actually taught but also about whether he really intended to found a new religion. In any case, Buddhism spread to China and Sri Lanka, as well as Tibet, but declined in its native land to the point of near extinction. It is only fairly recently that the great Buddhist shrines in India have been returned to Buddhist care. Even in the fourth century BC and later, under the great Buddhist emperor Ashoka, there never was a 'Buddhist period' when Buddhism was the religion of the majority in India; the majority always seem to have followed some form of Brahmanical Hinduism, which was itself constantly evolving under the pressures of the new cults and changes in philosophical outlook.

The fortunes of Buddhism and Jainism were closely allied to the degree of royal patronage that each received, although most Indian monarchs, once having embraced a religious system, remained tolerant towards the others that were espoused by their subjects. This long history of Indian religious tolerance and theological syncretism has no parallel in European history.

Alexander the Great

A key date in Indian history is that of Alexander's invasion, because it can be fixed unambiguously, without any of the uncertainty that surrounds other significant events during this period. Alexander wasn't the first invader from the west, for the Persians had captured territory before him. He arrived in 326 BC, after a triumphant progress through the Persian Empire. He crossed the Indus, and advanced towards the city of Taxila; no Western invader had ever crossed the Indus before, for this river was the western boundary of the sacred land of India. Little was known about the lands to the east of the river in Alexander's day, and what stories there were were mostly fabulous.

The Greek invaders were received with honour and gifts by the Taxilans, and after resting in their lands, the Greeks continued their eastward march, this time against King Poros, ruler of the lands

between the Jhelum and Chenab rivers, both tributaries of the upper Indus. Poros gave battle in traditional
Indian style, with a large army supported by
war elephants. He was defeated, and taken, badly
wounded, into Alexander's presence; Alexander was
so impressed by the Indian king's proud bearing,
even in defeat, that he treated him generously.
Alexander continued eastwards, with more victories,
but eventually the discontent of his army, who had
been away from their homelands for many years,
and who were faced with the completely unknown
lands and kingdoms of north India, forced him to
retreat. He left Poros as his viceroy over his Indian
domains, and died at Babylon in 323 BC.

After Alexander's death, a young Magadhan named
Chandragupta led an attack on the Macedonian-
officered garrisons in the Indus basin, and defeated
them. He is hailed in some modern Indian histories
as having 'liberated the country from the yoke of
the Greeks'. The adventurous young man also led a
revolution at the capital, Pataliputra (near Patna in
modern Bihar), and overthrew the ruling Nandas.
Chandragupta's counsellor or preceptor was the
wily Kautilya, variously known as Chanakya and
Vishnugupta, the author of the treatise on statecraft
called the *Arthashastra;* it can be compared to
Machiavelli's *The Prince*.

The rise of the Mauryan Empire

Chandragupta proceeded to build an empire, and
by his death, around 298 BC, ruled all India north
of the Narmada river and most of what is now
Afghanistan. Accounts of life at court and in the
empire have come down to us through the writings
of the ambassador Megasthenes, representative of
Seleukos Nikator of Babylon. Towards the end of
his life at least, Chandragupta became a devout Jain,
and is said to have abdicated and travelled south
with the religious teacher Bhadrabahu. The former
emperor ended his life in the approved Jain fashion
near the great shrine at Shravanabelgola; that is, he
slowly starved himself to death there.

He was succeeded by his son, Bihudasara, who
enlarged the empire that he had inherited, and whose
reign lasted until 273 BC, when he was in turn

succeeded by his son Ashoka, one of the greatest figures in Indian history.

Ashoka   Buddhist legends like to exaggerate the excesses of Ashoka's early reign, to make his transformation after conversion the more dramatic; however, it is certain from Ashoka's own record, left in his rock and pillar edicts all over India, that he underwent a great change of heart after waging an aggressive war of conquest against the Kalingas, who inhabited a region roughly corresponding to present-day Orissa. Ashoka was so appalled by the horrors of his war, by the destruction of life and by the sufferings of the survivors, that he resolved never again to conquer by force of arms; he abolished the hunt and other bloody royal pursuits, and embraced Buddhism with a remarkable fervour.

Ashoka did not become a pacifist, and he did not abolish the army or the death penalty; what he did do was try to mitigate the harshness of many judicial penalties, and he embarked on a great campaign of missionary work, his conquest by righteousness. He devoted himself to the well-being of his people, declaring that they were all his children, and he encouraged all manner of humanitarian projects from the planting of shade trees along roads to the building of rest-houses for travellers – especially pilgrims making their way to or from the Buddhist holy places. Animals were protected, and the slaughter of some species forbidden altogether. Ashoka was the first Indian monarch to embrace unequivocally the doctrine and practice of *ahimsa*, or non-violence; and although he was a devoted Buddhist he remained tolerant of other faiths.

The edicts   Perhaps the most important of Ashoka's acts was the ordering of the seven pillar and fourteen rock edicts, in which the great emperor declared and explained his philosophy of universal love and brotherhood, and exhorted others to follow it also; these inscriptions were mostly in the ancient Brahmi script, and aided the later interpretation of these precursors of the modern Sanskrit characters.

Ashoka is certainly one of the most fascinating and admirable monarchs in the world's history, and he is too little known in the West. In his edicts, he enjoins three fundamental principles; showing reverence (from children to their parents, for instance, or from pupils to their teachers), respecting animal life, and telling the truth. His edicts also preach religious tolerance, pointing out that those who persecute other faiths debase themselves and their own religion, while those who are tolerant exalt both.

The popularity of Buddhist (and Jain) principles, and the encouragement given to them by imperial patronage, no doubt account for the growing distaste for the traditional bloody Brahmanical sacrifices that seems to have developed around this time. (Bloody animal sacrifices were very important in early Brahmanism; in the horse sacrifice, or *ashvamedha*, a horse was released and allowed to roam for a year, followed by a band of priests; wherever the horse went became the realm of the king who had instigated the sacrifice, and the horse was ritually killed at the end of its year of freedom. All great or aspiring Indian monarchs indulged in this sacrifice, usually after a period of successful conquests; it could hardly have encouraged good relations between neighbouring kingdoms.)

Ashoka's patronage had profound effects on Buddhism itself, transforming it from a north Indian sect into a great faith that spread far beyond its homeland. Many foreign missions are recorded, and during this period Sri Lanka was converted by a close male relative of Ashoka's, one Mahindra. Sri Lanka has remained firmly Buddhist to this day, with the significant exception of the Hindu Tamil minority. The great Buddhist shrines, such as Sarnath near Varanasi, where the Buddha preached his first sermon in the deer park, were enriched by the emperor, and *stupas*, the hemispherical mounds dressed with stone which contained relics of the Buddha, were raised all over the country. These *stupas* are in fact the earliest permanent religious structures that have come

Effects on Buddhism

down to us, and predate the earliest Hindu temples by many years.

Buildings No buildings from the Mauryan age survive because they were built of wood instead of stone; this was even true of the royal palace at Pataliputra, and does not suggest that they were crude or lacking in luxury. Some stone carving has survived, notably the capitals of some of the pillars which Ashoka caused to be raised. The pillar from Sarnath is perhaps the most famous, and the design of the capital has been adopted as the national emblem of modern, independent India. It consists of four lions back to back, with beneath them, on the abacus, the Buddhist wheel of the law (the *dharma chakra*), flanked on the right by a bull and on the left by a horse.

The Sunga dynasty The empire declined after Ashoka's death in 232 BC, and in 185 BC the throne was usurped by the commander of the army, a brahman named Pushyamitra Sunga, who founded what became known as the Sunga dynasty. Pushyamitra was an orthodox brahman, and revived the ancient Vedic sacrifices and practices; under the Sungas, the centralized empire further decayed into a collection of more or less autonomous states. The Sungas were in their turn overthrown in about 73 BC by Vasudeva, who founded the Kanva dynasty.

The Kanva dynasty This was an age of disintegration and invasion; from the north-west came Bactrian and Indo-Greek invaders, and finally the descendants of the nomadic horde that had called themselves the Great Yueh-Chi. This horde had been driven out of western China, displaced another tribe called the Sakas and took their lands in Bactria. The Yueh-Chi lost their nomadic habits, and settled in the regions to the north-west of India, from where they eventually invaded under the leadership of Kadphises I, king of the dominant tribe called the Kushans.

The Kushan rulers Kadphises I died in about 77 AD, and was succeeded by his son, another Kadphises. Kadphises II moved out of the north-west provinces, and successfully conquered much of northern India.

There is then a period of uncertainty, between Kadphises II and the great Kanishka, whose power was such that he is sometimes styled Emperor Kanishka; like Ashoka before him, he became a great patron of Buddhism, and it was in Kanishka's time that the religion underwent another period of transformation, both in doctrine and iconography. The dates of Kanishka's rule are usually given as 120 AD to 162 AD, and he was the greatest of all the Kushan kings, with lands from Central Asia to the Ganga plain under his rule.

The early Buddhists had never dared to represent the Lord Buddha in any work of art, and his presence was usually signified by a pair of footprints, an elephant, an empty chair, or some other generally recognized symbol. During the age of the Kushans, the Gandharan or Graeco-Buddhist school grew up, and it was these artists who first began to represent the figure of the Lord Buddha, with momentous effects for Buddhist iconography thereafter. These early statues of the Buddha obviously owe much to Hellenic influence; they are graceful, delicately robed, and elegant. Many Buddhist buildings were constructed under royal patronage, and the famous cavetemples of Central India begun. The veneration that Buddhist historians accord Kanishka is second only to that they give to Ashoka himself.

Changes in Buddhism

These iconographical changes were accompanied by changes in doctrine; the veneration of the Lord Buddha as a still living saviour, who could usefully interfere with the course of events on behalf of his followers, rather than as a great religious teacher whose worth lay in precept and example, grew into Great Vehicle or Mahayana Buddhism. Nonetheless, the older and historic form, the Lesser Vehicle or Hinayana Buddhism, still flourished, and representatives from both sects were at the great council summoned by Kanishka.

**The south
and the
Tamil states**

The history of the south of India is very hard to piece together. Some of the earliest mentions of Tamil kingdoms are in Ashoka's edicts, but it is only in the early centuries AD that Tamil history emerges from obscurity and confusion. Traditionally the Tamil lands were divided between three great kingdoms, those of the Pandyas (centred on Madurai), the Cholas (centred on the Madras coast), and the Cheras (on the Malabar coast, incorporating the modern state of Kerala).

The early centuries AD were a great age for Tamil literature. Aryan influences were strong in the Peninsula, but, drawing upon their own traditions, the Dravidians were making their own contributions to the development of Hinduism.

The Guptas

The Guptas succeeded in restoring a great empire centred on ancient Pataliputra, the capital of Ashoka. The man who became Chandragupta I owed much of his success to marriage with a princess from the powerful Lichchavi tribe, and to his control of Magadha, nucleus of the Mauryan Empire. His reign was short, ending in about 330 AD, when he was succeeded by his son, Samudragupta, who was not only a great warrior but a poet and musician. Samudragupta had a long and successful reign lasting some forty or fifty years, and he celebrated the *ashvamedha* (horse sacrifice) after a succession of military triumphs that left him master of much of India north of the Narmada river. The king even mounted a military expedition into the Peninsula, whence he returned laden with tribute, but he never permanently annexed any of the southern lands. In the north, however, he created a true empire.

*Chandra-
gupta II*

The age of his son, Chandragupta II, who acceded to the throne in 380 AD, is considered to be a golden age for India in all respects. In particular, this was the great age of Sanskrit literature, with authors like Kalidasa, Vishakhadatta (the author of the play entitled *The Signet of the Minister*, dramatizing events in the Nanda court at Pataliputra some seven hundred years before, when another Chandragupta was about to depose the Nanda king), and Sudraka. Most of the writings called the Puranas (see 'The religions of modern India') date from the Gupta period, although they contain very old material. Hinduism proper now appeared, transformed by the years of Buddhist dominance.

An account of life under the Guptas has been left by the Chinese traveller Fa-Hien, who travelled through Chandragupta II's domains from 399 AD to 414 AD, as a pilgrim to the great Buddhist shrines. Most of Fa-Hien's observations are connected with monasteries and shrines, but he does mention the state of the country at large from time to time. A Hindu renaissance was under way, but most of the people still followed Buddhist precepts, and to Fa-Hien, the land ruled by the Guptas seemed very peaceful.

In the last years of the reign of Chandragupta II's son, Kumaragupta, the empire was invaded by the people known as the White Huns. Although the invaders were driven off, and the empire saved, it was seriously weakened; more invaders appeared around 500 AD, and by 550 AD the Gupta empire no longer existed. The rulers of the empire are sometimes known as the Imperial Guptas to distinguish them from the Guptas who ruled in Magadha until the eighth century.

The empire's end

The last paramount ruler of northern India before the Moslem invasion was Harsha, who ruled from 606 AD to 647 AD, and whose reign started somewhat unpropitiously after the death of his father and the murder of his brother. Harsha had to fight for survival, and showed himself very adept at it; he eventually subdued much of northern India. His one defeat was at the hands of the Deccan kings, the Chalukyans, who drove him back and obliged him to accept the Narmada river as his southern frontier. Another Chinese pilgrim, Hiuen Tsang, who came to India to do the Buddhist sites like his fellow countryman Fa-Hien, appeared in India during Harsha's reign, and he too left an account of his

Harsha

travels, including his experiences at Harsha's court.

Harsha founded no dynasty, dying without an heir, and his empire collapsed soon after his death. From Harsha's death until the Moslem conquests in the late twelfth century there was no political unity in the north.

Peninsular India

While the north split into warring kingdoms that were to be a relatively easy prey for the Moslem invaders, power in the south was centred on two dynasties; the Chalukyan, ruling from Badami near modern Bijapur, and the Cholas of Tanjore. The Cholas were under something of a cloud until the mid-ninth century, when they defeated the Pallavas of Kanchipuram and re-established themselves as the dominant power in the south-east.

The Pallavas had been great patrons of art and culture, and the remains of their rock-hewn temples (the so-called Seven Pagodas) and huge rock-cut reliefs are still to be seen at Mahabalipuram, a small village south of Madras. The most famous Pallava remains are the shore temples in the same village, which are only a few metres from the sea and are one of the most beautiful and romantic sites in India.

The greatest Chola rulers were Rajaraja (985–1014 AD) and Rajendra I, who turned the Chola kingdom into an empire. Both kings had considerable naval power, unusual for Indian monarchs, and Rajendra I even conquered parts of the Malay peninsula. The Chola empire suffered badly at the hands of later Chalukyan rulers, and finally came to an end in 1310 AD when Malik Kafur invaded the south.

The Moslem invasions

On the eve of the Moslem invasions the Hindu chiefs and kings of northern India were hopelessly divided. They had long been a law unto themselves, used to fighting almost as a sport, and were not equipped to deal with the new invaders and their military efficiency. A powerful Moslem kingdom was established at Ghazni, in Afghanistan, in the ninth century. The Amir Subuktigin made the first attack on India, but left the real damage to his son, Mahmud of Ghazni.

From about 1001 AD, Mahmud (now styled sultan) made a yearly foray into India during the cold season, the time for campaigning, and returned as the hot season began, laden with looted treasure and slaves. Mahmud's rape, plunder, and murder expeditions must have been terrifying beyond belief for those who were caught up in them, for the Moslems seemed unstoppable. Great damage was done to temples, especially the Temple of Somnath in Saurashtra, and those in Mathura, the holy city of Krishna. Modern Indian critics of British rule often say that the British used Hindu–Moslem antagonisms to promote a policy of divide and rule, but even the most ardent apologist for the Moslem community in India must surely admit that their early co-religionists' activities under Mahmud were not the best public relations exercise run by Islam. Mahmud is said to have made about seventeen of these trips in all, and all of them involved slaughter and plunder; Mahmud liked treasure, of course, but it was all the better that it belonged to idolaters whose killing was a meritorious act.

The first true Moslem invasion of India came in 1191 when Muhammad Ghuri, who had already made himself master of the Sind and Punjab, advanced into the lands to the east of the Indus. A hasty confederacy of Hindu princes was organized against him, and the Moslems were defeated in the First Battle of Tarrain by an army led by the Rajput Prithvi Raj Chauhan. Unfortunately the Moslems returned the following year, and this time, in the Second Battle of Tarrain, the Hindu army was defeated and their leader captured and killed. This battle, fought in 1192, is the decisive event in the history of Moslem India, and marks the end of the old order.

Someone had the good sense to stab Muhammad to death in 1206, but by this time he had done incredible damage in India. Because of the sensitivity of the communal issue – that is, the uncertain relationship between the Hindu and Moslem communities in contemporary India – many Indian writers virtually lie about the depredations wrought by the Moslems, and save all their venom for the European invaders, especially the British. The Moslems' own accounts of their activities stand as testimony against this hypocritical and dishonest apologetic; furthermore, although Buddhism was in serious decline by the time Mahmud's men arrived at the monasteries in Bihar, sacking them and destroying their libraries didn't help; neither did putting the monks to the sword. Sarnath was sacked at about this period.

The Delhi Sultanate   Mahmud left the task of conquest to Qutub-ud-din Aibak, who was technically a slave. This man became the first sultan of Delhi, and founded the dynasty known as the Slave Kings, which lasted from 1206 AD to 1290 AD, and ended with Qaiqabad, who was murdered. The Delhi Sultanate controlled large areas of north India, but its fortunes waxed and waned with the sultans' personalities; the sultans were also distracted from further internal conquest by various external threats, especially that from the Mongols during the sultanate of Balban (1266–86).

The Delhi Sultanate continued with Jalal-ud-din Khilji, a senior official who was placed on the throne by the nobles, and who was an agreeable old gentleman (one feels that by this time the long-suffering Indians deserved one) of seventy. Unfortunately he was murdered by his ambitious son-in-law, Ala-ud-din, who ruled from 1296 to 1316. Ala-ud-din pursued a policy of expansion and conquest, and took Moslem arms down into the Deccan and beyond; he also conquered Gujerat, and had to repulse Mongol attacks. The Tamil lands were not annexed, but were subjected to a series of damaging raids; Malik Kafur, Ala-ud-din's general, returned to Delhi from his southern expedition laden with treasure and booty.

The reign ended in confusion, and some stories say that Ala-ud-din was helped to paradise by the hand of Malik Kafur himself; whether this is true or not, the latter set an infant son of the former sultan on the throne, and exercised true power himself. Malik's rule lasted but a short while, for he was assassinated by his own guards. Another son of Ala-

ud-din was then wheeled out, and he became Sultan
Qutb-ud-din Mubarak. This young sultan was wholly
given over to homosexual and alcoholic extrava-
gances, and the only good thing about his reign
was, as Professor Vincent Smith observed, that the
Mongols didn't attack. The sultan was sometimes
said to have appeared in company dressed as a female,
a habit which did not endear him to a Moslem court,
and he was murdered.

His murderer usurped the sultanate, but sadly was
little more to the liking of the nobility than his
predecessor; so he too was killed, by Ghazi Malik,
who was then offered the sultanate himself. He
accepted this, and took the name of Ghiyas-ud-din
Tughluq; he is sometimes known as Tughluq Shah.

The Tughluq dynasty Tughluq Shah was the first
of the Tughluq dynasty, which ruled from about
1320 to 1412. He was an efficient and energetic ruler,
and did much to restore the prestige of the sultanate.
He died in 1325, and was succeeded by his son
Muhammad bin Tughluq. The latter was a strange
man, with great personal gifts and great weaknesses.
One of his more eccentric proceedings was the
removal of his capital to Dualatabad, near Aurangabad
in what is now Maharashtra. Muhammad was not
content with moving the capital in name with the
court; the stories say that he also forced the entire
population of Delhi, including cripples, to go too.
Needless to say, everyone suffered great hardship *en
route*; those who survived must have been thoroughly
exasperated with their sultan again when he decided
to go back to Delhi a couple of years later.

Timur During the reign of the last Tughluq, Sultan
Mahmud, the Mongol Moslem conqueror Timur (the
Tamburlaine of English literature) descended on
India. Mahmud was defeated, Delhi was taken, and
a general massacre of the inhabitants undertaken.
Timur then made off home to Samarkand with a
huge train of booty and captives. He left behind him
chaos and famine.

The strength of the sultanate was all but destroyed

by Timur's visit, but some semblance of order was restored by Khizr Khan, who was the first of the Sayyad dynasty that lasted from 1414 to 1450. This was succeeded by the Lodhi dynasty, which lasted until 1526 when Ibrahim Lodhi was defeated by Babur, the first Moghul emperor (as he was to become), at Panipat.

Bahmani and Vijayanagar

The Bahmani kingdom was founded by disaffected Moslem nobles in 1347, but much later, in 1489, it split into the separate kingdoms of Berar, Golconda, Bijapur, Ahmadnagar, and Bidar. These Moslem kingdoms produced some fine architecture, notably at Bijapur and Golconda. They were in a state of more or less permanent warfare with the last great Hindu empire of India, Vijayanagar, which had been founded in 1336 by the brothers Harihara and Bukka. The city of Vijayanagar was once huge, and contemporary descriptions of it have been left by Middle Eastern and European travellers. Now all that remains are the monumental ruins scattered for miles around the Karnatakan village of Hampi, on the banks of the Tungabhadra river. Vijayanagar waged successful wars against the neighbouring Deccan sultans, but in 1565 the last Vijayanagar king, Rama Raja, was defeated at the Battle of Talicota by a confederacy of Deccan (Bahmani) sultans, and the great city was sacked.

The Moghuls

After the confusion and bloodshed of earlier Moslem ages in India, the Moghuls produced another golden age of Indian culture, and one of them, Akbar, is a figure who rivals Ashoka.

Babur and Humayun

The first Moghul was Babur, a king of Kabul, who invaded India in 1526 with a ludicrously small army compared with that of the sultan of Delhi, Ibrahim Lodhi. At Panipat, Babur won the day, and the sultan was killed on the field; Delhi and Agra were then occupied. Much of Babur's reign from his capital at Agra was spent in fighting other enemies, such as the Hindu Rajputs. He died in 1530, and was succeeded by his son Humayun. Humayun was defeated by Sher Shah in 1540, and for a time Moghul rule was extinguished; however, Humayun restored Moghul power in 1555, but died in the following year.

Jalal-ud-din Muhammed Akbar, Humayun's son, became the greatest of the Moghuls. He was a learned and broad-minded man who pursued a policy of religious toleration towards his Hindu subjects to the extent of encouraging them to occupy high official positions. Akbar was also something of an amateur theologian, and invented a religion of his own that allegedly combined the best aspects of every faith known to the emperor. Alas, it never caught on. *Akbar*

Akbar's long reign ended in 1605, when his son Jehangir came to the throne. Jehangir's main passion was the Kashmir, and he was responsible for some of the most beautiful of the formal gardens there. He died *en route* to the Kashmir, his last wish being for 'only Kashmir'; anyone who has travelled to Kashmir on a video coach will sympathize with the dying emperor's feelings. *Jehangir*

After Jehangir's death in 1627, Shah Jahan came to the throne. He is the Moghul responsible for most of the great buildings in Agra and Delhi, including the Taj Mahal (which was built as a memorial to his beloved wife, Mumtaz), the Red Fort, the great mosque – the Jami Masjid – in Delhi, and the Agra fort in which he was to spend his last years as a prisoner of his own son, Aurangzeb. *Shah Jahan*

Aurangzeb came to power in 1658, and although he pushed the boundaries of the Moghul Empire to their furthest limits, he was the last great emperor and is often blamed for sowing the seeds of decay. He was a stern man, devoutly religious, whose private life was simple and austere; unfortunately, a part of his religious zeal involved the chastising of infidels, and he lost the support of his non-Moslem subjects. Aurangzeb had a habit of knocking down *Aurangzeb* temples and building mosques on their foundations, the most notorious example being in the Hindu holy city of Banares (Varanasi). Aurangzeb expended a lot of energy in trying to crush the rising power of the Marathas; he died in 1707, and after this the empire declined rapidly.

Later
Moghuls

Descendants of the Moghuls lived in Delhi up until the time of the 1857 Indian Mutiny, when the last Moghul king of Delhi was sent into exile to Rangoon, where he later died. During the nineteenth century, the sovereign in Delhi had little real power, but could still be the focus of popular nationalism. Events in the Mutiny proved this when the eighty-one year old Bahadur Shah II became an unwilling rallying point for the Indian rebels.

Non-Moslem
powers – the
Rajputs and
the Marathas

The Rajputs

The Rajputs were the inhabitants of what is now known as Rajasthan, 'the land of kings'. The Rajputs were a loosely federated group of tribes or clans, with strong links to the White Hun invaders of later Gupta days. They were fiercely independent, and had a strong martial tradition. They clashed with the Moslems, for the Rajputs were Hindus, and so effective were they at prolonged and bloody defensive warfare, often against the most incredible odds, that the Moghuls found it better to have the Rajputs on their side, and often made use of them as military commanders. The Rajput officers also provided useful links with the Hindu population who then, as now, form the overwhelming majority of the Indian people. Even Aurangzeb had a Rajput commander, Raja Jai Singh; however, he was plainly not greatly attached to his Hindu officer, because he publicly rejoiced when he heard that Jai Singh had been poisoned by his own son.

A curious Rajput institution, and one that made them fearless and fearful enemies, was the *jauhar*. When a Rajput fortress (Rajasthan is the land of Indian fortresses, some of them wildly romantic half-ruins on hilltops) could hold out no longer, and conquest was imminent, the men would don saffron robes and ride out of the gates to certain death; behind

them, the women and children would immolate
themselves on a huge communal pyre. This is not a
legend, for there are many well-attested instances of
the inmates of a beleaguered fortress committing
jauhar. The most famous are perhaps those at
Chittogarh; the first was when Ala-ud-din Khilji
attacked in order to seize the beautiful Padmini, and
the last when Akbar himself sacked Chittogarh in
1568.

The Marathas were Hindus, and they too waged   *The Marathas*
ceaseless war against the Moslems, but their methods
were different. The region from which the original
Maratha fighters were drawn was the rough hill
country of the Western Ghats in present-day Maharashtra, and their method of fighting was something
like guerrilla warfare, rather than the doomed chivalry
and bravery of the Rajputs.

Shivaji The first great Maratha leader was Shivaji,
who remains one of India's most popular heroes,
holding a place in popular folklore akin to that of
Robin Hood in England. He was born in 1627, and
was a sudra; that is, a member of the lowest caste.
This has added to his popular appeal over the years,
for Shivaji showed that you didn't have to be a
brahmin to get on in the world; all you had to do
was be a resourceful and brave leader.

   Shivaji's first exploits were frankly little more than
banditry, and he retained something of the dacoit all
through his life. He was not content to be a robber
chief, however, and a great following grew around
him, attracted by his success, his personality, and
the fact that he was a Hindu successfully resisting
Moslems. His power spread through the Ghats, the
coastal Konkan plain, and into the Deccan. His
troops, who knew the country well and were skilled
guerrilla fighters, were more than a match for
the well-drilled Moslem forces sent against them.
Eventually Shivaji became such a nuisance that a
sizeable army was sent against him, under the
command of one Afzal Khan, who was murdered
by a trick; Shivaji pretended to parley, and ripped

open Afzal Khan's belly with a claw-like appendage attached to one hand. The Moslem army was then ambushed and routed.

Many other exploits are told of Shivaji and his men, and they are true; Shivaji really was a strange mixture of military genius, bandit, and chivalrous leader. Even Aurangzeb finally came to the conclusion that it would be better to treat with Shivaji than to wage permanent and hopeless warfare against him, and received him honourably at the court in Agra. Shivaji died in 1680, by that time having declared himself an autonomous king (that is, one whose office was not held by virtue of a commission from the Moghul emperor) of a wide area of central India.

The Peshwas   The Marathas went on growing in power after Shivaji's death, and continued to be a thorn in the Moghuls' side. The leadership eventually passed into the hands of the Peshwas, who had originally been high ministers with the title of 'Peshwa'. In the days of the third Peshwa, Balaji Baji Rao (1740–61), the Maratha empire reached its height, even incorporating parts of Orissa in the east. Malwa, Gujerat, Bundelkhand, and parts of the Punjab were all under Maratha rule.

Nadir Shah   Moghul power continued to decline, and suffered a devastating blow in 1739 when Nadir Shah of Persia invaded northern India and defeated the imperial army at Karnal, not far from historic Panipat. The Moghul, Muhammad Shah, was treated with mercy and courtesy when he surrendered, and the two sovereigns entered Delhi together; unfortunately, an uprising by some of the population prompted a general massacre, at the direct order of Nadir Shah, who watched the citizens being slaughtered from a mosque near the Chadni Choak. The city was then plundered, and the famous peacock throne carried away by the invaders. It was through Nadir's invasion that Afghanistan was lost to the Indian crown.

Like other invaders before him, Nadir Shah left chaos and misery behind. To some extent the

Marathas filled the power vacuum, but their expansion came to an abrupt halt when they were defeated at the Third Battle of Panipat (1761) by Ahmad Shah Durrani of Afghanistan. Later, Maratha power was to fall in the struggle with the British.

British India – origins and expansion

The first European presence

Europeans first arrived in India as traders, prepared to use military force in their competition with the Arabs for the rich cargoes of ports such as Calicut, on the Malabar coast. First to arrive were the Portuguese in 1497, under Vasco da Gama, who sailed his four small ships round Africa and opened the sea-route to India. The Portuguese returned later in force, had a stormy relationship with the ruler of Calicut, the Zamorin, and entered into open warfare with the rival Arab traders. The Portuguese won, by virtue of their superior naval forces, and soon (1510) Alfonso de Albequerque occupied Goa, which became the first modern Western settlement in India. The Dutch and the English were the early rivals of the Portuguese, the former establishing trading posts at Pulicat (north of the modern Madras) in 1609, and later at Surat. The English too established a post at Surat in 1613, in spite of violent Portuguese opposition. All this was the fruition of Queen Elizabeth I's charter of 1600, granting exclusive trading rights with India to 'the Governor and Company of Merchants of London trading into the East Indies'; this was what was to become known as the East India Company.

British acquisitions

The English moved to the east coast too, and founded posts on the islands at Armagaon (north of modern Madras) and at a number of other places. Because of the problems caused by local officials, the English on the Coramandel coast eventually moved to the north of the old Portuguese settlement of San Thome, in 1639. Francis Day, the head of Armagaon, bought the land from the Raja of Chandragherri for 12,000 Pagodas (that is, almost £600). Only Europeans were to be allowed to live in this enclave, and most important, the English were allowed to fortify it. This small piece of land became the first real British territory on Indian soil, and the fort was called Fort St George. It still exists, on the Marina in Madras, and its church, St Mary's, is one of the most fascinating remains of the British occupation, containing memorial plaques ranging from one to the Reverend William Walter Posthumus Powell, late of Worcester College Oxford, and sometime garrison chaplain, to an unfortunate but not forgotten subaltern, who was 'killed in an encounter with a tiger'. In 1653, the Agency (as this settlement was known to the Company's directors in London) was raised to the status of a Presidency; that is, it was superior to all of the company's other settlements on the Coramandel and Bengal coasts.

Bombay and Calcutta were founded somewhat later; the British acquired the site of Bombay from the Portuguese as part of the dowry of Catherine of Braganza, who married Charles II of England. The king later granted it to the East India Company for a small annual rent. The actual city was founded by a governor, Gerald Aungier, who was in office from 1669 to 1677. Eventually Bombay became the British headquarters on the west coast, and eclipsed Surat, which had been much damaged by Maratha raids. In time, Bombay became the Bombay Presidency, one of the three historic administrative divisions of British India.

Calcutta was founded in 1690 by Job Charnock, and like Madras it was chosen for its defensible position. A fort was constructed here and named Fort William after the English king. In the early years of the eighteenth century, a rival trading company called the 'English Company Trading to the East Indies' was founded, but eventually differences were settled and a new, single company was formed, 'The United Company of Merchants trading with the East Indies'. This is the true East India Company, and was responsible for the spread of British power in subsequent years. Three of the four great metropolitan centres of India are British creations, Madras, Bombay, and Calcutta; only Delhi corresponds to a great pre-colonial city.

The period from 1740 to 1818 marks the decisive expansion of British power, when instead of trading by imperial permission the Company became the patron of local princes and nawabs, and rival European power – mainly that of the French – was eliminated. The Company had initially derived its legitimacy from permission from the emperor in Delhi; with the decline of Moghul power, this permission became more and more meaningless, but the behaviour and disposition of the local rulers became increasingly important as they became laws unto themselves. This was one factor that dragged European traders into local Indian power politics, and ended up with them sponsoring the claims of one of a number of rival rulers and potentates. The other factor that led to local involvement was European rivalry; local rulers would be solicited as allies, hostile ones would be overthrown, and so on. Indian histories of the popular and nationalistic variety like to portray the Indian rulers as trying to get on with a difficult job, and being impeded in their good work by wicked and Machiavellian Europeans. Again, like so many of these attempts to explain away unpalatable aspects of the writers' own history, this is at best rubbish, at worst a lie. One of the main factors that helped European expansion was the complete lack of any sense of national cohesion between the local rulers, and of the least sense of solidarity against the Europeans. The Indians rulers were prepared to use European patronage against one another, especially if that patronage took the form of military assistance. The breakdown in imperial authority contributed to the confusion, of course, but the fact remains that Indian rulers were more interested in their own power struggles than in resisting foreign domination. During this period there was absolutely no sense of a single Indian identity, as some Indian historians like to pretend.

In the early days of the trading stations (or 'factories' as they were called) the patronage and good will of the local ruler was essential to the success of the enterprise. The final result of this, when the power of the Company had grown relative to that of the native princes, was the sponsoring and support of rulers by the Company rather than vice versa. Eventually, when power had passed from the Company to the British Crown, this developed into the practice whereby those rulers considered incompetent or unreliable were retired and their territories taken under direct administration.

Anglo-French rivalry

The French were the main European rivals of the British, with their Compagnie des Indes Orientales. This was somewhat different in conception to the East India Company, being state run; it never achieved the volume of trade of its British rival, in spite of some very able men like Dupleix, the governor of Pondicherry. Up to the War of the Austrian Succession, the British and French traders had maintained an amicable policy of neutrality in times of war between their two countries, but by the mid-eighteenth century the rivalry between them for the Eastern trade led to open hostilities in south India. It was during this time that the first major manipulation of Indian rulers to serve European interests took place. The French were successful under Dupleix and La Bourdannais, and took Madras in 1746; the city was given back to the British in the Treaty of Aix-la-Chapelle, which concluded the hostilities in Europe and elsewhere.

Dupleix had made a bid for a French south Indian empire; during the Anglo-French struggle the Indian rulers had turned from patrons into clients as it became apparent that the intervention of well-armed, well-drilled European troops was a decisive factor in their quarrels. The final struggle between the English and the French in the south came during the Seven Years War, which started in 1756. In 1760 the French general Lally was defeated by Coote at Wandiwash, and Pondicherry was taken in 1761. This spelt the end of French power in India. Pondicherry was returned to France in the peace of 1763, but its status was that of an open port.

The decisive events for the future of British rule took place in Bengal, where the problem of the breakdown of imperial authority was most apparent, for the local ruler was in principle a Moghul governor. By the mid-eighteenth century the rulers of Bengal had become effectively free of imperial control, and ruled over not only Bengal but Orissa and Bihar also. In 1756, a young man named Siraj-ud-daula became nawab. His position was somewhat precarious, because he was engaged in a dynastic squabble with his cousin; he was also alarmed by the growing power of the European settlements, some of which, notably the English, had fortified themselves. The English gave further offence by harbouring a political refugee, and this precipitated the attack on Calcutta that led to its fall and the notorious and largely apocryphal Black Hole episode.

The British general Robert Clive was sent against the nawab with a relatively small force, and the clash between the Company's and the nawab's armies took place at the celebrated battle of Plassey, in 1757, which is often taken as signalling the advent of 'British India'. The nawab was decisively defeated, and later killed; the English helped Mir Jafar to assume the title of nawab, thus turning the ruler of Bengal into a British client and establishing a precedent for future policy in the north. Mir Jafar was later replaced with his son-in-law Mir Kasim.

The new nawab tried to disentangle himself from the foreign power in Calcutta, with the result that he too fell foul of the British; a campaign was fought that involved the British, Mir Kasim, Shuja-ud-daula of Oudh, and the wandering Moghul emperor Shah Alam. The fighting ended with a British victory at Buxar in West Bihar in 1763, after which Shah Alam and Shuja-ud-daula came to terms with the foreigners. The British were granted Diwani of Bengal, Orissa, and Bihar, that is, the right of the Company to collect revenue from these territories.

This agreement secured British supremacy in the north-east, and paved the way for the next wave of expansion. Once the process of interfering with local rulers to safeguard trading and revenue rights had begun, it couldn't stop; there was an irreversible involvement with Indian dynastic politics and of course any new territory always had borders across which there could be another difficult or unsympathetic ruler.

Tipu   In the north, there came a period of inconclusive struggle with Maratha power; in the south came the succession of Mysore wars, in which French forces became embroiled. First Haider Ali, then his son Tipu (the man who had the famous clockwork toy of a tiger eating a British soldier) inflicted defeats on the British forces in the south. Tipu was a brilliant military leader, and it was not until 1799 that he was finally defeated and killed fighting in a breach of the walls of his capital, Sriringapatna near Mysore.

The British liked to present Tipu as a tyrant, but he was an enlightened and benevolent ruler; as an English officer observed (a copy of his letter is still to be seen in the museum in Tipu's summer palace), so beloved was Tipu by his men, that in long years of campaigning and ultimate defeat, there were hardly any desertions from his forces. In place of Tipu's line (his sons were incarcerated in the fortress at Vellore) the British set a Hindu puppet king over the Carnatic, the descendants of whom became the maharajas of Mysore, the Wodiyars.

Changes in administration   The almost casual manner in which the British, through the East India Company, had been acquiring what amounted to imperial control over vast tracts of India had long been a cause of concern in Britain itself. Newly acquired territories not only had to be defended, they had to be properly administered. In the eighteenth century, suspicion about the motives and competence of the Company's officials grew, and culminated in a number of reforms. Pitt's India Bill was amongst these, in 1784, and it is interesting because it expressly states that 'to pursue schemes of conquest and extension of dominion in India are measures repugnant to the wish, honour, and policy of this nation.' The *raison d'être* of British power in India was to be trade, and trade alone. The reforms

"Then we come to the ones that got away in India . . ."

also changed the manner in which power was exercised in India itself; the governor-general was appointed by the directors of the Company, but could be recalled by the Crown. A new Board of Control was set up to work alongside the directors of the Company, and this body was composed of unpaid privy councillors.

Nonetheless, the territory under British control continued to grow; for instance, after the defeat of Tipu, governor-general Wellesley found himself with vast areas of south India at his disposal. One method of dealing with these was to set up sympathetic rulers who were dependent on British power. Such rulers were bound by what were known as subsidiary treaties that allowed them to maintain a British force in their territory, so long as they paid for it, and this gave the governor-general the right to intervene in the event of maladministration by the native authorities. Obviously maladministration could, and often did, mean anything that was opposed to British interests. Thus many native rulers enjoyed only a nominal independence, being in reality dependent on British patronage.

The nineteenth century up to 1857

The Marathas were subdued (after a long history of conflict with not only the British but also everyone else) and a large part of the territory of the last Peshwa was annexed in the so-called General Settlement of 1818. Much of the Maratha territory became part of the Presidency of Bombay, and the city began its period of rapid expansion as the great sea-port of western India. The Peshwa was sent away to Bithur, on the Ganga, but he had a last fling through his son Nana Sahib, who was active against the British during the Mutiny of 1857, and who is often held responsible for the massacres of European women and children at Kanpur (Cawnpore), an event that was used by the British to justify the brutal repression of not only the mutineers but the Indian population in general.

The British fought the Burmese from 1824 to 1826, and took over Assam. The Sind was annexed in 1843. The Punjab followed in 1848 after the two Anglo-Sikh wars, and the Second Burmese War of 1852 resulted in the annexation of Rangoon. Coorg, in the south, was annexed in 1834; the administration of Mysore was taken over in 1831; and 1853 saw the annexation of Nagpur. By the time of the Mutiny the British controlled all of India, either directly, or through the rulers of the 'Princely States' who were bound to the British by treaty, and whose territory could be annexed if they misbehaved themselves in the eyes of the paramount power. The so-called 'Doctrine of Lapse' was also used, whereby the territory of any Indian ruler who died without issue was taken under direct British rule. This often flouted long-established local customs concerning adoption and inheritance, and caused much resentment, which eventually boiled over during the Mutiny.

The Indian Mutiny and its aftermath

The British expatriates and the Indians had long been growing apart; by the 1850s, the days were gone when someone like Sir William Jones, who arrived in India in 1783 as supreme court judge in Calcutta, threw himself into a detailed study of the Indians, their history, languages, and customs. In the early days, the British made an invaluable contribution to Indian culture by rediscovering its lost or dim past; men like Colonel Tod, Jones, James Prinsep, and many others were responsible for rediscovering India's forgotten or garbled history. Ironically, it was this foreign reawakening of its history that eventually led to a heightened sense of Indian nationalism in the closing years of the last century. The efforts of the British antiquarians and enthusiasts led to the translation of Ashoka's edicts, the establishment of Buddhism's Indian roots, and the rediscovery of priceless works of art like the frescoed caves at Ajanta and Ellora.

Background to the Mutiny

By the middle of the nineteenth century, much of this attitude had been lost; all too frequently the young officers and Company employees were inclined to regard the Indians as beneath contempt, and their culture and religions as not worthy of serious consideration. British rule had also produced great social changes that were regarded with regret or open hostility by the generally conservative Indian people. Apart from measures to eliminate quaint and venerable Hindu institutions such as widow burning (called *suttee* by the British, from the term *sati* that was applied to a woman who had immolated herself on her husband's pyre, and which meant 'honourable'), the British had brought things like the telegraph and the railways; by the time of the Mutiny, 200 miles of railway track had already been laid. The penetration of Western technology and ideas created an atmosphere of great distrust amongst the Indians, who feared for the future of their own traditions and institutions. The Princely States were havens of conservatism, but all too often they were upset by interference and annexation.

The general disquiet amongst the Indians found expression in extraordinary rumours that the British were about to effect the forcible conversion of the entire native population to Christianity, and one of the first ploys towards this goal would be to subvert caste by subtle defilement; it was suggested that crushed and burned cows' bones were mixed up in the flour that was sold, for this, of course, would spell defilement to any caste Hindu. The obvious proselytizing zeal of the British, who had passed beyond the phase during which they didn't care what the Indians believed so long as a handsome profit was made, to visions of a quasi-religious imperial mission, didn't help to allay Indian distrust. Missionaries had originally been forbidden to operate in India, but by the middle of the nineteenth century, they were quite common.

Finally, there was an aspect of the Mutiny that is always underplayed by traditional British historians and exaggerated by Indian ones, and that was a quite genuine desire on the part of many Indians to free themselves from alien rule. In spite of this, there was no sense in which the Mutiny was a well-planned, coordinated war of independence; it was rather an expression of frustration and anger at European contempt and arrogance.

Beginnings of the Mutiny The wild rumours finally found a focus when a new type of cartridge was issued to the native (sepoy) regiments of the Bengal Army for the new Enfield rifles. It was rumoured – perhaps with justification – that the cartridges were greased with animal fats that were unclean to either Hindus (who would be defiled were there to be cow fat in the grease) or Moslems (who would be equally defiled were there to be pig fat in the grease). Disaffection amongst the native regiments was very serious for the British – just how serious can be judged from the tiny contingent of 14,000 European troops amongst the 300,000 strong Bengal Army. The other two Presidencies maintained armies (the Bombay and Madras armies), but again these were composed mainly of native troops. The Queen's Army (that is, the regular British Army) had a contingent of only 23,000. Many of these were up in the troubled northwest, and were not on hand when the Mutiny broke. Feelings amongst the native troops had been running high over both the issue of the cartridges, and various changes in their conditions of service; in particular, the new requirement of serving beyond the Indus, if need be, was resented, for this too meant the loss of caste for many orthodox Hindus. The first signs of trouble came at Dum Dum barracks, near Calcutta, in early 1857; but the explosion came to the west, at Meerut, on 10 May of that year. In spite of assurances that the cartridges were not greased with offensive substances, and a new firing drill that avoided the biting of the cartridge, the native troops mutinied and shot many of their European officers, and a general massacre of Europeans took place. The mutineers then marched on Delhi, which they easily took, and again there was a massacre of Europeans. The descendant of the great Moghul line, Bahadur Shah II, was somewhat surprised to find himself hailed as a leader by the insurgents, but he undertook to command them in spite of his misgivings.

The Mutiny spread quickly, with similar episodes elsewhere; troops mutinied at Lucknow and Kanpur, and in both places the British community was placed under siege. At Lucknow, the siege became an epic and passed into legend, for it was to last from late June, when the Residency was surrounded, to late November when the final relief took place under Havelock and Campbell. Lucknow was in fact relieved twice, but on the first occasion the relieving force wasn't strong enough to break the siege, although its members fought their way through the mutineers' lines to the famous Residency.

Lucknow and Kanpur

At Kanpur, some of the most tragic and unfortunate events took place, not in terms of loss of life, because far more blood was to be shed later, but in terms of their effect on the British attitude towards the Indians. The British commander there soon became convinced that a long siege was impossible, and negotiated a safe passage for the garrison and the women and children with representatives of Nana Sahib, the son of the retired Peshwa of the Marathas, who had a great desire to become a Peshwa himself.

The garrison and the women and children left Kanpur
under the terms of the safe passage, but were
ambushed as they were about to embark on small
river craft on the Ganga at the Satichaura Ghat;
many were killed, and those who were taken prisoner
were subsequently murdered in the notorious 'House
of the Ladies'.

The responsibility for these excesses was never
clearly established, but blame naturally fell on Nana
Sahib. The murder of the defenceless women and
children had a strange effect on the British officers,
who afterwards seemed determined to inflict much
the same thing on helpless Indians who crossed their
path. The treatment of Indians, both mutineers and
villagers, was appalling, and far exceeded the horrors
of Kanpur. The diaries of many British officers reveal
a passionate and unforgiving hatred for the Indians,
and this found expression in their behaviour.

Progress of
the Mutiny

The mutineers were initially successful and soon had
a great swathe of northern India under their control;
but although they produced resourceful and brave
leaders like Tatya Tope and the Rani of Jhansi,
Lakshmi Bai, they suffered from a lack of command
and purpose. By September Delhi had been recap-
tured and Bahadur Shah taken; his sons were
treacherously killed by a British officer, Hodson.
Thereafter the Mutiny was a long string of defeats
for the mutineers, although they kept the British
Army busy until well into 1858. It was not until June
of that year that the Rani of Jhansi was killed fighting
in battle dressed as a soldier; after her death
she became one of the heroines of the Indian
independence movement. Tatya Tope was captured
and executed, and the old Bahadur Shah was exiled
to Rangoon, where he later died.

In fairness to the British, it must be said that once
the immediate military crisis was over, and red-
coated soldiery had ceased charging into battle yelling
'Remember Cawnpore!', they realized that further
harsh treatment of the Indians would result in a
permanent breach between the native population and
their colonial masters. The more perceptive officials

and soldiers realized that India could only be governed with the co-operation of the Indian people, and could not be held down for ever by military force; the British had not the resources for the latter course of action, even had they been inclined to attempt it. The Mutiny was therefore followed by extensive reforms to the Indian government and administration.

The East India Company (which had ceased to exist as a trading organization in 1833, yet retained responsibility for the administration of India) was abolished. The Government of India Act of 1858 replaced the Company's Board of Control with a secretary of state for India, and the administration was overhauled. All treaties entered into with native princes by the East India Company were to be respected, and the integrity of the princes' territories guaranteed. The Indians were to be accorded the rights and protections of any other subjects of the British Empire. The British domestic interest in Indian affairs culminated with the declaration of Queen Victoria as empress of India in 1876.

The aftermath

The Mutiny did irretrievable damage to relations between the British and the Indians; although the period following 1857 was in a sense the golden age of the Raj, which has spawned a vast nostalgia industry, the events following the mutiny at Meerut created a rift between the Indians and the British that was never healed. The Indians were generally regarded by the British as incompetent and incapable of managing their own affairs; in Lord Northbrook's famous remark, made in 1880, 'No one in India could believe the Indians to be capable of responsibility.'

The British created a new middle class in India, and it was this, rather than an armed revolt, that was to spell doom for British rule. This new class, though superficially Westernized, was able to look back to its Indian roots and take pride in its Indian heritage, yet tackle the British on their own terms using Western principles of justice and equity. Eventually the arguments for Indian self-government acquired an overwhelming moral force.

The struggle for independence

The new middle class

The extensive railway network that was built in India stimulated the development of heavy industry; in the second half of the nineteenth century the Indian coal, iron, and steel industries grew up, as did the cotton mills and the jute industry of Bengal. This industrialization created new social conditions in which the new Indian middle class was born. Men like Tata, one of India's first and greatest industrialists appeared, and the Indian people had another class to speak for them, more articulate and more likely to be heard by British ears than the old aristocracy, dreaming of the past while eccentrically cultivating selected European manners and foibles in their palaces and Princely States.

The Hindu rivival

Hinduism began a great revival under men like the saintly Ramakrishna and Swami Vivekananda. Such men had the confidence to point out (following Ram Mohan Roy from earlier in the century) that Hindus didn't have to appeal to Western ethical standards to condemn the 'evils' of their religion that Western critics made so much of; widow burning, infanticide, and the crueller consequences of caste distinctions could all be condemned from within Hinduism itself, they argued, were appeal made to the great and pure spiritual tradition of the Vedas that had been corrupted by human frailty and wickedness. Westerners became ardent apologists for Hinduism, a notable example being Annie Besant, who brought Theosophy to India and became herself something of an Indian nationalist.

The Moslem reappraisal

Islam in India also began a reappraisal, under men like the great Sayyid Ahmad Khan, who had a long and distinguished career in public service and who visited England in 1869. He saw that Islam had to come to terms with Western power, if it was not to be absorbed by the majority Hindu community. He had theological interests, and like his Hindu counterparts became an apologist for his faith, reinterpreting it in a modern context, and forcefully answering European critics of Islam.

Unfortunately, the rivalry that grew up between the modernist Moslems and Hindus ended in the tragedy of partition and the creation of Pakistan in 1947.

The beginnings of the National Movement (as the campaign for independence came to be known) were in fairly modest demands by educated, middle-class Indians for a greater say in the government and administration of their country. Such demands were largely unsatisfied, although certain concessions were made; educated Indians were left with the feeling that though they could advance, sooner or later they would be told 'No further'.

Direct economic conflict with Britain arose over the issue of textiles. In 1879 all Indian import duties on cotton goods were abolished, and this had a serious effect on the domestic textile industry; this matter was later taken up (together with the salt tax) by Mahatma Gandhi as symbolic of British injustice to India, and he exhorted Indians to spin and weave for themselves and boycott imported cloth. This is the origin (in part) of Gandhi's famous spinning wheel, which once appeared on the Congress flag.

Congress For some years the National Movement was a middle-class, intellectual affair, and couldn't be described as a popular mass movement. The National Congress was formed in 1885, ironically with the help of a retired British official, and held its first meeting in Bombay in December of that year. It rapidly grew from its small beginnings into the voice of Indian opposition to colonial rule. From its early years it was plagued by serious divisions, between, for example, the 'extremists' who ended up by advocating violent opposition to the British, and the 'moderates' who favoured change by consti-tutional means; but in spite of such problems it grew in both numbers and prestige. By 1906, the annual Congress meeting was calling for *Swaraj*; that is, a kind of dominion status similar to that of Canada or Australia. Such reforms as were made did little to satisfy Indian aspirations.

The National Movement

The All-India Moslem League A portent of the future was provided by the ambiguous relationship between the Congress and the Moslem community. Initially many Moslems had treated the Congress with suspicion, fearing that democratic rule in India would mean Hindu rule and cultural absorption. Later they took fright when it became apparent that the Congress was recognized as a powerful force by the British, and that they too had to make their voices heard in any negotiations leading to reform or self-government; in 1906 the Moslem community sent a deputation to the governor-general, Lord Curzon, and the All-India Moslem League was founded.

Moslem opinion in India, which tended to be more sympathetic to the British than did the Hindu community, was alienated by the treatment of Turkey in the First World War. Shortly after the end of the war came the massacre in Amritsar of Indian demonstrators by British troops. By this time, the days of British rule were clearly numbered, and demands for full independence were being made.

Gandhi Mohandas Karamchand Gandhi came from the Gujerat, but lived for many years in South Africa where he practised as a lawyer. There he represented the interests of the Indian community, was a stretcher-bearer in the Boer War, and experimented with vegetarianism and pacifism.

He returned to India in 1915, and after the First World War rose to prominence in the National Movement. Gandhi's two great contributions were the non-violence that lent the Movement overwhelming moral force, and the involvement of the Indian people in general. Gandhi's background as a lawyer and his experiences in Africa enabled him to fight the spiritual and intellectual struggle on the Westerners' own ground when he chose to do so, and he soon became a strange species of living icon, revered not only by many Indians but by many Westerners as well. His threatening, and actually beginning, to starve himself to death whenever the British or anyone else did anything of which he disapproved

proved successful in disconcerting the British.

The Indian National Movement was taken into the villages, for Gandhi, with his simple life style, the fact that he closely identified himself with one of the most potent symbols of Indian religious feeling, the cow, and his spinning wheel, inspired the respect and trust of the Indian rural masses. He was known as the Mahatma – that is, 'great soul'.

During the Second World War, most Congress leaders were broadly sympathetic to the Allied aims, but were understandably angered that India had been taken into a war without the Indian people having had a say in the matter. Indian co-operation was vital, and was generally forthcoming, though revolutionary nationalists like Subhas Chandra Bose and others sympathized with Japan and helped to form an Indian National Army which fought against the British in Burma.

After the war, the British had neither the desire nor the will to maintain an Indian empire. It is interesting to speculate how successful Gandhi's proposed campaign of non-violent resistance and non-co-operation would have worked against the Japanese, had they broken through into India; against a worn-out, tired British empire it had been extremely effective.

The road to independence was blocked by the serious religious and communal divisions in India between the Moslems, represented by Mohammed Ali Jinnah, and the Hindu majority who adhered to the Congress, a leading figure in which was Jawaharlal Nehru. The Congress did not pursue sectarian policies – indeed, it was largely responsible for the successful secular Indian constitution – but the Moslems were frightened of being overwhelmed by the Hindu majority, and were demanding a separate state, Pakistan.

Various federal schemes short of outright partition were proposed, but this was by now against a background of growing communal strife; further-more, the British were anxious to be rid of India. In 1946 there were widespread communal disorders

Indepen-dence and partition

and riots, some of them bloody; Nehru and Jinnah
went to London for direct talks with the British
government, but no useful conclusion came from
them. Lord Wavell was replaced by Lord
Mountbatten as governor, and the British announced
that full independence would come in June 1948.

Jinnah remained immovable in his demands for a
separate state, and was given to passing unhelpful
remarks such as 'The Moslem League will not yield
an inch in its demand for Pakistan' and 'I will have
India divided, or have India destroyed.' Eventually
all parties saw partition as the only alternative
to full-scale civil war, and Mountbatten brought
independence forward to 15 August 1947. Pakistan
was carved out of the old north-western provinces
and East Bengal, creating a country that was itself
split into two; this was never a happy arrangement,
and ended with the war in 1971 that turned East
Pakistan into Bangladesh.

*Communal
violence and
sectarian strife*

Partition and independence were marked not only
by euphoria and Nehru's famous 'tryst with destiny'
speech, but by pain and violence. The Punjab was
reduced to anarchy as Moslems fled one way, trying
to get over the new line that had been drawn on the
maps to mark the boundary between India and
Moslem Pakistan, and Sikhs and Hindus fled the
other. The Punjab, the Sikhs' homeland, was split
in two, for the new border passed between their
holy city, Amritsar, and their old capital, Lahore.
Most of the Sikhs fled into India, and today Lahore
is almost an exclusively Moslem city. This exodus
was marked by appalling bloodshed and violence,
the most notorious incident, perhaps, being the
massacre of Moslem refugees at Amritsar railway
station. Thousands of people lost their lives in the
Punjab alone.

The partition in the east wasn't marked by such
bloodshed, but vast numbers of people fled over the
new border, and this too caused great suffering.
India was left with a large Moslem population, and
sectarian strife remains a threat to its social cohesion.
A further problem were the Princely States that had

not been part of the British Raj, but semi-autonomous; these were left with the choice of trying to go it alone, or of joining with one of the two new dominions. There were some absurdities like the Moslem Nizam of Hyderabad, ruling an island of Moslems in the middle of a sea of Hindus, who thought for a while of setting up his own state; but there were also tragedies, like Kashmir, which has been a source of conflict between India and Pakistan for the last forty years.

Kashmir   Kashmir was one of the Princely States, and although the population was mainly Moslem, the ruling maharaja was a Hindu with leanings towards India. He vacillated about which of the new states he should attach himself and his state to, until an undisciplined Pakistani force appeared, bent on annexing Kashmir in the name of Pakistan. Before they could reach the capital, Srinagar, the Indians moved in with a force of their own, and the distracted maharaja announced that he wanted incorporation into the new Indian state. The first Indo-Pakistani war followed, which ended with *de facto* partition of Kashmir under the auspices of the United Nations. Neither side acknowledged the other's claims, and to this day Kashmir is divided by what is known as the 'Line of Control'. Indian maps show the border as the old boundary of the state of Kashmir, and have footnotes about the 'illegal occupation of parts of Kashmir by Pakistan'. India was to clash with Pakistan over Kashmir in the 1960s, and today Indian and Pakistani special forces are fighting an undeclared and little reported war on the inhospitable Siachen Glacier.

While India has thrived since independence, and looks set to become at least a regional superpower, Pakistan has fared less well. There was always something of a temporary, makeshift air about the country, and the slide into political chaos has not helped to dispel this. While India has scrupulously followed a path of official secularism, Pakistan has moved towards Islamic fundamentalism.

**After
independence**

Gandhi was always opposed to partition, and was greatly saddened by the events of 1947. He did not assume any political office himself, the first prime minister of India being Jawaharlal Nehru. Gandhi was assassinated by a Hindu fanatic on 30 January 1948.

The modern state

India is officially styled a sovereign socialist secular democratic republic in the 1950 constitution. Politically India is a quasi-federal union of twenty-five states and seven other regions that are known as Union Territories. The whole is called the Union of India.

The national government resides in New Delhi, and is known as the Centre. The central legislature is bicameral, the lower house being called the Lok Sabha (the assembly of the people) and the upper house the Rajya Sabha. The two houses are often referred to as 'Parliament' in the Indian press, and many of the procedures and the style of rhetoric do bear some resemblance to the British parliament in its better days.

National government

The Lok Sabha is the more important and powerful of the houses, and its relationship to the upper house is similar to that of the Commons to the Lords in Britain. No fiscal legislation can be introduced or originate in the upper house, the Rajya Sabha; only the lower house has this power. Furthermore, no bill can become law unless it has been passed by the Lok Sabha. All fiscal measures passed in the Lok Sabha must go to the Rajya Sabha for approval; the upper house must return the bill to the Lok Sabha with its amendments or recommendations within fourteen days. The Lok Sabha is not obliged to accept these amendments, but is supposed to give them due consideration. After this process, a fiscal measure is deemed to have passed through both houses and is passed on to the president for assent.

The Lok Sabha

The Lok Sabha does not have such powers in the case of non-fiscal legislation, which can originate in the Rajya Sabha. Bills must pass through both houses

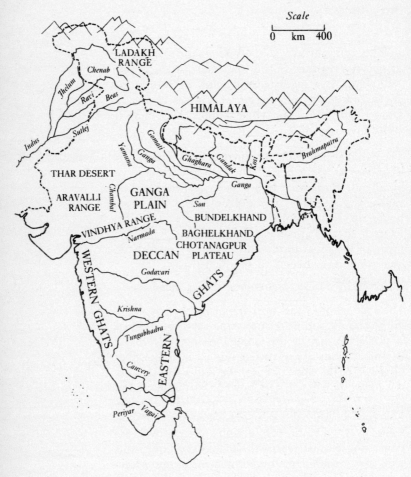

Figure 2

before they can become law, and if the agreement of both houses cannot be secured, then the president summons a joint session of both houses to reconsider it; since the Lok Sabha has a larger membership than the Rajya Sabha, it is the will of the lower house that will prevail.

The Lok Sabha has a five-year life, after which it is dissolved by the president and elections take place. The strength of the lower house is 542, of whom 530 are elected members from the states of the Union and twelve are elected members from the various Union Territories. The house elects two of its members as speaker and deputy speaker, and the president invites the leader of the majority party in the Lok Sabha to take the office of prime minister and submit recommendations for ministerial posts. Although the president has vital constitutional functions and is commander-in-chief, the day-to-day running of the government, the formation of policy, and major political initiatives are all taken by the prime minister. His or her relationship with the president is somewhat similar to that between the British prime minister and the Crown. The president is elected by an electoral college with a membership drawn from both houses of Parliament and the state legislative assemblies. He or she holds office for five years.

The Rajya Sabha has a maximum membership of 250, of whom 238 are from the states or Union Territories and are elected by the members of the state assemblies, and twelve are nominated by the president. The latter are usually distinguished figures from the worlds of science, literature, and art, or have made some outstanding contribution to the public good. One third of the membership of the Rajya Sabha is retired every two years, so the members effectively have a six-year term of office.

The Rajya Sabha

The map of India has changed considerably since independence, when there were but fourteen states. Many of these were later split up on linguistic grounds, such as the old state of Bombay, which

The states and Union Territories

became Maharashtra (where most of the people speak Marathi) and Gujerat (where most people, logically, speak Gujerati). The state of Mysore became Karnataka, and the north-eastern frontier, originally simply Assam, has now become no less than seven separate states, all divided on tribal or linguistic grounds.

The Union Territories are administered by the Centre, and are usually culturally or geographically distinct regions that deserve a separate identity, yet are not large enough to have full statehood conferred upon them. Delhi is a Union Territory somewhat analagous to the District of Columbia in the United States. Other Union Territories are enclaves like Pondicherry, which was a French possession only returned to India in 1954, or the Andaman and Nicobar Islands, which are geographically distinct from India.

State
government   Each state of the Union has a bi- or uni-cameral legislature and a governor, who is appointed by the president for a five-year term, and who is the chief executive head of the state within the Indian Union. The governor has the power of summoning or dissolving the state's legislative assembly, and the responsibility of ruling directly if the constitutional machinery has for some reason broken down. Normally, however, he or she acts on the advice of the chief minister of the state and the council of ministers, who are drawn from the legislative assembly.

The state governor Few government offices have suffered such tarnished reputations as that of state governor. The original intention, when the Indian constitution was framed, was that the governor would be even-handed, above party loyalties and factionalism, and perhaps not even a career politician but a great figure from some other sphere of life. Although governors of this stamp were once common – especially in the Nehru era – the recent tendency has been to use the gubernatorial office to reward burnt-out, time-serving, and unelectable politicians from the Centre. This has further led to the suspicion that President's Rule (that is, when the elected state assembly is suspended, and the governor rules directly in the name of the president) is sometimes used as a political weapon against state governments which are unpalatable to the Congress-dominated Centre. The imposition of President's Rule in Andhra Pradesh in 1984 led to widespread popular disturbances. The more the governors are seen as docile tools of the Centre, the less respect they command; this is perhaps one of the most serious causes of the widespread Indian disillusionment with career politicians.

The two houses   All states have a legislative assembly (Vindhan Sabha) composed of not more than 500 and not less than 60 directly elected members from territorial constituencies, and some have an upper house, the legislative council (Vindhan Parishad). The latter has limited powers, and has a role subordinate to that of the lower house. The chief minister and the council of ministers are drawn from the majority party in the legislative assembly, and they are appointed by the governor.

The legislative assembly has a five-year life, while the legislative council is permanent, one third of its members retiring after two years, thus giving a six-year term to each member. Members of the council are also directly elected. The legislative council has no fiscal powers, and only has staying powers on bills presented to it by the legislative assembly. One of the most common causes of constitutional crisis in state politics is the breakdown of shaky opposition (that is, non-Congress) coalitions; this is a frequent precursor of President's Rule.

Members of the New Delhi Parliament are usually called MPs in the press, but members of state legislatures have the initials MLA (member of the legislative assembly) or MLC (member of the legislative council) appended to their names.

The states are divided up into districts, with representative democracy extending down to the village level through the village councils, the *panchayats*.

Local administration

The states of the Indian Union

State	Capital	Population	Area (km²)
Andhra Pradesh	Hyderabad	53,549,673	275,068
Arunachal Pradesh	Itanagar	631,839	88,743
Assam	Dispur	19,896,843	78,438
Bihar	Patna	69,914,734	173,877
Goa	Panaji	10,086,730	3,814
Gujerat	Gandhinagar	34,085,799	196,024
Haryana	Chandigarh	12,922,618	44,212
Himachal Pradesh	Simla	4,280,818	55,673
Jammu and Kashmir	Srinagar	5,987,389	222,236
Karnataka	Bangalore	37,135,714	191,791
Kerala	Trivandrum	25,453,680	38,863
Madhya Pradesh	Bhopal	52,178,844	443,446
Maharashtra	Bombay	62,784,171	307,690
Manipur	Imphal	1,420,953	22,327
Meghalaya	Shillong	1,335,819	22,429
Mizoram	Aizawl	493,757	21,081
Nagaland	Kohima	774,930	16,579
Orissa	Bhubaneswar	26,370,271	155,707
Punjab	Chandigarh	16,788,915	50,362
Rajasthan	Jaipur	34,261,862	342,239
Sikkim	Gangtok	316,385	7,096
Tamil Nadu	Madras	48,408,077	130,058
Tripura	Agartala	2,053,058	10,486
Uttar Pradesh	Lucknow	110,862,013	294,411
West Bengal	Calcutta	54,580,647	88,752

Union Territories

Territory	Headquarters	Population	Area (km^2)
Andaman and Nicobar	Port Blair	188,741	8,249
Chandigarh	Chandigarh	451,610	114
Dadar and Nagar Haveli	Silvassa	103,676	491
Delhi	Delhi	6,220,406	1,483
Daman and Diu	Daman	78,981	112
Lakshadweep	Kavaratti	40,249	32
Pondicherry	Pondicherry	604,471	492

The division of power between the states and the centre

The Indian Constitution lays down those matters which are the responsibility of the Centre and those which are the responsibility of the state legislatures. There is also what is called the Concurrent List; that is, matters which are shared between the two. The so-called Central or Union list includes defence, foreign affairs, transport, banking, and other such matters. The state list includes education, public health, police, agriculture, and some forty-three other entries. The Concurrent List includes trade and industry, social and economic planning, and social security.

The judicial system

The highest court in the land is the Supreme Court, which consists of the chief justice and a maximum of seventeen other judges. All are appointed by the president. The Supreme Court is not only the highest court of appeal, but also presides over disputes between states of the Union, and between the Centre and states. Every state has a high court, which has both judicial and administrative functions. Within the state, it is the final court of appeal.

The Indian judicial system is slow and ponderous, and it can take years – literally – for cases to be heard. Indian lawyers seem to model themselves on the British, and in consequence are equally fond of wrapping up their activities in strange jargon.

Political parties

Indian party politics is almost incomprehensible to an outsider, and it is their preoccupation with domestic affairs that make Indian newspapers such limited reading. You might, for example, think that you know all about the Congress Party; but what are the Cong(I) and Cong(S)? You might consider yourself something of an enthusiast, and know that since 1967 the political life of Tamil Nadu has been dominated by the Dravida Munnetra Kazagham (DMK); but what are the AIADMK and the Jayalalitha Faction? You can read all about them in the papers and be none the wiser, in spite of the vast amount of newsprint expended upon them. On the left there's not only the Communist Party of India, or CPI, there's a CPI(M); a cursory glance through an Indian paper reveals that almost any political party comes in several flavours, denoted by some letter in brackets after its initials.

At independence there were really only two well-organized parties, the Congress and the Communists, although a total of fifty-one parties contested the first election in 1951, of which only twenty-one secured seats in the Lok Sabha. In these early days there was never a serious challenge to the might of the Congress, and the Nehru period, which lasted from independence until his death in May 1964, was the beginning of what some have thought to be an almost dynastic rule by the Congress.

Party splits

A two-party system never appeared in India, even when the Congress split down the middle. The opposition parties have usually been as hostile to each other as they have to the dominant Congress, and this has made the forging of electoral pacts very difficult. Furthermore, when a new party is created, it very soon splits into two or more violently opposed factions, each of which claims to be the true and only standard-bearer of whatever ideal the party espoused in the first place, and brands its rivals as venal heretics.

The first of the major party splits came in 1964, when the Communists divided into the Communist Party of India (CPI) and the Communist Party of India (Marxist). The former was a more moderate party than the latter, which is still rigid and doctrinaire. Gorbachev has caused them acute problems; the CPI(M) finds his criticism of Stalin hard to stomach. Saroj Mukherjee, CPI(M) politburo member, has said that 'We were brought up under the Stalin regime. We respect him a great deal. He was so kind to the colonised world.' As Arun Prokas Chatterjee CPI(M) member said, 'Why should we follow them blindly? Our communism is a lot purer than that of Deng or Gorbachev.'

The Left Front

Although the Left shows the same readiness to fragment itself as other political groups, it has been able to produce fairly durable alliances that have gained control of the state governments in West Bengal, Kerala (which had, in 1957, the world's first democratically elected communist government), and the small north-eastern state of Tripura. The other components of the Left Front, apart from the CPI and the CPI(M), are the Revolutionary Socialist Party and the Forward Block. The Naxalites were a Maoist group who favoured a violent, nihilistic rural revolution, and who took their name from the village of Naxalbari in Bengal.

Electoral
alliances

Becoming part of an electoral alliance is always a problem for the Left, for if such an alliance is to present a serious threat to the Congress, then it must include elements to the right of the government. The Right is dominated by the Bharatiya Janata Party (BJP), which is a descendant of the Jana Sangh; the latter had connections with the All India Hindu Mahasabha, which, with the Rashtriya Swayamsevak Sangh (RSS), was implicated in the murder of Mahatma Gandhi.

The paramilitary RSS (whose members dress up in khaki uniforms and drill in a manner not dissimilar to the Hitler Youth) and the BJP are best described as Hindu revivalist parties. They often invite the pejorative description of 'communal'; that is, they not only seek to assert the interests of one section of the national community, they seek to assert them at the expense of others. The RSS is also accused, with some justification, of being neo-fascist. Although it is a powerful force in some states, it had only two MPs in the Lok Sabha following the 1984 general election.

Congress

The Congress Party split in 1969, one section being led by the late Mrs Indira Gandhi (Nehru's daughter, and no relation of the Mahatma), and the other by the party's president, Nijalingappa. Mrs Gandhi's party carried the day in the 1971 elections; later, in 1981, Mrs Gandhi's party became known as the Congress(I), while the heretical group went through various metamorphoses from Cong(U) to Cong(J) and finally to Cong(S). The latter is now largely confined to pockets in Kerala and Assam, but it can still confuse you when you're reading the papers.

What might be called the middle ground of Indian politics is occupied by the Cong(I), which at present is the majority party in the Lok Sabha, and from whose ranks Mr Rajiv Gandhi and his ministers come; the Janata Party, composed of what are best described as agrarian romantics; the Lok Dal(B) (there are other Lok Dals but they might as well be ignored if anyone is to finish reading this); and some regional parties that are strong enough to have an impact on national politics.

Regional parties tend to make an appeal to the interests or sympathies of linguistic groups, and therefore to be strong in a particular state; notable examples are the Telegu Desam in Andhra Pradesh (which is almost like a fan club for the chief minister, the former film star N.T. Rama Rao) and the Dravida Munnetra Kazagham (DMK) in Tamil Nadu. These two parties have an obvious appeal to Telegu and Tamil speakers, but cannot hope to form a nationwide base; they are therefore often ready to enter into pacts and alliances, but problems always arise when it comes to choosing a leader. The great men of the regional parties are just as ambitious as those from the national ones.

Regional parties

The events of the summer of 1988, when V.P. Singh was trying to forge an electoral coalition or even a new party to challenge the Congress, showed the basic weakness of the Indian political system. Singh managed to get four parties, the Janata, the Lok Dal, the Cong(S), and his own creation, the Jan Morcha, to agree in principle on a merger into something to be called the Samajwadi Janata Dal (that is, the People's Socialist Party). There was also much horse-trading with other parties, notably Rama Rao's Telegu Desam, about forming a National People's Front. Policies were hardly discussed; negotiations seemed to be about who would hold high office in a party that didn't yet exist, about whose emblems would be used, and about whose idea it had all been

Attempts to challenge Congress

in the first place. With tears of sincerity in their eyes, time-serving old politicians appeared from the woodwork to relate how, after nights of doubt and spiritual struggle, they had come to one conclusion, and one that would be shared by any other patriotic Indian; and that was that they should lead the new party.

What made it worse was the general feeling that the Rajiv Gandhi administration was indeed very tired, and an alternative should be sought after; yet there can be no credible alternative without a more united opposition, who are not obsessed with personalities, and who have some ideological moorings, or at least some political convictions. The only thing that all opposition politicians seem to agree about is that Rajiv Gandhi must go; they are very silent about what will happen after this, except for vague promises of a return to 'people-based politics' and the like.

Elections   Indian elections are overseen by the Election Commission, a body which has the responsibility of ensuring that they are conducted fairly, without any duress being applied to voters, and that votes are properly counted. The Commission also maintains a register of parties; those which are 'recognized', that is, which obtained at least 4 per cent of the votes cast in any one state, are allotted emblems. These emblems are very important, for much of the Indian electorate is illiterate, and the emblems or party symbols are the only means by which they can identify a candidate. The list of 'recognized' parties is revised after each general election, and a party which achieves recognized status in more than four states is classed as a 'national party'; recognized status in less than four states leads to classification as a 'state party'. India has had eight general elections since independence, the last being in 1984 when Rajiv Gandhi and the Cong(I) achieved a landslide victory with 401 seats in the Lok Sabha.

The ballot boxes in remote Indian villages, the largely illiterate rural electorate, the lack of substance of the safari-suited politicians' utterances, all make

Indian democracy seem fragile and vulnerable; and yet it has an underlying strength that somehow overcomes these problems, as was demonstrated in the government's defeat in the 1977 election.

The Indian Constitution

The Indian Constitution was adopted by the Constituent Assembly, the forerunner of the Indian Parliament, on 24 November 1946, but did not come into force until 26 January 1950. The Rajya Sabha and the Lok Sabha share the power of amending the Constitution, and many such amendments have been added in the years since independence. The Supreme Court has the responsibility of enforcing the fundamental rights enshrined in the Indian Constitution, and so, to a lesser extent, do the high courts of the states.

Fundamental rights

Seven fundamental rights are guaranteed. These are:

1 The right to equality; that is, the recognition that all persons are equal before the law and have the right to the protection of the law without exception on grounds of race, religion, sex, or caste. The Indian Constitution formally abolished untouchability, and the conferring of titles by the state except for military and academic awards.
2 The right of freedom; that is, freedom of speech and expression, freedom to assemble peacefully and without arms, freedom of association, including trade unionism, freedom of movement within India, freedom to reside and settle in any part of India, and freedom to choose any legal trade or occupation or practise any profession.
3 The right of freedom of religion; that is, the freedom to practise any religion.
4 The right against exploitation, which prohibits slavery, the trade in human beings, and child labour in mines and factories.
5 Cultural and educational rights, which guarantee India's many minorities the right to preserve their cultural heritage (language, for instance) through maintaining appropriate educational establishments.

6 The right to constitutional remedies; that is, the right to move the Supreme Court or one of the high courts to enforce constitutionally guaranteed rights.

7 The right to property.

These fundamental rights have been greatly qualified by the 56 amendments to the Constitution. Like many other grand-sounding Constitutions, its proof is in its enforcement – or in its enforcibility. It is one thing to abolish untouchability on paper, and quite another to eradicate the powerful social barriers in rural communities. Bonded labour (whereby indebted agricultural labourers end up as what can only be described as the serfs of landowners) and the widespread exploitation of children make nonsense of other fundamental rights. Nonetheless, the Indian Constitution is a brave and optimistic statement, and has survived remarkably well considering the inconvenience that it has occasioned the government from time to time.

Composition of government, and the franchise

The Constitution further prescribes the composition of the houses of the Indian Parliament and the legislative houses of the states, their powers and their lifetime. It defines the office of president, vice-president etc., and sets out the relationships between the branches of government; the executive is subordinate to the legislature, but the judiciary functions as an independent unit. All Indian citizens of twenty-one years of age and above are entitled to vote in general and regional elections.

Languages

Some articles of the Constitution are of especial interest. Article 343 provides that the official language of the Indian Union shall be Hindi (the northern language that bears a relationship to Sanskrit like that of modern Italian to Latin) in the Devanagari script. English was to be a joint official language until 26 January 1965, but it proved to be impractical to eliminate it so quickly; the main reason for this was India's own linguistic diversity.

The adoption of Hindi as a national language was not well received in the southern (Dravidian) states, especially Tamil Nadu. On a wall in Madurai, in Tamil Nadu, I have seen scrawled (in Engish) 'English ever, Hindi never!', and 'Death to Hindi!' The language question was often the focus of regional nationalism in India, and states were formed on the basis of linguistic divisions; many Indians regard the precedent set by the partition of the Telegu-speaking regions of the old Madras state to form Andhra Pradesh in 1953 as being little short of disastrous.

In 1956 the radical reorganization of the states on linguistic lines took place, and there seems to be no end to the process. In some regions, notably Tamil Nadu, local nationalism has been strong enough to spawn separatist movements.

The Indian Constitution recognizes fifteen languages under its eighth schedule, and any of these may be used for official purposes in addition to Hindi. These languages are: Assamese, Bengali, Gujerati, Hindi, Kannada, Kashmiri, Malayalam, Marathi, Oriya, Punjabi, Sanskrit, Sindhi, Tamil, Telegu, and Urdu.

Domestic politics since independence

The most obvious feature of post-independence India has been the dominance of the Congress and Nehru's family. Indira Gandhi was Nehru's only daughter, and Rajiv is his grandson. In spite of the democratic institutions, India has slipped into something dangerously close to dynastic rule. Nehru's successor, Lal Bahadur Shastri, survived him by only nineteen months, dying of a heart attack during the 1966 Tashkent talks with Ayub Khan of Pakistan. Indira Gandhi, who had held ministerial office in his government, and who had been president of the Congress in 1960, became prime minister shortly afterwards.

The death of his elder brother, Sanjay, in a plane crash, and his mother's assassination by her Sikh guards in 1984, catapulted Rajiv Gandhi into office; he won a landslide victory in the 1984 election. Now, however, his popularity (and that of the monolithic

Congress) seems to be crumbling, in spite of the ineffectual opposition.

Nehru   After the convulsion of the partition, the murder of the Mahatma, and the settlement of the floods of refugees, the Nehru government began to try to reconstruct Indian society through the National Planning Commission and the first of the Five Year Plans. Nehru inclined towards socialism, but shied away from the rigidity of the state control imposed by communist governments. A mixed economy was envisaged, in which much heavy industry was controlled by the state (steel, oil, electricity, ship-building etc.), but some remained in private hands (textiles, for example). In the First Plan, however, the emphasis was placed on agricultural development, with the eventual aim of making India self-sufficient in foodstuffs.

A succession of plans followed, and there have been six to date. The Second Plan concentrated on the development of the heavy industrial base, while the Third, which lasted from 1961 to 1966, was to have created a self-sustaining economy but foundered; it ended with a large foreign debt and an economic crisis in which the rupee was devalued. One of the factors that held India back was its rapidly growing population; from 320 millions in 1947, it had grown to 439 millions by 1961.

Many social reforms were implemented under Nehru. A reservation system for members of sched-uled castes and tribes was introduced ('scheduled castes' is a euphemism for untouchables; 'tribals' are members of India's aboriginal tribes, such as the Bhils or Gonds), in a move that anticipated affirmative action programmes in the United States. The position of women had been improved with the passing of the 1955 Hindu Succession Act and the 1956 Hindu Marriage Act, the former giving women equal rights with men with respect to the inheritance and holding of property, and the latter providing for divorce in the event of marital breakdown, with maintenance and alimony. Untouchability had already been out-lawed in the Constitution. With these, as with all other reforms, the problem was one of enforcement in an overwhelmingly rural country. The Nehru period also saw the growth of regional nationalism, with the redrawing of state boundaries on linguistic lines. True to the Constitutional declaration that India is a secular state, communal strife – that is, fighting between the members of India's many religious groups, and particularly between Hindus and Moslems – was kept under control if not entirely eliminated.

Green Revolutions Although the sixties were an unhappy time economically for India, a notable success was the Green Revolution of 1967–8. This arose from improved methods of cultivation and the introduction of new, high-yielding strains of Mexican wheat and dwarf rice. This first revolution was confined to the Punjab, Haryana, and some parts of Uttar Pradesh, but 1983–4 witnessed a second, caused by improved management and services to farmers. Foodgrain production of 152 million tonnes was achieved, and India has not only become self-sufficient in this respect, but stored enough to see it through the disastrous monsoon failures of 1986 and 1987.

Mrs Indira Gandhi came to power in 1966. The three things that will long be associated with her are the birth control programme, the Emergency, and the Punjab crisis which ultimately led to her assassination at the hands of her own guards.   *Indira Gandhi*

The birth control programme India's exploding population had been causing alarm for some time, but the intervention by Mrs Gandhi's son, the late Sanjay, was little short of calamitous. These were the days of free transistor radios for Indians who had vasectomies, of what amounted to forced sterilization, and of wild rumours of piratical gangs of sterilizers roaming the countryside that made peasants afraid to go out at night.

Although it had a blackly comic side, the sterilization campaign made the Gandhis very unpopular.

Much propaganda was produced to promote the joys of the two-child family; many of the posters and wall paintings are still to be seen, with messages such as 'Planned family is happy family', 'Small family is happy family', and so on.

The Emergency   The Emergency was Mrs Gandhi's response to a deteriorating social and economic situation, and, it must be said, to serious political difficulties of her own. In 1975, the Allahabad High Court declared Mrs Gandhi guilty of corrupt electoral practices; there had already been a wave of protest at alleged government corruption, and the Allahabad verdict was a gift to the vocal opposition. Instead of resigning, Mrs Gandhi chose to declare (through the president) a state of emergency on the grounds that the state was under threat from a widespread conspiracy. Exactly who these conspirators were, or what they planned to do, was never clearly explained, but many of Mrs Gandhi's opponents and critics ended up having a hard time, some of them in prison, so one can only conclude that plotting against the state and plotting against Mrs Gandhi amounted to the same thing. Some extreme political groups were banned, such as the RSS, the Jamat-i-Islami, and the Anand Marg. The government produced a stream of hysterical propaganda to justify its actions, accusing all of its opponents or potential opponents of plotting against the state, suggesting that the whole country was being ruined by corruption and black-marketeering, and telling the people that the only way through all these difficulties was the Emergency. The president of the Congress came out with his immortal line, 'India is Indira, and Indira is India.'

Indian opinion still seems to be divided about the Emergency, in spite of its excesses; the judiciary and the press were strictly controlled, as the authorities assumed arbitary powers of arrest. Many Indians still say that the Emergency was the only way in which India's hopelessly inefficient bureaucracy could be goaded into life, and that the extraordinary powers assumed by the state were the only means by which the racketeers and the corrupt could be dealt with;

that their very existence made a mockery of the law, and they had to be punished. Other Indians who lived through those times say that the Emergency had the opposite effect to that which was intended; corruption and extortion became worse, not better, because of the new powers held by the police and government officials. The Emergency did see a degree of economic recovery, but whether this was because of, or in spite of, Mrs Gandhi's measures is something else about which Indians disagree.

The Emergency was relaxed in 1977, and normal political activity resumed. A loose coalition of non-communist opposition parties, including the Congress(O) and the Bharatiya Lok Dal (the Indian People's Party), campaigned against the Congress as the Janata (that is, the People's) Party. They won a huge majority in the 1977 general election, holding 296 Lok Sabha seats to the Congress's 153. Mrs Gandhi was now out of office.

Although the Indian people had shown that they could use their votes to turn the government out, what followed highlighted perhaps the greatest weakness of Indian political life. The Janata Party had devoted so much thought and energy to getting rid of Mrs Gandhi and the Congress, it had become so rarefied in the rhetorical flights against her imperial style of rule, that its leaders had had no time to think about what they would do were they to form a government themselves. This proved to be a serious embarrassment to them, and the difficulty was compounded by the usual personality clashes and internal strains to which political alliances are subject. The first problem, of course, was who should be prime minister; the mantle fell on the ancient Morarji Desai, a seasoned politician of the old school who was deeply concerned with prohibition and the welfare of cows. Although the Janata government was responsible for some policy successes, it fell apart because of the internal rivalries of the hastily assembled coalition. After only three years, another election was called, and this time Mrs Gandhi was swept back into power, with 353 Congress seats in the Lok Sabha.

The Punjab crisis The eighties were marked by tragedy for the Gandhis. Indira's eldest son and heir-apparent, Sanjay, was killed piloting a private plane at a New Delhi airfield. Sikh disaffection in the Punjab turned into violence and outright terrorism under men such as Sant Jarnail Singh Brindranwale, who was killed when the Indian Army stormed the Golden Temple, Amritsar, in Operation Bluestar in 1984. It was in response to this that Mrs Gandhi's own Sikh guards murdered her in the garden of her New Delhi home later in that year, and this was followed by some of the worst communal violence since partition; in many cities in north India (including Delhi), Sikhs were lynched and their homes and businesses looted.

The Punjab was created in 1966, when the old state was split into two. The region where there was a majority Hindi-speaking population was turned into a new state, Haryana; this and the new Punjab shared a capital, the Corbusier horror of Chandigarh. Unfortunately, the two states ended up sharing more than a capital; in particular, they had to share an ambitious irrigation scheme to harness the waters of the Ravi and the Beas, both of which flow mainly through the Punjab. The Punjab was one of the cradles of the Green Revolution, and through hard work and good planning, the Sikhs have turned their state into one of the major foodgrain producers in the Indian Union. The Punjab also has a number of thriving industries; Ludhiana, for example, is the home of those magnificent 'Hero' bicycles.

In spite of their success, the Sikhs were left with the feeling that they were not reaping the rewards themselves, but were in effect subsidizing others; in particular, Hindi-speaking and Hindu Haryana next door. The issue of the joint irrigation project brought all this to a head, the feeling amongst Sikhs apparently being that Haryana was stealing their water. In the background more sinister forces were at work, which transformed the problem from one that could have been settled by negotiation into an apparently unbreakable cycle of terrorist violence. Although Mrs Gandhi had given the Sikhs a Punjabi-speaking homeland when the state was created in 1966, some Sikhs wanted more than this; they dreamt of an independent Sikh state. Most Sikhs, of course, had no such ambitions, believing that their grievances could be redressed while their state remained part of the Indian Union. The secessionists' demands were made not so much for economic as for sentimental and religious reasons; those who dreamt of the independent Sikh state dreamt of Khalistan, the Land of the Pure, and many (if not all) of them were religious zealots – like Brindranwale.

The situation was further complicated by alleged Pakistani support for the militant separatists; the Punjab occupies a vital strategic position straddling the route to Kashmir, and any hint of Pakistani involvement was unwelcome news in New Delhi. The terrorists began a series of outrages, such as the murder of the editor of the Hind Samachar group of newspapers, Ramesh Chandra Chopra, and they began to use the holy shrine, the Golden Temple in Amritsar, as a base. Because of the sanctity of the Golden Temple, the Indian security forces hesitated to pursue them there; eventually the complex was being used not just as a refuge, but as a headquarters and armoury.

On the advice of her security chiefs, Mrs Gandhi took the decision to storm the temple and flush the terrorists out; this was the famous (or infamous) Operation Bluestar of 6 June 1984. The terrorists fought hard, and tanks had to be brought up against them. The temple was seriously damaged, including the second most sacred shrine, the Akal Takht. It is generally believed that either the Indian commanders underestimated the opposition they would face, or that they misled Mrs Gandhi; she was appalled when she saw the damage that had been caused to the Sikhs' most holy shrine, and she must have realized that there would be a backlash. The Golden Temple had been desecrated, and Sikhs throughout the world cried vengeance – despite the reasons why the place had been attacked in the first place. (Much later, in 1988, when the security forces entered the temple a second time in Operation Black Thunder, the bodies of informers or businessmen who had failed to pay protection money were found buried in a pile of earth; many had been mutilated and tortured.)

Mrs Gandhi paid for Operation Bluestar with her life, on 31 October 1984. Moderate Sikh opinion had been outraged by the desecration of the temple, and now Indian public opinion was outraged by the assassination of the prime minister. The crowds vented their fury on the Sikh community in many northern cities, including Delhi. Hundreds were said to have been killed in these communal riots, many of them burned to death.

The Punjab has remained a seemingly intractable problem ever since. It has been without a government, having been under president's rule since 1984. Rajiv Gandhi nearly implemented a settlement with moderate Sikh leaders, but drew back because he was apparently afraid of offending Hindi-speaking voters elsewhere. The terrorists wage open war not only against the security forces but against Hindu and Sikh villagers; the former to cause yet more communal strife so that they can present themselves as the protectors of an embattled and persecuted people, the latter to eliminate political opponents. Behind all the rhetoric there is, as with many terrorist organizations, a strong financial incentive; the extremists are adept at robbing banks and extorting money from villagers at the point of a gun. The terrorists themselves come, like everything else in Indian politics, in several flavours; perhaps the worst and most brutal are the so-called Khalistan Commando Force. Every day the Indian papers carry news of yet another murder or murders in the Punjab, and it is long since they made front page news. The continued violence and unrest are having a serious effect on the state's once thriving economy, and the involvement of Pakistan hasn't helped India's already precarious relationship with its Moslem neighbour. The Pakistanis can have no real interest in Khalistan, except for the trouble caused to the Indians, because recent maps released by separatist extremists show more and more territory included within the bounds of the Land of the Pure. Large sections of Pakistan are now included. Big cities in India (like Delhi) would be renamed after great Sikh gurus. There really appears to be no limit to Khalistan.

The dynastic nature of Indian – or at least Congress – politics was demonstrated when Rajiv Gandhi, Indira's young son who had but four years parliamentary experience, and had not even held ministerial office, was sworn in as prime minister on the same day that his mother died. Rajiv was greeted warmly by the press and the public, in spite of his inexperience, and he was untainted by any scandal or allegations of corruption – unlike his dead brother. The Indian press liked to call him Mr Clean, and he won a landslide victory in December 1984 when the Congress gained over 400 seats in the Lok Sabha.

Rajiv Gandhi

Now it seems that nothing good can be said about poor Rajiv. Here is an extract from a feature article from a leading Indian paper, *The Hindustan Times*; 'The Congressman of yore used to be a dhoti-kurta or pajama-kurta clad common man with a Gandhi cap. Today Congressmen rarely wear a Gandhi cap, many or most leaders have taken to safari suits, take pride in smoking cigars and pipes like burra sahibs, and invariably seek the sanctuaries of the air-conditioned five-star hotels while attending plenary sessions of the party. . . the masses of India cannot be faulted for being xenophobic towards the proponents of the "modern day Congress culture".' In another article where Mr Gandhi's habit of going away on endless foreign jaunts was being severely criticized, the journalist suggested that the prime minister felt more at home abroad than in India because he was married to a foreigner (his wife is an Italian lady name Sonia). Again and again this matter comes up, that the prime minister is married to a foreigner; somehow Rajiv Gandhi has touched a latent xenophobia.

Industrial liberalization One of the few success stories of Rajiv Gandhi's government has been the industrial liberalization policy. The Indian tradition has tended towards nationalization, central planning,

Call to ban sex with foreigners

By A Staff Reporter

NEW DELHI, June 8: Should Indians have sex with visiting foreigners and NRIs, given the AIDS situation abroad?

The Indian Council of Medical Research says no. In fact, it had suggested legislation to ban sexual intercourse between Indians and visitors from abroad. The intention was to check the menace of AIDS from spreading in India.

However, though several ministries viewed the proposal favourably, the law ministry shot it down as it felt that it would be violative of the Constitution, particularly the fundamental right to privacy.

The idea of introducing such a ban is the brainchild of the director-general of ICMR, Dr A. S. Paintal. Speaking at the ICMR award distribution function today, he said that the ICMR had proposed such an act under which only Indians would be punishable for having sexual intercourse with foreigners and NRIs. No foreigner will be punished. He said that he was "shocked" when the law ministry turned down the proposal which was "favourably viewed by most ministries".

Dr Paintal further said, "after this disappointment, I discussed the matter casually with the famous lawyer, Mr Fali Nariman, and he said that India could not have a constitutional right that would destroy the nation. He agreed with me that the provision needed to be modified. Several other lawyers also thought the same. Very recently I have received great encouragement from our attorney-general, Mr. K. Parasaran".

Undeterred by the rejection of the law ministry, the ICMR and the Union ministry for health and family welfare ministry have jointly decided to hold a nationwide debate to elicit public opinion on "would legislation prohibiting Indian residents from having sexual intercourse with foreigners and visiting NRIs be violative of the constitutional right to privacy". The debate will be at the college and university level with the national debate to be held on January 21, 1989, in Delhi. The winners would be awarded prizes.

Dr Paintal said that it had also been decided to sponsor workshops and seminars "among the legal fraternity" to elicit their opinion. Finally the ICMR proposes to place before parliament the "recommendations of the nation" during the budget session next year.

Several observers felt that as a debating point the subject was not bad. But the idea of having such legislation was ludicrous. They said that the government was unable to implement so many other acts and legislations, and wondered if it would really get into private bedrooms to implement this legislation, if ever it was passed. It would be violative of constitutional rights, besides being impractical, they said.

However, a health ministry official pointed out that even if no legislation was brought forward, the national debate would help in creating awareness on the dreaded disease and would also possibly throw up suggestions on how to control the spread of AIDS in India.

It may be mentioned here that the debate is being held as part of the national AIDS control strategy.

Source: *The Times of India*, 9 June 1988

and massive government intervention. Industrial
planning was surrounded by complex licensing regulations which inevitably involved the cumbersome
Indian bureaucracy. These have been relaxed, and
the government is trying to introduce efficiency
through competition. Large industries will still come
under the control of the Monopolies and Restrictive
Trade Practices Act and the Foreign Exchange
Regulation Act, but the delicensing has made it much
easier to set up smaller industrial concerns.

Unrest and alleged corruption   The negative side of
the Rajiv Gandhi administration is provided by the
continuing regional unrest, especially in the Punjab,
and the serious allegations of corruption that have
been made against some of the prime minister's close
associates.

Other allegations of high-level graft and corruption
have surfaced in the press, and some of them have
come uncomfortably close to the prime minister
himself – the general feeling seems to be that far
from his being a Mr Clean, corruption, graft, and
cronyism have flourished under Rajiv Gandhi as
never before. As an Indian paper's editorial expressed
it, 'Whether he is part of it or not, the corruption
scourge will continue to plague Rajiv unless he acts
to change the image of cronyism that has come to
characterise his four-year-old reign.'

The fixed point in Indian foreign affairs is the mutual
distrust between India and Pakistan. The countries
have fought three wars, the first just after independence, the second in 1965, and the last during 1971.
The third war gave Indira Gandhi what was perhaps
her most triumphant moment, when she announced
Indian recognition of the new People's Republic of
Bangladesh to the tumultuous cheers of both houses
of Parliament. While the first two Indo-Pakistani
wars were indecisive, the last was a dismal defeat for
Pakistan in both east and west, although the Pakistani
airforce made a good showing. In the east, the Indian
Army marched into what was then East Pakistan,
defeated the beleaguered Pakistani Army, and helped

**India and
the world**

*Indo-
Pakistani
relations*

to create the new state of Bangladesh. There was much popular and official rejoicing in India over this defeat of the old archenemy.

Indo-Pakistani relations continue to be strained, with both sides making allegations that their rivals are indulging in threatening military build-ups, covertly arming with nuclear weapons, or interfering in their internal affairs and encouraging insurgency. In the case of India, this means accusing the Pakistanis of helping the Sikh extremists (which the Pakistanis certainly do), and on the Pakistani side it means accusing the Indians of fomenting the racial strife in Sind or of being implicated in the death of President Zia. The part played in Pakistani national life by the army, and the country's general instability do little to make the Indians feel secure.

Indo–
Chinese
relations

India fought a short and disastrous war with China in 1962. The cause of this was the disputed McMahon line, the frontier agreed in the Simla Conference of 1913–14 between the imperial British authorities, the Tibetans, and the Chinese. The Chinese claimed that they had never agreed to this frontier, and so the ownership of some remote and mountainous northern areas was at best uncertain, and at worst disputed. In 1959 the Chinese took over Tibet; the Dalai Lama fled to India, where he was offered sanctuary. This caused some offence to the Chinese.

The Indians then discovered that the Chinese were building an all-weather road across the Askai Chin plateau, an area to which the Indian government laid formal claim. Nehru ordered the Indian Army to step in, and they were crushingly defeated; it was also a personal defeat for Nehru and a great blow to India's prestige. For a time, it seemed that India might be invaded by the Chinese, but they declared a unilateral ceasefire and withdrew, evidently satisfied at having humiliated the proud new Indian state.

India still lays claim to territory occupied by the Chinese, and this is the subject of very pointed footnotes in tables of statistics and on maps – 'No information is available for those areas under illegal occupation by Chinese and Pakistani armed forces.'

Nehru was the architect of the early Non-Aligned Movement. In the first years of Indian independence, few of the African states were free from colonial rule, and India saw itself as the crusading voice of anti-colonialism. This could have led to closer ties with the United States, but Nehru was astute enough to realize that the power of the dollar was overwhelming and kept his distance. Nehru therefore avoided alliances and power blocs, and cultivated communist China and Russia as much as the West. In those days, the Mahatma's moral authority seemed to have attached itself in the world's eyes to the doings and sayings of almost any Indian; Nehru was feted as a visionary who had succeeded in a precarious balancing act between East and West, and was to some extent a mediating force in the world.

The Non-Aligned Movement

Much of this was lost after Suez and the Russian invasion of Hungary; the former Nehru condemned in the most extreme words, the latter was commented on in a mild and somewhat ambiguous manner. Later came the collision with China, and the shift in power as new African states became the world's main producers of moralistic, anti-imperialist rhetoric.

India had to arm itself, given the troubled nature of its land borders, and for this it turned to the USSR. The Indian airforce is almost wholly equipped with Russian-built aircraft. This close military relationship has been reinforced by the American support for Pakistan; the United States supplies the Pakistanis F-16s, the Russians supply the Indian Air Force the new Mig 29. The Indians remain deeply suspicious of the United States, which they believe to be engaged in interference in their internal affairs.

Indo-Soviet relations

India now has close ties with the Soviet Union; although there seems to be little affinity between the two countries, and although you never read of anyone in the 'matrimonials' columns who is looking for a 'smart young man' who is preferably a doctor with permission to reside in the Soviet Union, the degree to which Soviet propaganda has penetrated India is remarkable. This is the result of a deliberate effort on the part of the Soviets. For instance, a casual visit to the Rangacharlu Memorial Hall in Mysore reveals a USSR book fair; there are cheap primers for all of the major Dravidian languages, low-cost textbooks on physics, engineering, and mathematics; and of course a political section, the show-piece of which is a series entitled 'The ABC of Social and Political Knowledge'. These invaluable guides to the modern world contain such gems as 'In October 1956, International Imperialism and Reactionary Forces launched a counter-revolution in Hungary' and 'The DPRK (Democratic People's Republic of Korea) is a state with a multi-party system.' The last piece of information would come as a shock to Kim II Sung: I hope someone has the courage to tell him about it.

Indian students also receive education and training in the Soviet Union, and India has launched satellites with Russian help. (India now has a launcher programme of its own, though the flight of the ASLV-D2 vehicle in July 1988 was a failure.) An Indian has been into space, Squadron Leader Rakesh Sharma on 3 April 1984, courtesy of the Soviet Union.

The armed forces

India is beginning to flex its muscles as a regional superpower, and this is reflected in the growth in its armed forces, especially the navy. During the Indo-Pakistan war of 1971, the United States angered the Indians by sending a fleet into the Straits of Malacca; the fleet did nothing in the end, but if it had, there would have been little the Indians could have done to stop it. India now has the world's seventh largest navy, including two ex-Royal Navy carriers that are equipped with Sea Harriers. India recently took delivery of a Russian nuclear-powered submarine for evaluation – much to the distress of Pakistan, which wants one of its own.

The Indian Army is enormous, with some 960,000 men (compared to Pakistan's 450,000); the airforce is the world's fifth largest, and is very well equipped. India is now the Third World's fourth largest producer of armaments, after China, Brazil, and Argentina. It is capable of building its own warships, and plans to build an aircraft carrier in the Cochin construction yard before the end of this century. Behind all the talk of Gandhian principles, it is fair to say that the Indians have a realistic attitude to their armed forces; they maintain them in order to use them when they see fit.

India has become involved in the Sri Lankan conflict. This is a civil war between the Sinhalese majority and the Tamil minority in the island, and its history is depressingly familiar to anyone who has followed the growth of local nationalism. The two communities are distinct, the Tamils speaking (of course) Tamil and following their traditional Hindu religious beliefs, and the Sinhalese using their own language and following their traditional Buddhist faith. The Sinhalese are in the majority, and the Tamils have felt, with considerable justification, that they and their culture were being discriminated against. As usual, demands for concessions on local autonomy and language rights turned into a movement advocating outright secession, which in its turned spawned terrorism.

The Sri Lankan conflict

The Tamils produced a number of militant organizations, of which the most important are the Liberation Tigers of Tamil Elam (the LTTE), the Elam Revolutionary Organization (EROS), the People's Liberation Organization of Tamil Elam (PLOTE), and the Tamil Elam Liberation Organization (TELO). These organizations devoted much effort to fighting each other, as well as the Sri Lankan army, and the LTTE emerged as the dominant force. The war with the Sri Lankan regular forces was expanded, and the Sri Lankan government received help from outside – from the UK, the USA, Pakistan (which wanted to enter into a treaty of peace and friendship), and China. In other words, the conflict took on an international dimension, involving all of India's archenemies.

The Indian attitude towards the civil war has always been a little ambiguous, because Indian Tamils have also demanded secession at times; the Tamil party, the DMK, was secessionist in its early days. There were therefore obvious hazards in encouraging the growth of militant Tamil separatism, but there were also dangers in not supporting it in Sri Lanka, for all of India's own Tamils were clamouring for intervention. Many Tamil refugees made their way to the mainland, and have caused serious problems in the state of Tamil Nadu; to finance their operations, they engage in crime. Thus, while it was hardly in India's interests to encourage militant separatists in neighbouring states, the government risked offending their own Tamils by not doing so.

The compromise was to make threats, and give sanctuary to the refugees. India violated Sri Lankan sovereignty in May 1987, by air-dropping supplies to the beleaguered Tamils in the Jaffna peninsula. India played a role as mediator between the Jayawardene government in Colombo and the Tamil militants, and eventually an accord was worked out whereby most of the major Tamil demands would be met and the militants would be disarmed by an Indian Army force. Soon the Indian Peace Keeping Force (IPKF) was bogged down in a bloody war with the Tamils themselves, and this is still going on; elsewhere in the island, atrocities are regularly committed by both Sinhalese and Tamil extremists.

Nuclear power   Finally, India is a member of the exclusive 'nuclear club'. An 'atomic device' was exploded at Pokram in Rajasthan on 18 May 1974; India also has a number of nuclear power stations. Although the Indian government insists that it only develops nuclear technology for peaceful purposes, it nonetheless has the ability to manufacture and deliver nuclear weapons. This must cause much soul-searching in Islamabad, and the Pakistani response has been to try to make a bomb of their own.

The modern people

Few countries can hold as many racial, cultural, and linguistic groups within their borders as India. The 1981 census gave the official population as 685,184,692 (see tables in 'The modern Indian state'); the sex ratio was 933 females to every 1,000 males, the literacy rate was 36 per cent (that was an average of two figures – nearly 47 per cent for males and only about 25 per cent for females), and an overwhelming majority of the population (522,000,000) lived in rural areas. What lies behind these figures?

First of all, there is no more a single Indian people than there is a single Indian language. A group of people that includes the predominantly Aryan northerners, the pre-Aryan Dravidian races of the south, and ancient aboriginal hill tribes such as the Bhils of Maharastra, can hardly be said to share a common descent; neither do they share a common language. Ironically, in spite of popular patriotic fervour and official disapproval, English is almost a first language for many educated and professional Indians.

Then there are all the other divisions in Indian society, some of which are brutally obvious and simple, and some of which are subtle and hard to understand. In the first category comes the stark division between rich and poor; as stated in the introduction, rich men tend to be overweight and wear safari suits or other Western clothes, poor men tend to be thin and wear traditional dress. In the second category come all the caste and religious distinctions; and there are very many of them. It is a fiction that there are but four castes; the total number must run into the thousands. Furthermore, the caste structure is fluid, because caste is associated with profession.

Population and peoples

"Yes, Miss Gupta, the pay isn't much and the hours are hard. But you've got to admit it's nice, steady work."

One of the most important things for a Westerner to appreciate is that India is *not* a poor country; it is a very rich country with a very large number of very poor people living in it. The wealthy, predominantly urban middle classes outnumber the entire population of France, and some of them have really big money and lead luxurious lives. Then there are the slums and shanties, which are found in every Indian town or city. Many of the Bhopal victims (killed when a Union Carbide storage tank began to leak poisonous gases on 3 December 1984) lived in shanty towns built close to the chemical plant; people stream into Bombay from the country, the city bursts at the seams, and instead of success they find Mahim, said to be Asia's biggest slum. A visit to Mahim is a must for any Westerner; and before you go, read some of those accounts of the slums written by Western or Westernized authors, about the vibrancy of the people's lives, about how they have something that Westerners and Westernized Indians have lost, about how their dignity is stripped away not by their material circumstances but by the Westerners' horror of them, by the Westerners' ignorance of their inner life. Even V.S. Naipaul was unable to resist a little of this cant in his book about India, *An Area of Darkness*.

Rich and poor

Mahim in Bombay is on the north of the peninsula upon which the main city is built. It is really an unreclaimed swamp; most of Bombay is built upon reclaimed swamp. Hundreds of thousands of people live in makeshift shelters, without running water, without sanitation of the most basic kind, and with little medical care. Nearby is the famous church of St Michael's, which seems to be permanently crowded; here the halt, the lame, and the dying lie hearing mass. The main railway line from Victoria Terminus and Bombay Central runs through the middle of this huge, squalid reflection of 'bustling Bombay, India's economic powerhouse'.

Or there is Nand Nagri in Delhi. Here the people might have vibrant and intense lives, but during the monsoon of 1988 they also had polluted drinking water; the tube wells from which they drew their water supply were close to large communal lavatories, and sewage had seeped into them. The result was a cholera epidemic that claimed hundreds of lives.

Then there is rural India; this can sometimes be idyllic, and sometimes as squalid and terrible as the city slums. Gandhi was much concerned with the squalor and heaps of excrement to be found in the villages, and was moved to say (in another context) that the one thing that India could learn from the West was the science of public sanitation.

The biggest divide in Indian society is probably that between the cities and the rural masses. Although many country people gravitate to the cities in the search for work, they remain on the margins; and the cities are the stamping ground of the English-speaking, educated, wealthy middle classes. An Indian upper class remains, of course; this means old money, estates, perhaps even a palace or two – or three. Although the privy purses and special privileges of the former princely rulers were abolished in 1970, many Indians still have a great affection for the old aristocracy; indeed, they are surrounded by a social snobbery that is disconcertingly similar to that in the United Kingdom. Many of the former ruling houses have found a new place in Indian society by involving themselves in politics – for example, the Queen Mother of Gwalior became a leading light in the right-wing Bharatiya Janata Party (BJP).

The middle classes
The middle classes are, like the middle classes anywhere else, composed of military men, businessmen and businesswomen (India has a growing number of highly successful businesswomen and female entrepreneurs), and those from the professions and the government bureaucracy. Generally, these people are highly educated, speak English as well as one or more Indian languages (for instance, educated northerners traditionally speak both Hindi and Urdu), and are very well informed.

The old middle class The older generation of this class have a strange split between a nostalgic affection for things British, and a strong pride in independent India. The Anglophilia can be disconcerting at times, because the picture many of them have of Britain is very out of date; comments of the 'Of course, in London you can always trust the bobby and the cabby' type really are made, and, if you have just fled from contemporary Britain, will leave you speechless. Such attitudes do not compromise these Indians' attachment to their own traditions; they will stoutly defend them, and in doing so will often betray further unrealistic and stereotyped views of the West. For instance, an Indian millionaire, with a large Mercedes outside and a son at college in the United States, will tell you, with a twinkle, that the Indians care about *people*; the implication being that Westerners don't. The West, especially America, might be a big money pile into which you dip a hand from time to time, but it's soulless and people don't care for one another the way Indians do.

It is fairly easy to see what he means; family ties and bonds are much stronger in India than they are in the West, and the Hindu undivided family – that is, parents plus married children – is a recognized legal entity for taxation, amongst other purposes. Yet there is a catch; in spite of the official prohibition of caste and untouchability, they remain powerful forces, especially in rural India. Strong familial bonds don't necessarily imply a strong respect for the rights of those outside the family, and the millionaire would do well to remember that Gandhi was much concerned to encourage the Western ideal of social service in India. It is no answer to suggest that all these noble ideas of social reform are implied, or even explicitly stated, in ancient scriptures. The point is that, stated or not, such ideals were not common amongst Indians until the reforming movements of the nineteenth century; and these were catalysed by the impact of Western ideals upon India. It is Gandhi who took the message of social action, and social service, to the Indian masses, and his great achievement was to make something uniquely Indian out of it when he combined it with his traditional beliefs and the very Indian ideal of *ahimsa*, or non-violence.

The new middle class The younger middle classes are very different to their elders. The phenomenon of quick money, and the expanding market offered by liberalization and the new spending power, has led to a new kind of creature called the Puppy. A Puppy is a Punjabi Urban Professional; they are looked down on. Old money views them with distaste. Here is a thumb-nail sketch of a Puppy given to me by a professional Indian couple, over dinner:

'Puppies? Oh, they all live in Karol Bagh and Punjabi Bagh.'

'He is the sort who probably has a small factory or sells saris or something.'

'*I* would never let a daughter of mine marry the proprietor of a sari shop.'

'They probably bought their house for cash – what? Oh, it would cost about 200 lakh.'

'And *she* would go round covered in make-up and her two or three lakh worth of jewellery. You see them outside Nirula's ice-cream shop in the evening, they've no money or breeding, just a lot of quick money.'

This new class lacks the educated, informed sympathy of their elders for both their own culture and that of the West; for them the West means a fast life style and consumer luxuries, and India is somewhere to make money (if possible). Perhaps surprisingly, this class can also be aggressively nationalistic; they are great believers in free markets and the dawn of the Asian century. They are very different to the traditional Indian industrialist, a highly educated man who has all the social graces, and is equally at home in India or the West.

Conservatism A strongly conservative element still exists in the Indian middle class; this might be typified by, say, a government official or civil servant, probably an orthodox and devoted Hindu, perhaps a little wary and distrustful of foreigners. It is hard not to have great sympathy with such people, for they try to hold fast to the gentle dignity displayed by Gandhi and other leading members of the National Movement. Sadly, they are no longer fashionable; India will be the poorer without them.

Hospitality The Indian middle classes are, like most other Indians, very friendly and hospitable. If you are entertained at someone's home, then you will be received as an honoured guest and friend, fed enormous meals, introduced to people, asked all about yourself, and treated with remarkable generosity. Even if they don't always use them, most Indians will adopt Western customs when entertaining Western guests, a politeness which is rarely reciprocated. It is only in a very traditional or orthodox household that you would be expected to remove your shoes or eat with your fingers.

A difficulty of being asked out to dinner in India is that the meal is often a hurried affair that happens late in the night; it is prefaced by vast amounts of social drinking and conversation; and the drinking *is* social, you are expected to go on talking and to make sense and not to fall out of your chair. Treat the servants in the same way as the Indians do; that is, let them do everything for you. Westerners are often very guilty and awkward about this, but don't be; if the servant wants to open the door for you, let him; if he wants to rearrange your glass and cigarettes for no apparent purpose, let him go ahead. If you don't, he will only think the less of you. Great men and women *expect* to be waited on.

Even in Westernized households, you might sometimes find that the women retire to another room while the men sit around and smoke and drink. Western women can be treated in various ways under these circumstances. If you are a professional, you would be treated as (so to speak) an honorary man for the purposes of drinking; if you have a consort or are part of a couple, you would probably retire with the other ladies.

Rural India is like another planet. Although foreign travellers are quite common, you will find that you

Rural India

can still be greeted with amazement and curiosity in Indian villages. Why, the people's faces seem to say, has this strange person, with those unattractive white legs sticking out of those strange shorts, come all this way to see how *we* live? Women travelling alone are particularly fascinating – here is the explanation of this from one Indian: 'In India, if a girl travelled round like that on her own, it would mean she was free and available. Of course no decent girl would. She would travel with a family member, or she would be married and be with her husband. So the villagers wonder what all those Western girls are up to.'

Hospitality   It is in the villages that you can run up against some of the paradoxes of Indian life. Here you will still find people who regard you as polluted and untouchable (you have no caste), yet who are also bound by their traditions of offering hospitality to travellers; anyway, they are fascinated by foreigners and will want to know all about you. The main problem in a village will be one of communication; there could well be few or no English speakers. On the other hand, people will always try to help, you will always be offered water, and often food. In a village you would certainly be expected to remove your shoes before going into someone's house, and if you eat, don't dip into the communal dishes in which the food is served; wait for someone to serve you, because your touch might well be held to have polluted (in a ritual sense) the meal. Don't forget to use only the *right* hand for eating; the left is unclean, being used for sexual caresses and wiping your backside.

Indian villagers are also amazed that Westerners want to do things for themselves, instead of getting someone else to do it for them. Why do they want to carry those heavy bags round in the heat? This can, in fact, knock visitors down from their pedestal, because if they were truly great, then of course they would never think of carrying their own bags. Such an idea!

Public behaviour   Public displays of affection between the sexes can be highly offensive to many Indians, in both towns and villages; Western visitors should respect this. In the large cities, such as Bombay, you will see Indian boys and girls walking along hand in hand, or with their arms round each other. This is the exception rather than the rule, and it is in general quite difficult for Indian boys and girls to be alone together. The extravagant physical displays that many young Western couples indulge in can not only cause offence, they can also excite curiosity; so if you choose to go in for that sort of thing, don't be surprised at the consequences. The same comments apply to revealing fashions worn by Western women.

Most Indians love foreign-made luxury items, for the simple reason that they have traditionally been very hard to buy in India itself. The economy has long been geared towards the development of heavy industry and agriculture; the manufacture of consumer goods always took a very low priority. Sanjay Gandhi made a disastrous attempt to produce a 'people's car', that was to be called the Maruti; this ended with a Japanese rescue, and now the car is available as a Maruti-Suzuki. In general, however, luxury items such as cars, washing machines, and fridges have been quite expensive and hard to obtain. Imports were strictly limited and subject to high rates of duty to preserve India's reserves of foreign currency.

The consumer boom

Things have changed recently, and nowhere is this more apparent than the video screens that have appeared in public places in India, especially railway stations, and advertise TV sets, washing powder etc. *ad nauseum*.

I once saw exactly the same adverts over and over again, in a station waiting room where they also showed a public information video about how dangerous it was to race trains to level crossings in bullock carts. Few of the people in that waiting room could have afforded a TV set; and I doubt that many of them were going to rush out to buy washing powder. The sudden consumer boom amongst the upper and middle classes is exposing the poorer Indians – and there are millions of them – to advertisements that portray life styles and luxuries

Minimum wages for farm labour fixed

By A Staff Reporter

BANGALORE, July 15:

The state government has fixed the minimum daily wages for agricultural workers ranging from Rs 12 to Rs 17.65.

According to an official release, workers engaged in cattle-grazing are entitled to a minimum daily wage of Rs 12. Those engaged in works like digging, harvesting, etc. are entitled to payments ranging from Rs 12 to Rs 16.40 per day.

Workers making jaggery, processing grapes, cultivating tobacco, arecanut and coconut, are entitled to daily wages, ranging from Rs 5.20 to Rs 17.65.

Workers in farm households should be paid a monthly salary of Rs 287, if food and clothing are provided, they should be paid a monthly salary of Rs 227. For overtime, they should be paid double the amount of salary.

Source: *The Times of India*, 16 July 1988

that they simply cannot aspire to; one can't help wondering whether this will eventually cause extreme frustration and discontent amongst those who know that the TVs, the Maruti-Suzukis, the refrigerators, and the new high-tech washing machines are forever beyond their reach.

Many Indians fear that liberalization and the drive for greater efficiency will create unemployment – as well it may. If you are in an office, or a hotel, and wonder why ten people are doing the work of one, a possible answer is that there are ten people and not one person to be employed. Inefficient as some Indian methods appear to be, they at least provide employment; and there is a fear that the drive for efficiency will dispossess the lower classes and the peasants. The following slogan was daubed on a wall in Bangalore: 'Computer kills jobs! Death to computer!'

Hindi and English remain joint official languages in India, and are used by the Centre and for interstate communication. The fifteen languages recognized by the Constitution are official languages within various states; for example, Tamil in Tamil Nadu. The name of the state will usually tell you what the official language is. The great Hindi belt is in the north, embracing states such as Uttar Pradesh; sometimes this region is called the Hindi heartland or the Hindi cowbelt (from the reverence paid by devout Hindus to the cow). Hindi has many dialects, and although it is helpful to learn a few important words, you will have to devote a lot of energy to its study if you want to converse easily. The script, called Devanagari, is quite easy to learn, and this knowledge can be very useful. Urdu is closely related to Hindi, but has many borrowed Arabic and Persian words, and uses the Perso-Arabic script.

Languages

Indian languages fall into two main groups, the Indo-Aryan, to which Hindi and Sanskrit, (the great classical language of India) belong, and the Dravidian. Of the languages listed in the constitution, Bengali, Marathi, Gujerati, Oriya, Punjabi, Assamese, Kashmiri, Urdu, and Sindhi belong (with Hindi and Sanskrit) to the Indo-Aryan group, and Telegu, Tamil, Malayalam, and Kannada to the Dravidian. Malayalam is the language of Kerala, Telegu that of Andhra Pradesh, and Kannada that of Kanartaka, formerly the state of Mysore. Most of these languages have ancient literary traditions, but the Dravidian languages are hard to learn. Tamil has an alphabet with over two hundred characters, and is sometimes known as Indian Chinese. Unfortunately, it is in the far south that notices are often in the local language only; trying to read a bus timetable in Tamil can be a formidable task unless you have an enthusiasm for complex languages.

Portuguese is spoken in Goa, but the French have left little of their culture behind; the traffic police in Pondicherry wear something that looks vaguely like a kepi, but that's about all. Many Indians take the trouble to learn other European languages apart from English, and you will sometimes meet official guides (in temples and the like) who can also speak French, German, and Italian.

Education Education in India is as variable as everything else. Some village schools are simply classes held under trees, without books, blackboards, and in some cases teachers. At the other extreme are the elite private schools, run on the lines of English public (fee-paying) schools, which provide a first class (and expensive) education.

Basic education for the Indian people was always one of the priorities of the National Movement, and since independence, great efforts have been made to eliminate illiteracy. At independence, the literacy rate

Cow's 'mischief'

Bombay (PTI): Members of the Maharashtra Legislative Assembly were stunned when the Education Minister Kamalkishore Kadam disclosed in the house on Wednesday that several answer books of students, who appeared for SSC examination this year, were found to be missing, stolen and chewed away by cow and that a moderator had approached a sadhu to seek his advice on the missing answer papers. The Minister said it was observed that irregularities were committed by examiners and moderators in 460 answer books and the results in these cases were withheld. It was found that in some cases 30 to 40 marks were increased or decreased indiscriminately and in other cases the answer books were either rewritten or supplements detached from the answer books, Mr. Kadam said.

Source: *Indian Express*

for men was around 25 per cent, and that for women around 8 per cent. The present rates (about 47 per cent for men and 25 per cent for women) show that great improvements have been made, especially in women's education, but there is still a long way to go. In 1986 the government promulgated its National Education Policy, which attempted to establish a national curriculum, and access to education for all students irrespective of caste, creed, or sex. The problem was the usual one of actually getting the required resources out to where they were needed.

School education is the responsibility of the state governments, and in theory runs in a grade system similar to that of the United States. Classes I to VIII cover the age range from six years to fourteen years, and this education is provided free in most states and Union Territories. Although many states and Territories have passed legislation making elementary education compulsory, this is hard to enforce in a country where the labour of children is both a traditional part of the family economy and of considerable value.

India has over a hundred universities, twenty-four agricultural universities, and four medical institutes. The Indian institutes of technology (IITs) in Kharagpur, Bombay, Madras, Kanpur, and Delhi are prestigious centres of scientific training and education; they are intended to supply world-class research facilities to postgraduate students and established Indian scientists.

The family remains central in the life of most Indians. Age and grey hair are still respected, and many Indians show what can only be described as reverence for their parents. Marriage fits into this scheme in that it is seen not so much as a relationship between two people as an alliance between their families. This is true amongst all of India's religious groups, including the Christians. The Western boy-meets-girl love affair plays a very minor role in determining marriage partners.

The family, marriage, and death

Source: *Hindustan Times*, 26 June 1988

Source: *Indian Express*, 24 July 1988

Indian weddings can be very variable, depending on the religion of the bride and groom. Hindu weddings can be somewhat awkward, because a propitious time for them is chosen by the family Pandit, a sort of domestic chaplain-cum-astrologer. The propitious time could well be in the middle of the night or the small hours of the morning. The ceremonial can be long-drawn-out, and the bride (looking virginal or trying to) and groom (looking self-conscious) sit side by side in throne-like chairs while everyone else has a large meal. The actual marriage takes place when the couple make their vows, exchange garlands, and the groom fastens a thread round the bride's neck (the *mangalasutra*, or *mangalathali* in the south). This thread is the mark of a married woman. Toe rings are sometimes worn as well, but the thread is the significant ornament. Ankle bracelets are widely used by all Indian females, including young girls, and have no connection with marital status.

Sikh and Moslem weddings are less complicated. The former usually take place in the mornings, either at a gurdwara (Sikh temple) or at the bride's home. If you are invited to such an occasion, men are expected to cover their head with a *clean* white cotton handkerchief (not knotted at the corners as if you were on the beach at Brighton, but just neatly folded and covering the top of your head) and women are expected to wear a headscarf. Moslem marriages are mercifully brief, and usually take place in the early evening.

There can be very great regional differences in ceremonial at Hindu weddings, and if you are invited to one, try to find out what to expect. Indians are always very happy to explain their customs and practices to anyone who shows a polite interest. The general advice to Westerners seems to be to dress decorously (especially Western women – don't expose too much flesh, and do wear a long dress at a wedding), don't forget to remove your shoes before entering the place where the wedding is being held, and if it is Sikh or Moslem do cover your head (both sexes).

Funerals   The Sikhs and the Hindus cremate their dead, on piles of sandalwood (if the relatives can afford it) in the open air, while the Moslems go in for burial. The Parsis have the custom of sky burial on the Towers of Silence; that is, the corpse is exposed on these special structures (well hidden from ghoulish, would-be spectators) and the flesh is stripped away by vultures. It is very unlikely that you would ever (as a foreigner and a non-family member) be asked to share any of the funerary rites of these faiths unless you were an intimate friend of an Indian family to begin with; and in that case, you wouldn't need the advice of this book.

The custom of cremating the dead publicly always seems to fascinate Westerners (they all go to stare at the burning bodies at Varanasi, egged on by the enthusiastic guides), so a few words about it seem appropriate. The pyre is supposed to be lit by the eldest son or the eldest surviving male relative of the deceased. The mourners (who would only be close family at this stage, in an ordinary funeral) pour ghee (clarified butter) on to the wood. Then the corpse burns, and as it does, the family leave. The colour of mourning in India is white, not black.

Caste   Caste is a term coined by the Portuguese, and is not an Indian word. It comes from the Portuguese word *casta*, which means breed, race, or kind. Almost everyone from the West who visits India has heard of caste and untouchability, of the great social evil that they were and are, and of how the Mahatma struggled against their strictures and named the untouchables 'Harijans', Children of God. Visitors are therefore often puzzled when they don't see any obvious evidence of caste distinctions or differences.

The caste   A common misconception is that caste is an ancient,
system   monolithic institution with four major divisions, the Brahmans or priestly caste, the Kshatriyas or warrior caste, the Vaishyas or mercantile class, and the Sudras or labouring class. It is more realistic to say that existing castes can be classified under one of these four heads. So, what is a caste? A caste is a group

of people who are united by custom and endogamy (marriage within the group), but above all by a common (hereditary) occupation. Castes have rules for ceremonial purity which not only bind a caste together, but serve to separate it from others. The number of castes in India runs into the thousands – 3,000 is the figure usually quoted in the authoritative works – and is constantly changing. Those beyond the pale of the caste system will develop their own castes, castes will split up into subcastes (a purely relative term) because of a change of occupation. The complications of caste are amazing; castes are subdivided into exogamous units called *gotras*, there are castes that are matrilineal and hypergamous, like the Nayars, and so on. It is impossible to give a detailed examination of caste in a book like this, but the works cited in 'Further reading' should help interested readers to find out more about it.

The aspect of caste that is worth mentioning is its significance in modern Indian politics. It was the hope of the reformers in the heady days after independence that caste barriers would eventually be broken down under the pressures of education, Gandhian ethics, and changing economic circumstances. This hope has not been fulfilled, and caste plays a major role in determining the way the Indian electorate votes; that is, people tend to choose whom to vote for on the basis of the candidates' castes rather than their political beliefs. Parties therefore feel obliged to fish around for candidates who will attract those sections of the electorate whose votes are vital if they are to win. Caste loyalty can (and often does) come before party loyalty, and although the importance of caste is declining in most spheres, it has a distorting effect on Indian political life.

Caste's affect on politics

Special provision has long been made for what are called the scheduled castes and tribes; that is, those who really have no caste. A quota system is operated whereby a certain number of places in India's medical schools (for example) are reserved for members of these groups. This has caused a lot of resentment amongst those from the more privileged castes, because it has made it more difficult for them to get into higher education. A Brahman or a Rajput has to obtain ridiculously high marks in his or her examinations to get into a medical school, whereas a member of a scheduled caste or tribe can get away with much lower ones. Both end up with the same qualification. The objections raised against the reservation and quota system in India are much the same as those raised against similar schemes elsewhere, but in India they have become a major political issue that has occasionally spilled over into violence. An example of this is the riots in Ahmedhabad in 1984, where high-caste Hindus set on Moslems and untouchables; many were killed.

Caste in
rural India

Caste still has a hold over the daily lives of the rural Indians. Bihar, for example, is often plagued by caste warfare, Untouchables are massacred, reprisals are taken, more people are killed, and so on – and on and on. Bihar was the site of the ancient empires of the Mauryas and the Guptas; now it is one of the most wretched and depressed regions in the whole of India. Caste distinctions can also surface without warning; Christians obviously have no caste, nor should they recognize caste distinctions – in theory; yet there are stories of caste structures amongst Christian communities, and of worshippers being reluctant to take communion from the hands of a 'low-caste' priest.

Attempts at
reform

Occasionally Harijans are barred from temples, although this is illegal. The religious leader Swami Agnivesh, who is waging a running battle against the more conservative Hindu spiritual leaders (such as the Shankaracharya of Puri), recently tried to take a party of Harijans into the Nathdwara temple in Rajasthan. The police stopped him and his followers on the grounds that their actions would endanger public order, a move that was widely condemned in the Indian press. The Shankaracharya of Puri is a conservative and a Hindu revivalist; he has made statements that lend support to *sati*, the self-immolation of widows on their husbands' funeral

Agnivesh, followers detained

Udaipur (UNI): Arya Samaj leader Swami Agnivesh and his followers, consisting mostly of Harijans, were on Tuesday detained by the police at Negadia village, 12 km short of their destination—the famous Shreenathji temple of Nathadwara—for violating prohibitory orders. The Deputy Inspector General of Police said. Swami Agnivesh and his followers would be taken to Chittorgarh and let off there. They would be provided vehicles for going to their respective places if they desired.

The district administration had imposed prohibitory orders in Negadia village in apprehension of breach of peace. Swami Agnivesh, who began a two-day padayatra from Udaipur on July 10, and the batch of Harijans seeking entry into the Shreenathji temple, were taken into custody when they tried to proceed to the temple, in defiance of the prohibitory orders.

Source: *Indian Express*

pyres. Swami Agnivesh is one of the many Hindu religious leaders who are actively trying to alleviate the still wretched lot of many Harijans; this movement is very widespread, although it is only the tales of caste massacres in Bihar that hit the Western press. In the south, for example, many of the formerly conservative and orthodox religious fraternities, the Hindu mutts, are not only accessible to Harijans but have launched welfare programmes for them.

Beggars

India has a large number of beggars, and you can't avoid them. They come in all shapes, colours, and sizes, and you can't give money to all of them because soon you'd have none left yourself. On the

Harijans enter Nathdwara temple

Express News Service

New Delhi, Aug. 10: Welfare Minister Mrs. Rajendra Kumari Bajpai announced in the Lok Sabha today that a group of local Harijans had entered the Nathdwara temple in Rajasthan in the morning around 11 a.m.

Replying to a question from Mr. Bhattam Shriramamurthy (Telugu Desam), she said she had just received a report from the Rajasthan Chief Minister that the local Harijans, including safai karamcharis, had entered the temple. She said they were received by the elder son of the head priest.

While opposition members did not seem satisfied by the answer, several members from the ruling Congress-I cheered her announcement by thumping the desks.

In order to complete the answer and supplementary questions, the Speaker extended the Question Hour by more than 10 minutes.

The Minister said the country was ruled by the Constitution and Article 70 of the Constitution bans untouchability.

She did not reply to the demand from opposition members to arrest the Shankaracharya of Puri for his statements regarding entry of Harijans in temples. She said that the Shankaracharya had denied the earlier statement.

She also read out from a recent letter of the head priest of the Nathdwara temple saying that the Vaishnavite temple never practised untouchability. This sparked off shouts and protests from opposition members.

Replying to Mr. Jaipal Reddy, she denied that Swami Agnivesh had been arrested. He wanted to know why instead of arresting the Shankaracharya, the State Government arrested Swami Agnivesh. She said there was brickbatting on the group led by Mr. Agnivesh and this resulted in tension. In order to avoid trouble Swami Agnivesh was persuaded to withdraw.

She reiterated that the State Government had given all protection to Swami Agnivesh.

Mr. Basudeb Acharya (CPM) said for all these years the State Government had not taken any action and was a silent spectator to the denial of the right of entry into the temple.

Source: *Indian Express*

other hand, it is hard to just walk past, because (stage devices aside) many of them are obviously in a bad way.

Begging in India is a profession; when people beg, they have an act designed both to catch your attention and to excite your sympathy. Quite extraordinary devices are used. Stumps and withered forearms are suddenly pushed under your nose, attended by churchyard groans; small girls are sent out with babies, and they will trot along beside you, plucking at your clothes with their free hand as they mumble, 'Baby, baby, baby, to feed baby!' Even those who have lost limbs can still follow you, and limbless cripples propelling themselves along by their hands, upon large boards with wheels attached, are no uncommon sight. Maimed beggars go kerb-crawling in these strange vehicles, and will cruise along beside you heaping praises upon your august person, 'Lord, master, great one, please sahib, rupees, rupees, only five rupees, sahib, lord, captain, please captain!' Others have acts with broken down snakes and mongooses, and then you might be asked for 'cobra baksheesh' or 'mongoose baksheesh'; whole families will follow you up the street, the parents in front and behind, and the children all around you, tugging at your hands and clothes. Indian beggars are always very determined, and have only one object; to extract money from you. Sympathy doesn't come into it, they don't want to tell you their life stories. If they can get you to part with money by panicking you, then they will.

The best response, then, is never to feel cornered or panicked, or if you do, never to betray it. A firm 'No!', perhaps repeated a few times, then complete indifference, will do the trick. The beggars are professionals, and know when they aren't going to get anything; but if they detect hints of weakness or sympathy, then they'll stick like leeches. If any readers think that this is callous, it is the advice that's been offered to me by Indians themselves.

If you want to help beggars, the best thing to do is to allocate a certain amount to charity each day or week, and stick to it – somewhat in the manner of the Aga Khan. You can also make a point of giving away your small change. If you get carried away making donations, you'll find that it is surprisingly expensive. Be prepared for some very unpleasant experiences with child beggars; some of them carry bits of paper explaining that they have been mutilated by parents or relatives, and whether this is true or not, many of them are indeed tongueless, fingerless, or deficient in other bodily parts.

Shopping The Indians are used to haggling, and do it very well. Most Westerners are not, and this puts them at a disadvantage that Indian traders are only too happy to exploit. As an Indian friend said, an Indian shopkeeper can size up a customer in a split second, and can judge just how much he can inflate his prices and still retain their interest. Many shops, of course, have fixed price goods; the problem is that many of the places that sell the sort of things you might want to bring back home do not. All of the states run 'craft and cottage industries emporia' (so-called), and you'll find these in most of the major cities. The prices in these establishments are regulated and generally fair, and you do not have to bargain or haggle. The quality of the goods is usually excellent; that is, silk scarves are actually made out of silk, the sandalwood carvings are actually sandalwood, and so on. The places to treat with the deepest suspicion are the shopping arcades of the big hotels; these are usually just a rip-off.

If you bargain over a price, always remember that because you're a Westerner, the starting price asked by the shopkeeper is probably ludicrously high, and don't hesitate to offer something ludicrously low. Making as if to walk off sometimes leads to a dramatic fall in prices. If you are buying something expensive, and if the quality or genuineness of the goods are in question, try to take an Indian friend along with you (if you have one); in the end, most Indians are far better at this sort of thing than most Westerners.

Business dealings The Indian passion for business and entrepreneurial dealing would delight Mrs Thatcher, and Indian business people can be very tough and hard to deal with. In common with other Indians there will be the lack of a sense of privacy and the insatiable curiosity; then there will be the lavish hospitality that can, of course, be used as a weapon; and finally there is the Indian sense of time, which is best described as non-existent.

The curiosity can be trying; friendly interest is one thing, but the barrage of unashamed personal questions is quite another. If you are divorced, this is of absorbing interest; if you are travelling with a member of the opposite sex, they will want to know all about the nature of your relationship. This can induce a sense of mild panic, because it is quite relentless, and will go on and on and on until your interrogator is quite satisfied.

Curiosity and criticism

Then comes the problem of India. Indians *love* to criticize India, but beware; they are really (and with considerable justification) proud of it. A foreigner laying into Indian inefficiency or corruption is something quite different from an Indian saying the same words, and can cause serious offence. To be with an Indian who is telling you that India is a hell-hole is rather like being with someone from a very close family who is telling you that his father is a right bastard. You are not supposed to say yes, you are supposed to say something nice. People can criticize their own parents, but they don't expect others to join them, it would cause hurt and offence; similarly, Indians can criticize India, but foreigners are not expected to join in.

The lavish hospitality has a dark side, because it can, of course, be used to put you under an impossibly burdensome obligation. It can also be used to relax you and throw you off guard. The proper response to vast meals and endless entertainment is not to refuse them, but to *return* them. This neutralizes the obligation; indeed, it can reverse it.

Hospitality

The Indian sense of time is different to that of the West. This is not meant in any philosophical or metaphysical sense, it simply means that if you arrange a meeting with an Indian he or she might well fail to turn up, but have a quite sincere belief that they were there in the Indian sense – that is, they went to the wrong place, three hours late. It is no good waxing indignantly angry about this, it is how things are done. If someone wants to see you, then eventually you'll meet. If he or she doesn't,

The sense of time

then you won't. Appointments are irrelevant, except in so far as they make Westerners feel better. Remember that arrangements made over the phone are even more likely to go astray than others.

Pressure and politeness

Attempts to pressurize you can be blatant and insistent. Ploys can include calling on you in your hotel for an unscheduled meeting at odd hours of the day or night. Never allow such things to throw you off balance, and *never* lose your temper. Patience is essential.

Indians are also experts at evasive charm; if they don't want to give you a straight answer, then nothing will extract one. (Americans seem to find this particularly annoying, and it tends to make them babble and lose their tempers.) Don't be provoked, *be patient*; also remember that complicated family relationships might intrude into business dealings. A businessman might be evasive or disappear for a day because he has to consult his father before he can agree to something. The best response to the evasive charm is to return it, like the hospitality; never lose your temper, never become visibly impatient.

Indians often say things out of politeness and out of a desire not to disappoint; this doesn't imply a commitment. You'll find the same thing on the streets, when you ask for directions; if you simply ask 'Where is the station?', and the man you're asking doesn't know, instead of saying so, he will wheel round and point down the street. Frame questions in such a way that the reply has to be a definite commitment; in the case of the way to the station, for example, instead of asking 'Where is the station?' you should ask 'Is this the way to the station?' This principle extends to other dealings with Indians.

Face

There is also the matter of face. Indians seem to find it particularly hard to admit they're wrong, and can become evasive to the point of vanishing altogether if they are placed in a situation that requires an admission of error or inefficiency. Make allowances for this, and help things along by inventing face-saving formulae (but without compromising yourself) that avoid outright confrontation. This will be greatly appreciated, but beware of implying that you were at fault. This is weakness, and weaknesses are there to be exploited.

Because so much is left unsaid, and because Indians rarely say no directly but engage in the most elaborate circumlocutions, it is very helpful to have a friendly Indian business contact who can guide you through the maze. He or she will be able to read the signs that you can't, and will be able to interpret the mood of the opposition. The rule is, as always in India, *be patient*; don't expect things to happen quickly and don't expect immediate decisions, but be ready for pressure when they have made up their minds and want a commitment from you.

Dress counts for much; on formal occasions, be smartly dressed. A tie is a kind of talisman for the Indian professional classes, so men should wear one. Women should avoid overtly sexy and revealing fashions; don't try to wear a sari unless you can do it gracefully – most Western women can't.

Clubs and visiting cards

The great private clubs play a pivotal role in the lives of influential, professional Indians. They are part of traditional British life set in aspic; the Ooty Club, in Ootacamund in the Nilgiri Hills, has Colonel Jacko's riding crop in a glass case; the Colonel was obviously something of a hunting man. Legend has it that a British deputy high commissioner was blackballed at the Madras Gymkhana for turning up to his interview with the membership committee wearing casual dress.

Many of the clubs have arrangements for temporary membership, or have treaties with foreign clubs. If you are going to be in India for business or professional purposes for any length of time, it is well worth joining one, for they are not only interesting socially, but very useful for making professional contacts. The otherwise inaccessible and mighty bureaucrat will greet you as one of the chaps if you are at the same club. You will also meet the cream of India's business and professional

community. The private clubs also have some of the
best (and sometimes the only) sporting facilities
outside the five-star hotels. Many of them have tennis
and squash courts, and first class swimming pools.

Every great city has its great clubs. There are the
Gymkhanas in Delhi, Madras, and Bombay, the
Willingdon in Bombay, and the Bengal and Tolly-
gange (the former only allowed Indians to become
members in 1960) in Calcutta; there are clubs in the
hill stations and cricket and yacht clubs. The Taj
Group of hotels runs 'The Chambers', a sort of
dining club for senior executives. The big cities also
have American Clubs, which are open to any US
citizen who happens to be passing through. It is in
the clubs that you'll meet the eccentric Indian
Anglophiles who'll tell you how reliable cabbies and
bobbies are, shed a tear over pounds, shillings, and
pence, and tell you that 'Of course nothing here's
been the same since the Indians started running the
place.'

Finally, take some visiting cards. If you don't have
your own, use someone else's. When you are
introduced to clubland Indians you are invariably
asked, 'Oh, can I have your card?' Your reputation
will suffer if you can't produce one.

The religions of modern India

India is officially a secular state, and there is therefore no established religion. The Constitution confers rights on citizens without discrimination on grounds of faith or creed. Again, the problem is one of enforcement; the divisions between India's religious communities run deep, especially that between the Moslems and the Hindus, and there has been an alarming tendency in recent years for communal (that is, religious) divisions to spill over into violence again; in all the major Indian faiths there has been a movement towards fundamentalism and revivalism.

Secular India

The table gives India's main religious groups, their places of worship, their religious books and the percentage of the population who adhere to each.

The Jains and the Buddhists are much smaller communities, each being only a few million strong. There are a small number of Jews (numbered in the thousands), and the Zoroastrians or Parsis, a declining community now limited to Bombay and regions of the Gujerat. In addition there are animistic religions followed by the hill tribes. As the table shows, the

India's main religions

Religion	Place of worship	Sacred books	% population
Hinduism	Temple	Vedas, Mahabharata, Bhagavad Gita, Ramayana	83
Islam	Mosque	Koran	11
Christianity	Church	Bible	2
Sikhism	Gurdwara	Guru Granth Sahib	2

Hindus are in an overwhelming majority, and
although there is no state or official religion, it is
not unreasonable to describe India as a Hindu
country. India has, however, one of the largest
Moslem populations outside Pakistan, and the spectre
that haunts the Indian authorities is a major collision
between the two communities.

Hinduism The early history of Hinduism has been traced in
the chapter on 'History and the development of
religions'. To briefly recapitulate this, there are
intriguing hints of later Hindu beliefs and practices
in the early Indus valley civilizations, including
Proto-Shiva, yogic practices, and many features of
the later heterodox cults of Jainism and Buddhism.
Then come the Aryan invasions, and early Brahmanism down to around 500 BC; this period saw
the early sacrificial cults transformed by mystical

"Why can't she just be sacred and thankful for it?"

speculation upon the meaning and significance of sacrifice, which blossomed into the Upanishads. After that came the Gupta period up to about 600 AD, which saw the development of something like the Hinduism that is found in India today. The medieval and modern periods saw Hinduism responding to the impact of other faiths, notably Islam, and Christianity as expressed by India's colonial masters, the British.

To those outside it, Hinduism seems hopelessly complicated. Gods blur into one another, they have many names and epithets, the stories told about them seem contradictory and sometimes downright stupid, the whole affair seems anarchic and incomprehensible. This is compounded by the Hindu ability to absorb other people's gods, often mistaken by Westerners as some sort of charitable or tolerant attention bestowed on other faiths.

Syncretism

The reason for all this is that Hinduism has a long history of syncretism. It cannot look back to the sayings or doings of a divine or semi-divine founder; there is not a monolithic holy book, where all is laid down for all time. The Hindu scriptures are a vast mass of often contradictory mystical and metaphysical speculation, and there is no Buddha or Jesus Christ or Mohammed to whom to appeal. Because Hinduism has such a long history, and because it has been associated with theocratic societies, there is a tendency to assume that it is morbidly conservative and monolithic in its doctrines. This is not true, and Hinduism has shown a remarkable ability to adapt, to evolve, and to absorb new ideas precisely because it does not have a single founder whose authority, divine or semi-divine, is held to be absolute.

A distinction has to be made between popular Hinduism and the transcendental adventures of the religious virtuosos, the great holy men and yogis; yet it is fair to say that of all the great religions, Hinduism is the one that adopts an experimental and pragmatic approach to human spiritual experience, without overburdening itself with doctrines, theories, and telling people what they *should* experience –

something to which Christianity and Islam have an attachment. It is this exploratory, experimental approach that lends Hindus their apparent tolerance; as the Hindu saying goes, 'God is great and is known to the wise by many names.'

The
Upanishadic
period

The Upanishadic period represents the attempts of the priestly caste to divine the nature of the supernal mystery behind their sacrificial cult. The gods themselves had become secondary to sacrifice, for they depended upon it for their continued existence; this change went hand in hand with the atheistic cults of Buddhism and Jainism that were being developed at around the same time. The Upanishadic period also witnessed the growth of the idea of metempsychosis, or transmigration of the soul; this was to turn into the fully fledged concept of reincarnation.

The search for the absolute reality behind the sacrificial cult apparently led to the concept of Brahman; that is, a holy and absolute power that sustains the whole universe through every moment of its being. Brahman has an ancient pedigree; it is mentioned in the Rig Veda, and apparently means the supernatural power that is effectively manipulated by the priests and makes the act of sacrifice efficacious. Later, Brahman was seen as the ground of all being, a sort of impersonal absolute. The salvation offered by the Upanishads is not merely knowledge that the fullness of Brahman is contained within each person, in the individual soul or Atman, but in the living consciousness of this identity. Cerebral knowledge is not enough; salvation is the direct experience of the Brahman–Atman identity through spiritual training and discipline. This was the age of the ascetic cults, whose spiritual exercises led the devotee to transcendental and immediate knowledge of the absolute within. This is expressed in the words, 'Tat tvam asi'; that is, 'Thou [the Self] art That [the Universal Being].' Hinduism offers a spirituality vastly more sophisticated than that of the religions of revelation, and places far more responsibility on the devotee, who really does have to work out his salvation, but not in fear and trembling because of a threatening and capricious creator-god who is liable to take offence at the smallest insult to His majesty.

But what of the gods and the popular cults? A mass of priestly tales show how the relative positions of various gods shifted through the ages; myths grew up to rationalize the promotions and demotions or changes in relative status of the gods. Many of these stories are reminiscent of the naughtinesses of the gods of Olympus or Asgard, and are frankly very tedious. But behind the shifting pantheon was a powerful driving force; the search for a personal god, the attempt to transform the Brahman–Atman equation into something like fully fledged theism. The Classical Period therefore saw the development of the *bhakti* cults, which became centred on the gods Shiva and Vishnu (*bhakti* meaning devotion).

The bhakti cults

Shiva   Shiva has a long pedigree, perhaps reaching as far back as the Indus Valley Lord of the Beasts, depicted on the steatite seals (see 'History and the development of religions'). His Vedic forerunner was the uncertain and wild Rudra, and Shiva himself retains much ambivalence, for he is at once a creator and a destroyer, an ascetic and yogi and yet a haunter of burning grounds. His consorts too have this ambiguous nature. Somewhere in his long ancestry is a fertility god, for Shiva has long been associated with the phallic emblem, the *linga*, and is still worshipped in this form in his temples. Shiva is also a dancer, and as the Cosmic Dancer, Nataraja, performs his mystical dance of creation and destruction in the centre of a circle of flame. (This is a favourite subject for the south Indian school of bronze sculpture; at Chidambaran in Tamil Nadu there is a temple dedicated to Shiva as Lord of the Dance.)

Vishnu   Vishnu has a more sublime and less uncertain temper. He has been promoted from a somewhat obscure Vedic deity to one of the great gods of contemporary Hinduism. He is often equated with the supreme god and creator, with Brahma as a mere demiurge; Brahma appears from Vishnu's navel as he sleeps upon the coils of Sheshna, the great cosmic serpent, who himself floats upon the primal waters between the cycles of creation. (The Hindu cosmology envisages an endless sequence of creation, evolution, and dissolution.) Vishnu is often described as the preserver; he is a god who inspires love and devotion rather than awe.

Brahma   Most Hindus are either Shaivites (that is, devotees of Shiva) or Vaishnavites (devotees of Vishnu). Brahma, who is sometimes presented as a creator god and a third member of a Hindu Trinity, is far less significant, and occupies an almost insignificant place in popular devotion. The Hindu Trinity is known as the Trimurti, comprising Brahma the Creator, Vishnu the Preserver, and Shiva the Destroyer. However, this tidy categorizing never seems to have caught the imagination of devotees, and Brahma has but one temple devoted to him in the whole of India. The rest are devoted to Vishnu or Shiva (or their consorts) in one of their many forms.

Vaishnavites and Shaivites do not deny the god of the other sect, they merely regard the other deity as a secondary expression of the sublime and high god, of which the object of their own devotion is the highest expression. They can hardly be regarded as rival sects, for both seem to have the wonderful Hindu conviction that, in the end, everyone who believes in god is right anyway. Some attempts have been made to unite the two approaches in the figure of Harihara, who combines the main characteristics of both Vishnu and Shiva.

The *bhakti* cults had an enormous impact on Hinduism, and were heavily influenced by Dravidian traditions. The notion of salvation through devotion to a personal deity finds a magnificent expression in the Bhaghavad Gita, where Vishnu in the form of Krishna discourses on life, destiny, and human obligation to Arjuna on the great battlefield of Kurushetra.

The fundamental beliefs of contemporary and popular Hinduism can be summarized as follows. Each human being is possessed of an immortal, indestructible soul. This soul undergoes an endless cycle of rebirths in a none-too-pleasant world as a result of moral failings in past lives or incarnations. This spiritual and moral law of cause and effect is taken to be very real, not symbolic, and is called karma, a word now much overused in the West. It has an even more literal interpretation in traditional Jainism, where karma is conceived as a kind of subtle matter that adheres to, and thus impedes, the soul, as a result of desire and activity. It is the aim of a Hindu to break out of this chain of rebirths, and to be released into the bliss of union with the Absolute (conceived in terms of union with a personal god in many instances) by the correct observance of his or her dharma, or righteous duty, in his or her present life. Salvation can be achieved through devotion to a manifestation of the divine (*bhakti*), good works, or the hard though sublime path of the ascetic and religious virtuoso. The key point is that you must fulfil your dharma. This is made clear by Krishna in the Bhagavad Gita, for there Arjuna is losing his nerve on the eve of the great battle; he sees his kinsmen in the enemy ranks, and asks how he can raise his hand against them. The reply in essence is that it is his ordained duty, his dharma, and he must fulfil it for that reason and none other.

Contemporary Hinduism

Dharma has been held responsible for many of the less pleasant aspects of Hinduism; after all, if it is the righteous duty of a man to be an untouchable, and his only hope of bettering his lot is to be as untouchable as possible, he obviously isn't going to be an avid social reformer. Against this is the statement made by Krishna in the Gita; that no one who comes to Him in devotion will be turned away.

Temple worship is individual, not congregational; many temples have large public rites, when, for example, the image of a god might be thoughtfully put in his wife's shrine for the night, but these are not congregational acts in the sense that Christian worship is. Hindu temples make an interesting

Worship

contrast with Christian churches. The latter, especially the great Gothic cathedrals, give an impression of overwhelming grandeur and magnificence, of a grand approach to the majestic presence of the divine; Hindu temples become less grand and darker, more enclosed and womb-like, as the devotee approaches the shrine of the god, where the image resides in a small sanctuary. Hindu temples give the feeling of an inward journey, not the external journey into divine magnificence offered by the vistas of a great cathedral. This perhaps highlights the difference in the spirituality of the two religions. In Christianity, the enlightenment comes from a revelation that is imposed from without, by order of the deity; in Hinduism, though the divine is personified in the somewhat gaudy, Disneyfied idols (which can be a real shock and a disappointment when you first see them), the enlightenment is that of self-discovery.

Hindus attend a temple either individually or in groups to offer their devotion to the god, who, during certain rites, is held to be actually present in the sanctuary and the idol, much as Christ is held to be present in the eucharistic elements by Catholic Christians. Food is given to the priests (the white-clad Brahmins, who have the sacred thread over their left shoulders and beneath their right arms), who offer it to the god. Food thus offered is known as *prassad*; rice, coconut, bananas, a wide variety of foods are acceptable to the divine palate. The god is held to accept this offering, to consume some subtle part thereof, and to graciously leave the coarser and more corporeal elements of the offering to his devotees; some is given to the temple, and the rest is taken back home by the worshipper. The food is now consecrated, and is endowed with powers of an unspecified but spiritual kind. Such acts of devotional worship are called *pooja*.

The Hindu deities

The main gods and goddesses of the Hindu pantheon are Brahma and his consort Sarasvati, Shiva and his consort Parvati (who has the black aspects of Kali and Durga the demon-slayer), Vishnu and his consort Lakshmi (the goddess of wealth and fortune), and

Ganesha, the elephant-headed god who is the son of Shiva and Parvati. Jolly Ganesha is the remover of obstacles, and is generally appealed to at the commencement of any undertaking; for this reason, his image is often to be found near the entrances of temples; one approaches Ganesha first, before going higher up.

Hinduism has a strong monotheistic strain, in spite of the plethora of gods and goddesses, and it is this that gives it its all-embracing character; there is always the hint that all these deities are just reflections of a higher, supernal reality, and if this is true of the gods and goddesses of the Hindus, it may well be true of those of other faiths.

There is no Hindu equivalent of the Bible or Koran; instead there is a vast mass of religious writings. The four Vedas have already been mentioned; these are held to be *srutis*, that is, something received by direct spiritual inspiration. In effect, they are supernatural truth. Then come the collection of writings known as *smritis*, meaning that which is remembered. These are not held to be of divine origin, and give codes of conduct and government. The Epics are the Ramayana and the Mahabharata; the latter contains what is perhaps the most popular devotional work for Hindus, the Bhagavad Gita. Then there are the Puranas, which are of relatively recent composition but contain a lot of very old material. It is in the Puranas that many tales of the gods and goddesses are told, and in particular many stories relating to Vishnu's incarnations; whenever the world was slipping into evil and disorder, Vishnu, in his role as Preserver, appeared in some corporeal form to set it back to rights. He is held to have done this nine times, as a fish (Matsya), as a turtle or tortoise (Kurma), as a boar (Varaha), as a man-lion (Narasinha), as a dwarf (Vamana), as a man (Parasurama), as a man again (Ramachandra, the Rama of the epic), as Lord Krishna, and as the Buddha. This last was presumably invented to take the wind out of the Buddhists' sails. Vishnu's tenth and final incarnation (or *avatar*) is yet to come. This is the eschatalogical

Religious writings

Kalkin, who will appear on a white horse to wind things up at the end of this age of decay and degeneration.

Islam   Islam is a strictly monotheistic religion which holds that God (Allah) has revealed Himself and His will through a series of prophets of whom Mohammed was the last. The holy book is the Koran, in which the details of this revelation are set out. There is no caste amongst Moslems, but they have often been underprivileged and equated with the lower castes. Islam teaches that Allah is the One True God, and every Moslem should offer prayers five times a day, give alms, fast for one month during the year, and make the pilgrimage to Mecca at least once. The Moslems' strong feelings about graven images did even more damage to Indian architectural remains than the British search for ballast for their new railway tracks.

Sikhism   Sikhism was invented in the fifteenth century, in north-west India, by a religious visionary who came to be known as Guru Nanak Dev. His original intention was to unite the best aspects of Hinduism and Islam in a new faith. Sikhism has similarities to both faiths; it is monotheistic, casteless, rejects the idea of divine incarnations or *avatars*, and is in these senses similar to Islam, yet accepts the Hindu notions of karma, rebirth, the periodic destruction and recreation of the cosmos, and the cremation of the dead.

The gurus   Sikhs believe that their faith has been shaped by a
and the   succession of teachers or gurus, of whom there are
five Ks   ten. The last, Guru Govind Singh, instituted reforms that gave the Sikhs the unmistakable appearance they have to this day. In response to Moslem persecution, they were organized into a martial sect, and enjoined to display these five signs of their allegiance: *kesh*, the unshorn hair (hence the turbans, to wrap it in); *kangha*, the sacred comb; *kara*, the steel bracelet; *kirpan*, the sword; and *kachha*, a garment like shorts, which all Sikhs are supposed to wear beneath their

ordinary dress. Today the sword is often reduced to a symbolic role, being signified by a small ornament on the comb.

Sikh places of worship are called *gurdwaras*, and have a long tradition of offering hospitality to travellers. The holy book of the Sikhs is the Guru Granth Sahib, a heterogeneous collection of writings from various periods. Sikhs are supposed to abstain from the use of tobacco, and if you visit a gurdwara, don't take any in with you.

Worship and teachings

There are only about three million Jains left in India, and their numbers are declining. In its origins Jainism is a pessimistic, atheistical, and highly philosophical sect that developed during the same period as Buddhism; that is, about 500 BC. The Jains trace their origins back into fabulous times, through an impossibly long list of teachers called *tirthankaras* or ford-builders. The last two *tirthankaras* are historical figures, and some details are known about the life of the last, Mahavira (Great Hero).

Jainism

Jainism is bound up with the problem of pain, and of escaping from the endless cycle of reincarnation. A complex cosmology was developed, with a universe that was of amazing size (comparable to the astronomical distances of modern science) and ageless; there is neither creation nor creator, just a series of cycles of growth, development, and degeneration. Gods and goddesses were borrowed from Hinduism, but they play a subordinate role to that of the great teachers; indeed, the gods and goddesses are morally reprehensible, although some of them, so it is said, occasionally like to listen to the discourses and sermons of the great sages.

Beliefs

The object for every human is to escape from reincarnation, and to enter a state of isolated, blissful omniscience. The universe is held to consist of two types of material, *jiva*, which is living, and *ajiva*, which is not. The consequences of action and desire weigh down the *jiva* with karma, which is almost conceived of in material terms, and bind it to *ajiva*.

One sets oneself free by complete quietism and the practice of sometimes ferocious and extreme austerities. One of the actions of many Jains that has been held most noble has been to starve themselves to death; Chandragupta Maurya was supposed to have done this after retiring from the throne, and Mahavira too is said to have died in this way. Many contemporary Jains, however, are successful in commerce and business, and have presumably resigned their chances of liberation until the next life or two. Jainism is quite influential because of the commercial power wielded by many members of this sect.

Jainism has a strong monastic tradition, of which there are two branches; the *svetambaras* (meaning 'white-clad') and the *digambaras* (meaning 'sky-clad'). The latter group are so called because, in their zeal for liberation, they feel called upon to dispense with their clothing. Such men were known to the Greeks, who named them gymnosophists, or naked philosophers. Contemporary *digambaras* confine their nudity to their monasteries. Jains have a deep reverence for all living things, and monks take the most elaborate precautions to avoid accidentally killing even the smallest insect. All Jains are strict vegetarians.

Worship   A temple cult grew up around Jainism, and in effect popular, pragmatic Jainism sanctions the worship of the *tirthankaras*, although the very success of these spiritual giants has consigned them (according to orthodox teaching) to regions of bliss where they can no longer intervene in human affairs for good or ill. From the outside, Jain temples are similar to those of the Hindus; they are always very clean inside, and have Buddha-like images of *tirthankaras* in place of the Hindu images of the gods and goddesses. Jainism is a very gentle, unaggressive creed, with no recent history or tradition of proselytism.

Zoroast-rianism   Like the Jains, the Zoroastrians or Parsis are few in number, and are declining. Again like the Jains, their commercial success has given them a power and influence out of all proportion to their numbers; men like Tata, one of India's greatest industrialists, came from this community. The Parsis are noted for their philanthropy and generosity. There are fewer than 100,000 left, and most of them live in or around Bombay, though some isolated groups still live in Pakistan.

The Parsis came to India as refugees from Moslem persecution in Persia in about the seventh century AD. The name 'Zoroastrian' derives from the name of the founder of the religion, the prophet Zarathustra, who was born in what is now Afghanistan in about 660 BC. Zoroastrianism envisages a constant cosmic struggle between the forces of good and evil, a struggle in which humanity cannot remain neutral. Human beings can enter the fight on the side of the powers of good by following the path of good thoughts, good words, and good deeds. An omnipotent god presides over the world, and is named Ahura Mazda; the evil power is Angra Mainyu or Ahriman. Ahura Mazda is a god of light, and light, in the form of a sacred fire that is kept burning in the Parsi temples, is his symbol. The beliefs are laid out in the sacred text called the Zend Avesta.

Origins and beliefs

The Parsis have a doctrine concerning the purity of the natural elements, which must not be defiled by the decomposition of a corpse; corpses are therefore exposed on the Tower of Silence in Bombay, to be picked clean by the vultures. Modern Parsis produce elaborate and unconvincing apologetics for this practice, trying to argue that it is both 'scientific' (though in what sense is not made clear) and hygienic.

The ritual of the fire-temples is centred on the sacred fire, which is tended by priests; worshippers are not suffered to approach the fire, but give their offerings to the priests. Non-Parsis cannot enter fire-temples. Although the sect has a long history of working for the public good, it is very exclusive; you can only be a Parsi if both parents are Parsis, and this obviously precludes any proselytism.

Christianity

The Syrian Orthodox Church

Christianity has a long history in India. St Thomas (as in doubting Thomas) is said to have landed on the Malabar coast around 54 AD, and the very ancient Syrian Orthodox Church in Kerala regards him as its founder. St Thomas is said to have been rewarded for his labours with martyrdom, and to this day his tomb is displayed in the St Thome cathedral in Madras. (The cathedral was raised to basilica status not long ago.)

Whether these stories be true or not, the Syrian Christians caused the Portuguese, when they arrived in India, great distress, for the Syrian Christians had obviously been there for a long time but had never heard of the pope – a most serious omission from the martyred saint's teaching. Instead of looking to Rome, the Keralan Christians looked to Antioch. Moreover, they had become a corrupt and heterodox sect by this time, and had even developed something like a caste system amongst themselves. They reformed under the influence of the Jesuit missionaries in the sixteenth and seventeenth centuries; one group corrected St Thomas's absurd oversight and recognized the pope, while another remained true to the authority of Antioch. The Syrian Christian Church still exists today, and its churches and liturgy are fascinating; don't miss them if you visit Kerala.

Other forms

The Portuguese brought militant Catholicism, and saints like St Francis Xavier. At Goa there are huge churches, a cathedral, and a vast basilica, all rotting away in the palm groves and monsoon. St Francis Xavier's body is taken from the Bom Jesus Basilica once a year, which induces a state of near-ecstasy in the predominantly Christian Goans.

Otherwise Christianity is represented by quite a large number of born-again organizations, and some relics of the Anglican church. Missionaries have been hard at work in the north-eastern frontier, amongst the tribals, and in some regions Christians are actually in the majority.

Judaism

Kerala was also the home of a substantial Jewish community, which traces its roots back many centuries. Cochin was the centre, and still has some synagogues. Sadly, the community is in decline because of large-scale emigration to Israel.

The only group that absolutely forbids non-believers to enter its places of worship is the Parsis. Not all Hindu temples allow non-Hindus in, and those that do usually bar them from the sanctuaries. This can make visits to some famous temples very disappointing – the great Shiva temple in Varanasi, for instance, or the Lingaraj and Jagganath temples in Orissa. Most temples are closed during the afternoon; although opening times vary, they are generally open from about 5 a.m. to 12 a.m., then again from 4 or 5 p.m. to 10 p.m. You will be expected to leave your shoes at the gate, and there will be a stand for footwear with a watchman. If there is no set charge (it would only be about 50 paisa) you are expected to give him a tip when you leave. Be careful of burning your feet on hot flagstones!

Don't smoke in temple precincts, check on the rules governing the use of cameras (many temples charge an extortionate fee for a 'camera permit'), and beware of the guides. Most of the self-styled guides you meet in temples are ignorant and boring. If you want a guide, you can usually hire Government of India recognized ones through the temple office. They have identity cards, with a photograph; just as a bad guide or an outright imposter can ruin a visit to a temple, so a good guide can make it very interesting. The priests are usually very friendly, and will take trouble to show you round and explain things. They will of course ask for a donation for the temple.

The same rules about footwear apply to mosques. You can leave your shoes at the gate, or sometimes wear a sort of padded overshoe. Make sure that photography is permitted before you start pointing a camera at anything. The gates of all places of worship are gathering places for beggars; watch out for them. In general, common sense rules apply; behave decorously and respectfully, even if you have

Visiting temples, mosques, and churches

little sympathy for the faith to which the place is dedicated.

Festivals and the calendar

India has a large number of religious festivals, many of which are public holidays in addition to the three national holidays on fixed dates (26 January, 15 August, and 2 October): respectively, Republic Day, Independence Day, and Gandhi's birthday. The Hindus use a lunar calendar with intercalation (days inserted), and the Hindu festivals therefore do not fall upon fixed days but do fall in the same season year by year. The same is true of the Jains. The Moslems, however, use a lunar calendar without intercalation, and therefore the Moslem festivals slide through the solar year, occurring at quite different seasons after an interval of a few years.

January

Makara Sankranthi or *Pongal*, a harvest festival celebrated in the southern states of Tamil Nadu, Andhra Pradesh, and Kanartaka. Banks in these states can be shut on this day.

February/ March

Maha Shivaratri, a day-long fast dedicated to the god Shiva.
Holi, a sort of Indian Saturnalia to celebrate the advent of spring. It is a very happy and joyful festival, and people throw coloured water and powder over each other in the streets, presumably as an expression of their exuberance. This is a national holiday.

March/April

Mahaveer Jayanthi, a celebration of the birth of the last *tirthankara*, Mahavira. A major Jain festival.
Rama Navami, the celebration of the birth of the righteous prince Rama.

May/June

Buddha Purnima, a simultaneous celebration of the Buddha's birth, enlightenment, and entry into nirvana. Not even the Buddha was able to do all these things at once, but, no doubt with the convenience of future generations of worshippers in mind, he obligingly did them on the same day of different years.

Rathyatra, the great festival of cars in Puri, in which the Lord of the Universe, Jagannath, his brother Balbhadra, and sister Subhadra are taken from the Jagannath Temple in Puri and pulled through the streets on giant cars – the original juggernauts, beneath the wheels of which ecstatic devotees sometimes threw themselves. *June/July*

Naga Panchami, in honour of the serpent deity Shesha or Ananta, who supports the sleeping Vishnu on his coils during the interval between the dissolution of the universe and another creation. *July/August*

Raksha Bandhan, a festival for brothers and sisters. The sisters tie threads, called *rakhis*, round their brothers' wrists to ward off harm and evil through the coming year. *August*

Janmastami, the birthday of Lord Krishna.
Ganesh Chaturthi, the festival of the elephant-headed god, Ganesha.
Onam, a harvest festival in the State of Kerala, during which the famous 'snake boat' races take place. *August/ September*

Dussehra, also known as *Durga Puja* in West Bengal. This is one of the greatest of the Indian festivals, and lasts for ten days, as the conflict between the forces of good and evil are acted out in the Ramayana epic. The final triumph of the forces of goodness, personified by the hero Rama, bring the festival to a climax when huge effigies of the demon king are burned. In Mysore there is an especially magnificent procession; spectacular celebrations also take place in Delhi. *September/ October*

Diwali, a festival of lights, when houses are decorated with oil lamps. The festival has various associations, for the lamps are said to light the virtuous Rama home after his forest exile, but it is also associated with Lakshmi, goddess of wealth and fortune (especially in Bombay); and Kali (especially in West Bengal). *October/ November*

November *Guru Purab* or *Nanak Jayanti*, the celebration of the birthday of the founder of Sikhism, Guru Nanak Dev.

Govardhan Puja, a festival in honour of the cow, an animal sacred to the Hindus and the object of much popular veneration.

Pushkar Fair, which takes place in a small village near Ajmer in Rajasthan. It is a combination of cattle fair and pilgrimage and is spectacular.

The Christian festivals are also celebrated; Good Friday and Christmas Day can be local banking holidays. In regions with a large Christian population, like Goa, there are other local festivals like the feast day of St Francis Xavier (3 December) and those associated with the Virgin Mary (especially her immaculate conception).

The main Moslem festivals are Ramadan, which involves a dawn-to-dusk fast that lasts for thirty days; Id'l Fitr, which ends Ramadan when the new moon is first seen in the western sky; Id-ul-Zuahara (Bakrid), celebrating the Prophet Abraham's attempted sacrifice of his son Isaac and God's intervention to save the boy; and Moharam, a festival lasting ten days to commemorate the murder of Hussain, the Prophet Mohammed's grandson by his daughter Fatima and Ali. This festival has special significance for the Shia Moslems (most Indian Moslems are Sunnis, but there is a sizeable Shia community, mainly in and around Lucknow in Uttar Pradesh), who believe that Ali (not the Khaliphate) was the true inheritor of the Prophet's authority. Models of the tombs of Hussain and of his elder brother Hassan (these models are called *tazias* and *taboots*) are carried in procession and taken to the special buildings called *imambaras*.

The calendar For most purposes the conventional Gregorian (that is, modern Western) calendar is used. There are however, a number of Indian eras by which count of the years is made, including the Vikrama Era (traditionally founded by King Vikramaditya in 57 BC), the Shakra Era (traditionally founded by a

Shakra king in 78 AD), the Mahavira Nirvana Era
of the Jains (counted from 1527 BC), and the Hejira
or Mohammedan Era (counted from 579 AD). In
each of these eras, 1988 was thus 2045, 1909, 2515,
and 1409 respectively.

The original Hindu calendar was lunar, and this
reckoning is still used to fix the times of the religious
festivals. A solar calendar with twelve months, named
after the signs of the zodiac, appeared in Gupta
times, and a variant of this was adopted as the
'reformed' national calendar with a new year starting
on 22 March 1957. The Indian new year begins near
the vernal equinox, and the months are listed in the
box.

Month of Indian calendar	Gregorian equivalent
Chaitra (30 days, 31 in leap year)	22 March (21 March in leap year)–20 April
Vaisakha (31 days)	21 April–21 May
Jyaistha (31 days)	22 May–21 June
Asadha (31 days)	22 June–22 July
Sravana (31 days)	23 July–22 August
Bhadra (31 days)	23 August–22 September
Asvina (30 days)	23 September–22 October
Kartika (30 days)	23 October–21 November
Agrahayana (30 days)	22 November–21 December
Pausa (30 days)	22 December–20 January
Magha (30 days)	21 January–19 February
Phalguna (30 days)	20 February–21 March

For business and most official purposes, the
Gregorian calendar is used; that is, newspapers tend
to have (if they are in English) 'New Delhi, Tuesday,
August 16, 1988' written on them, not '25 Sravana
1910 S.E.'.

The signs of the zodiac are Mesha (Aries), Vrisha
(Taurus), Mithuna (Gemini), Kartaka (Cancer),
Simha (Leo), Kanya (Virgo), Tula (Libra), Vrishchika
(Scorpio), Dhanus (Sagittarius), Makara (Capricorn),
Kumbha (Aquarius), and Mina (Pisces). It is possible

to buy English language almanacs (*panchangs*) in many bookshops, and these give the details of the eras etc. and the dates of the various festivals for the Indian year.

Useful addresses

D.N. stands for Dadabhai Naoraji

**Foreigners'
registration
offices**

Special Branch (II)
Office of the Police Commissioner of Greater Bombay
D.N. Road
Bombay
(tel. 4150446)

Bombay

237, Acharya J. C. Bose Road
Calcutta

Calcutta

9, Village Road
Madras
(tel. 478210)

Madras

**Consulates
and
embassies**

UK – The British High Commission
Shanti Path
Chanakayapuri
New Delhi 21
(tel. 601371)
USA – Shanti Path
Chanakayapuri
New Delhi 21
(tel. 600651)

New Delhi

Bombay UK – Deputy High Commission
Hong Kong Bank Building
2nd Floor
Mahatma Gandhi Road
Bombay 400 023
(tel. 274874)
USA – Lincoln House
78, Bhulabhai Desai Road
Bombay 400 026
(tel. 8223618/8223611)

Calcutta UK – 1 Ho Chi Minh Sarani
Calcutta
(tel. 445171)
USA – 5/1 Ho Chi Minh Sarani
Calcutta
(tel. 443611)

Madras UK – 24 Anderson Road
Nungambakkam
Madras
(tel. 473136)
USA – 220 Anna Salai
Madras
(tel. 473040)

**Thomas
Cook and
American
Express**

New Delhi Thomas Cook
Hotel Imperial
Jan Path
New Delhi
(tel. 3328432/3328405/3328468)
Amex
Wenger House
Connaught Place
New Delhi
(tel. 344119/322868)

Thomas Cook
Thomas Cook Building
D.N.* Road
Bombay
(tel. 2048556/2043413)
Amex
Majthia Chambers
276 D.N.* Road
Bombay
(tel. 2048949)

Bombay

Thomas Cook
c/o Mirta Lina Private Ltd
Mezzanine Floor
12-B/1, Park Street
Calcutta
(tel. 298862/297537)
Amex
21 Old Court House Street
Calcutta
(tel. 236281/232133)

Calcutta

Thomas Cook
El Dorado Building
112 Nungambakkam High Road
Madras
(tel. 473092/475042)
Amex
Binny Ltd
65 Armenian Street
Madras
(tel. 29631/26978)

Madras

**Government
of India
tourist
offices
abroad**

21 New Bond Street
London W1Y ODY
(tel. 01–493-0769)

London

New York	30, Rockefeller Plaza 15 North Mezzanine New York NY 10020 (tel. 212–586-4901)
Chicago	201, N. Michigan Avenue Chicago Illinois 60601 (tel. 312-236-6899)
Los Angeles	3550 Wilshire Boulevard Suite 204 Los Angeles California 90010 (tel. 213-380-8855)

**Government
of India
tourist
offices in
India**

New Delhi	88, Jan Path New Delhi (tel. 320005)
Bombay	123 Maharshi Karve Road Churchgate Bombay (tel. 293144)
Calcutta	4 Shakespeare Sarani Calcutta (tel. 441402)
Madras	154, Anna Salai Madras (tel. 88685)

**Indian
Airlines
booking
offices**

Kanchenjunga Building   *New Delhi*
Barakhamba Road
New Delhi
(tel. 3310071/3310052)
Malhotra Building
Jan Path
New Delhi
(24 hours)
(tel. 3310646/3310454)

Air India Building   *Bombay*
Nariman Point
Bombay
(tel. 2048282)

Airlines House   *Calcutta*
39 Chittaranjan Avenue
Calcutta
(tel. 260731/263135)

Rajah Annamalai Building   *Madras*
Marshalls Road
Egmore
Madras
(tel. 478333/477098)

Further reading

Indian history

The Oxford History of India, V. A. Smith (OUP, 1958)
The Wonder that was India, A. L. Basham (Sidgwick & Jackson, 1954)
The Great Mutiny, C. Hibbert (Penguin, 1980)
India Discovered, J. Keay (Collins, 1981)

Indian religious and philosophical works

The Upanishads, trans. by Juan Mascaro (Penguin Classics, 1988)
The Rig Veda, trans. by Wendy Doniger O'Flaherty (Penguin Classics, 1988)
The Ramayana and Mahabharata, trans. by Romesh Dutt (Everyman, 1969)
The Ramaya, prose version by R. K. Narayan (Penguin, 1977)
The Bhagavad Gita, trans. by Juan Mascaro (Penguin Classics, 1962)
The Structure of Indian Thought, S. Sinari (OUP, 1970)
The Heart of Jainism, S. Stevenson (OUP, 1915)
Hindu Scriptures, trans. by R. C. Zaehner (Everyman, 1982)
Hinduism, K. M. Sen (Pelican, 1987)

General works

Caste in India, J. M. Hutton (CUP, 1946)
Into India, J. Keay (John Murray, 1973)
From Raj to Rajiv, M. Tully and Z. Masani (BBC Publications, 1988)
Indian Mythology, V. Ions (Newnes Library of the World's Myths and Legends, 1983)
Highness – The Maharajas of India, A. Morrow (Grafton, 1987)
An Area of Darkness, V. S. Naipaul (Penguin, 1987)
India – A Wounded Civilisation, V. S. Naipaul (Penguin, 1983)

Maps

The best general-purpose maps of India are those produced by Nelles-Verlag. They are on 1:1,500,000 scale, and consist of four sheets, north, south, east, and west India. Each sheet costs £4.95.

Bartholomews produce a convenient single-sheet map of the entire subcontinent.

Index